A PLACE CALLED BIRD

Books by Tony Parker

The Courage of His Convictions
The Unknown Citizen
The Plough Boy
Five Women
A Man of Good Abilities
People of the Streets
The Twisting Lane: Some Sex Offenders
The Frying Pan: A Prison and Its Prisoners
In No Man's Land: Some Unmarried Mothers
The Man Inside (ed.)
Three Television Plays
Lighthouse
The People of Providence: A Housing Estate and Some of Its Inhabitants
Soldier, Soldier
Red Hill: A Mining Community

A PLACE CALLED BIRD

Tony Parker

SECKER & WARBURG
LONDON

First published in Great Britain in 1989
by Martin Secker & Warburg Limited
Michelin House, 81 Fulham Road, London SW3 6RB

British Library Cataloguing in Publication Data

Parker, Tony, *1923–*
A place called bird
1. Kansas. Social life
I. Title
978.1'033

ISBN 0 436 37317 8

The six lines quoted on p. 335 are from
'A Walk After Dark' by W. H. Auden.
Reprinted by permission of Faber and Faber Limited
from 'Collected Poems by W. H. Auden.'

Photoset by Rowland Phototypesetting Limited
Bury St Edmunds, Suffolk
Printed by Butler & Tanner Limited
Frome, Somerset

For Margery
who was there

and for the people of 'Bird'
who so freely shared their lives
with me for a while

You won't find Bird in no guidebooks – but then you won't find Kansas either, least not in some guidebooks I've seen. That don't stop it being a neat little place to live and die in though.

Lester Gover, *Mayor*

He was as American as anybody out in the middle of Kansas.

Arthur Miller,
talking about his father.

Contents

Long after I'd chosen 'Bird' as the pseudonymous name of the town I'd stayed in in Kansas, I discovered that a much smaller place already exists, 21 miles from the northeast border between Kansas and Nebraska, called Bird City. I'd never heard of it and I've never been there, and that Bird isn't this 'Bird': they're of a completely different feather.

1 *Hi, Welcome to Bird*

Darsham railway station platform, Suffolk, at a quarter to eight on a bright August morning: a sunshine-blue sky with hardly a single cloud. I'm the only passenger waiting. Freshness and stillness, a sparrow twittering quietly somewhere unseen in a bush. Eventually in the distance the sight of the little yellow-fronted diesel train threading its way through cornfields, too far away yet to be heard. A rising sense of expectancy at the beginning of a new experience starts to grow as the train comes gliding down the final quarter-mile incline. It screeches to a halt; when I've got in and slammed the door shut behind me it gives a whoosh of air and a low groan, judders into motion again, and rumbles on.

The ticket collector appears in the carriage aisle, as always wearing his cap jauntily at an angle over one eye. 'Good morning sir, and where's it to be to today?'

'How far ahead can you book me to?'

'Ah well now, with these new printout machines they've issued us with, all the way as far as you could wish to go.' I'm glad he fell for it. I solemnly hold up the label on my bag, and he bends to read it. 'Howard Johnson Hotel' it says, 'Kansas City, Missouri, USA'. He straightens up again.

'Yes,' he says, 'I like it. I'll tell the missus that one when I get home tonight. So shall we say Ipswich then, will that be doing for a start?'

It'd begun two months earlier at lunch at the Grosvenor Hotel buffet in London with my publisher saying, 'How do you fancy doing a book about somewhere in the middle of America? Though wherever that might be I wouldn't know.' To the waitress when she came he said politely, 'Have you by any chance got an atlas?' and she responded levelly 'Certainly sir, large or small?'

'Large please,' he said, and when she went off I thought she'd misheard him and was going to come back with sweetbreads on a skewer. But within a few minutes she brought the huge Reader's Digest New Illustrated Atlas of the World, *clearing away most of the plates and cutlery so we could spread it open on the table. The middle of the United States was obviously Kansas: and after careful measurements with a butter knife and the handle of a soup spoon, the middle of Kansas looked to be somewhere around . . .* there.

'Why don't you go over and have a look?' he said. 'Tour round in a car for a week or so and see what there is.'

The first thing I learned about Kansas when I got there is that Kansas City, Missouri, isn't the capital of Kansas and nor is Kansas City, Kansas, which is just across the river. The capital of Kansas is Topeka.

In Topeka, after arriving late at night, the first Kansan I ever had a conversation with, on the telephone next morning, was a professional photographer. She'd had several expensive books published, of stunningly beautiful pictures of the prairie and its skies, of hard-working people and empty buildings and derelict farms. Her name was in the phone directory and I said I'd just arrived from England, and was hoping to find a small ordinary everyday town to try and write a book about: I didn't know anybody or where to start, but could she have lunch with me and give me some advice? No she couldn't she said, and if I wanted to talk with her the rate was 50 dollars an hour and I should ring her secretary to make an appointment.

I was in a cramped and shabby motel room in an alien country approximately 4,885 miles from home, and I felt like phoning the airport and asking the time of flights back to England. Her name was well it doesn't matter, and I still often look with great pleasure through the copies of her books I brought back. Her photographs of farms and buildings and people, and of the prairie and its marvellous vast skies are all stunningly beautiful and moving.

The same day in the afternoon I went to meet Chris Stanfield at the offices of the Travel and Tourist Division of the Kansas State Econ-

omic Development Department. He told me that Ms well-it-doesn't-matter had a reputation for being very much like that, and sat me down and gave me coffee. He also gave me maps, guides, itineraries, booklets, postcards, posters, pictures, photographs, accommodation lists, a pennant, car bumper stickers, T-shirts for my children and a souvenir beaker. He then gave me more coffee, photocopied lists of statistics concerning weather and population, demographic and ethnographic surveys, names and locations of 30 small towns, names and addresses and telephone numbers of at least two people in each one to contact, personal letters of introduction to all of them, and more coffee. And finally he told me very firmly that if there was ever anything else he could do, I wasn't to hesitate for a moment to get back to him. He also added that he hoped I'd not retain an impression I might have got that all Kansans were unfriendly.

I didn't and I've never met a single other than Ms who was.

In a ten-day 1,900-mile drive: Concordia, Jewell, Mankato, Smith, Downs, Lindsborg, Hiawatha, Seneca, Lucas, Norton, Eureka, Stockton, Riley, Bird, Baldwin, Beloit, Baxter, Fredonia, Garnett, Anthony, Augusta, Florence, Medicine, Cimarron, Kensington, Ulysses, Syracuse, Logan, Russell. Some were too small, some much too big, some indefinite and somehow intangible, and some had an identity that was still proudly European: Swedish, French, German, Bohemian. Which one could be almost a typical example of an ordinary everyday mid-American town? 'Well you sure couldn't get much midder than us here,' said the local newspaper editor in one of them. How would people there react to having someone from England coming and living among them, tape-recording interviews? 'Let's go ask a few,' she said.

Standing at the crossing of two state highways in the middle of what seemed a huge and limitless plain of prairie, Bird's population was just under 2,000. Viewed from a stance in the middle of the midday trafficless Main Street, the road to the north disappeared in a straight unbroken line off over the horizon. Turn round and look in the opposite direction, south, and it did exactly the same. A few well-used and not particularly large cars, and one or two high-mounted pickup trucks stood in front of a line of single-storeyed shops. There was a red brick church of the 1920s on one corner, and a 1960s First National Bank on the other. A filling station, a branch of East West Hardware, a laundromat, Ace Video Rentals, Dorothy's Cafe, Harris's Flower & Gift, a pharmacy, Gover's Supermarket, Loretta's Ladieswear. In side roads off Main Street a neo-Classical five-storey courthouse and a public library building with a wide modern extension: and trim rows of well-kept houses with mail boxes in front of them, and neatly tended front lawns with stone paths and shrubs. Not far away beyond the town's edge were wind-rippled wheatfields, grazing land with herds of cattle, and here and there isolated farms among clumps of trees.

It looked as though it might be it. I talked with people, drove and looked at other places, came back a few days later and talked with more people. Yes, it felt this was it.

April of the following year. Three hours after arrival, walking along Jackson Street and turning the corner into Main and almost colliding with a small young woman in a red T-shirt and jeans, with curly brown hair and glasses and suddenly a huge wide smile.

– Hi, welcome to Bird! So you finally made it eh, well great! I'm Irene Finney, we met in Dorothy's Cafe when you were here last August, remember? This is your wife? Well it's a real pleasure to know you, so how long are you planning on being here with us? My, really, you'll both be regular American citizens by then won't you! Well now listen, don't you forget this now: anything you're short of, anything you need, all you have to do's call me and you shall have it, I mean that, OK?

Three minutes later, coming across from the other side of Main Street, a short slightly plump woman of about 60 in a bright blue headscarf and an olive-green trouser suit.

– Say gosh you're the man from England aren't you, come here to write a book? I knew it, I just knew it: when I saw you from across the street I said to myself 'Mildred' I said, 'that man over there with that lady, he's that man who was here last year from England looking to write a book.' And this is your wife oh I'm so glad to meet you, my name's

Mildred Davies how do you do! Lester Gover he was telling me when I saw him yesterday you were due here today, and I said 'Oh I do hope I see them' I said, and what do you know now isn't that wonderful, now I have! And I hear you're giving us a programme tomorrow night at the library isn't that right, to tell us what you're going to do? Oh that'll be just great I know it will, Henry my husband and me we're so looking forward to it. Gosh it's so nice to have been able to visit with you, now you will remember won't you you're going to come and see my lovely home aren't you, one eleven North Washington don't forget.

– Excuse me sir would you be the gentleman from England? My name's Jody Stone, I'm in my freshman year at High School, I'd like to introduce myself and say I hope you enjoy your stay with us in Bird. Mr Westerman our principal told us yesterday you'd arrived, did you have a good trip? I guess you won't remember me but I was in the corridor of the school last August when you came. Is your wife here with you now, did she have a good trip too? I understand you're giving a programme tonight at the library, two of my classmates and I are going to come to hear that if that's OK? I hope you won't think it was rude, me coming straight up to you in the street like this?

– Heh how're you doing Tony? Surprised I knew your name aren't you: but don't be, I know most things there is to know around here. Augustus Boot, good to meet you, call me Gus same as all my other friends. So how's good old England then and Her Majesty The Queen? I wouldn't say exactly I've ever been in your country, but it's where all my folks come from. The Cheviot Mountain ranges, if you know where those are. Two hundred years back they were sheep dealers there, or sheep stealers more likely I should reckon. Heh all Englishmen like jokes don't they, do you know the one about the husband and wife who went to a counsellor because all the magic had gone out of sex for them? So he told them they should be more relaxed about it, do it in the daytime if they felt like it, not only always at nighttime in bed. Two weeks later when he saw them again he asked them were things better, they said fantastic, it was like a whole new life. For instance the Saturday before at their evening meal they'd felt like it while they were eating so they'd just broke off and done it right then and there on the floor. Only small problem was though, said the husband, the manager'd told them he'd never allow them in his restaurant again. How's that, that's a good one eh? See you around Tony, be looking out for you.

A programme is no more than a talk, and there were 62 people at the library to hear it: how over a period of three months I wanted to tape-record conversations with ordinary people, and try to get a more realistic impression of everyday America than the one conveyed by Dallas, Dynasty, The Colbys *and* Miami Vice. *Afterwards there was a flood of questions: one of them was did I get involved lastingly with people and places? Always, I said, the connection and interest seemed to continue for good. To take lighthouses for instance, which I'd done a book about ten years earlier: they still fascinated me . . . and indeed while I was in Kansas I hoped I'd see many of theirs. It was met with total silence.*

Afterwards a lady drew me aside as she was shaking hands on leaving. She'd enjoyed it, she said: but she did hope I wouldn't be offended if she pointed out there weren't any lighthouses in Kansas. I persisted, being an idiot: perhaps they ought to consider having some I said, then they wouldn't lose so many ships. 'Oh God' muttered my wife, 'Can't you ever learn?'

The next morning in the library Clare Oberlin the librarian said Mr Albert was waiting to see me: right over there look, in the photocopying section behind the glass partition. A tall thin elderly man, he held his hat in his hands and kept looking down at it when he spoke. He and his wife had been to the programme, it sure was an interesting idea to do, was a book. But it was sure going to be expensive though wasn't it, taking up all that time and coming all that way and my wife along too? Would 500 dollars help a little towards expenses?

No I wouldn't think of it I said, cold and English and making the idea sound faintly improper: and he bolted before I had time even to try and be better mannered about it and thank him.

Trundling a shopping cart slowly up and down the aisles in Gover's Supermarket, there was a sudden confrontation with a smiling group of three women and a softly spoken well-built young man in casual clothes. He drew himself up with a touch of formality. 'Good morn-

ing, I'm Gerry Meister, manager and proprietor of this store, and these ladies are some of our staff. I'm also this year's president of our local Chamber of Commerce, and everyone would like to welcome you to our town. We sincerely hope you enjoy your stay here.'

In Dorothy's Cafe, a short bright eyed man in his fifties came over to the table, his hand outstretched. He had on an open-necked check shirt and navy-blue trousers. 'Sure and didn't they tell me this was where you'd be this morning, and right enough now here you are. And straight away I must apologise to you that I wasn't at the library to listen to you last Tuesday, I'd every intention of it and then at the very last moment I discovered I was somewhere else. My name's Father Damien, and I know you'd never know it from the way I speak so I'll tell you at once I'm originally from Galway.'

On the rough-ground parking lot at the side of Gover's, instead of getting into his large white car a burly bearded man with a big badge on his shirt and a revolver prominent in its holster on his belt ambled across.

– Sheriff Jim Arnoldsen, heard you'd arrived in town, glad to know you, hi. Any problems, everything going OK? Good good, well if you have any difficulties any time or there's anything at all you need help with, now just you give me a call and it'll all be straightened out for you real quick. And as soon as you're settled in and've decided what you want to do, let me take you riding the County with me one day, show you around and give you an idea of the area. Be my pleasure to do it, give me a call soon as you like OK?

Item *Visiting with someone means merely talking with them, not visiting them at home.*

Item *Telling someone you'll give them a ring means you'll give them a ring. Ladies especially look puzzled, or even momentarily expectant. If you mean to tell someone you'll telephone them you say you'll call them.*

Item *If as you're leaving a store or restaurant where you've just bought and paid for something you say 'Thank you', the response you'll get is a clear polite 'Uh huh'.*

Item *There are no lighthouses round the coasts of Kansas. Despite this, they've had no recorded ship losses for several hundred years.*

2 *Riding the County*

Jim Arnoldsen, *Sheriff*

His office was on the top floor of the Courthouse. Don't be there much before eight in the morning he'd said, so's he'd have time to see if there was anything urgent in the mail his day'd have to be planned around. A heavily built middle-aged man with a thick short trimmed beard: his light blue eyes matched his uniform of short-sleeved shirt and smartly pressed trousers. He picked up his Colt Python Magnum in its holster from the top of the pile of correspondence on his desk, and carried it held in front of him sandwiched between his big hands as we went out to his private elevator. His voice was a soft slow drawl.

– I believe you call elevators 'lifts' in your country is that right? I've never been to England or Europe myself, I'd sure like to one day though. After you. So how's things going with you Tony, everything OK? Don't forget what I said now, any problems, let me know. OK, now through those glass doors down the end of the corridor, my automobile's in back. That's another different word you have isn't that so, you'd say 'My car's in back' right?

He swung the big white Chevrolet slowly out of the parking lot behind the building, and out along Main Street to the filling station. On the forecourt a small boy jumped out from between the pumps.

– No gas Billy, just gimme a windshield wipe real quick.

The boy sauntered away and came back with a bucket, a cloth and a rubber-bladed scraper. He worked over the glass carefully and unhurriedly. When it was finished the Sheriff gave him a nod.

– OK Billy you done a good job.

– Have a nice day Sheriff. You too sir.

– So now this here's Main Street, we usually say just Main. Might not be exactly Maple Street Los Angeles, but we like it well enough: least the prices aren't so high. All of the streets running across from north to south are named for American presidents – Washington Street this one, Jefferson Street the next one, one after that Lincoln, Grant and so on. It was the great idea of our Town Commissioners a few years back, they told us it'd give the town more civic pride. The way it was before, the streets were just plain First, Second, Third, Fourth through Tenth. That meant it was too easy to find your way around: so they changed it so's you gotta have a Bachelor's Degree in history and know whether Monroe comes before Jefferson, Grant precedes Garfield, or what. Neat idea huh?

This side, to the north of Main, some of the residences are smarter, ones that belong to folks with money. South of Main they're more the homes of ordinarily financially situated people. Not poor folk, there aren't too many of those in Bird. Out at Garland's mostly the place for that. That's about seven miles west, we'll take a ride there later.

Now this little store here we're passing, Harris's Flower & Gift, they have some good inexpensive things sometimes, artificial flowers on corn wreaths, arrangements, stuff like that. Gover's Supermarket on the corner there, I guess you'll be familiar with that already: they sure have a big array of everything you could think of to eat. They say if you can't get it at Gover's you can probably do without. Heh I'm getting to sound like I'm doing a TV commercial. Our bank there, a modern building, some folk like it and some not: there's not much else besides, not in the way of contemporary architecture here, other than that and the library. Look now, you see that good looking young woman walking along the sidewalk by the East West Hardware Store? That's Mrs Russburg: the prettiest lady you'll see between here and the Colorado border. Her husband's in a law firm in Bakersfield, he's a very nice person and so is she. That tall guy on the corner there look: that's Harold Albert, he's the richest man in the world, least around these parts he is. Wouldn't think it looking at him though would you? Very shy, but a real nice guy once he gets to know you.

At the end of Main he turned the Chevrolet right, then right again along Jefferson Street.

– This here's the High School, the Principal's Bernie Westerman. And that small bungalow over there with the white roof, that's where Arnie Marsh lives. Most often if it's a fine day you'll see him out sitting on his porch there in his wheelchair: guess it's too early yet for him. He'd be an interesting guy for you to visit with, he's always glad anytime someone drops by. This lady in the automobile up front of us, she's Betty Holt runs the Retail Liquor Store: on her way to work I guess. Huh-oh, that guy in the dirty old hat and the long black coat over there: take a good look at him as we go by so you'll remember him. He's one of the less precious adornments of our town. Gus Boot he's called. Steer clear of him, he's one big no good vagrant bum. Right now they say he's squatting in one of those run-down shacks by the old railroad warehouse, but the sooner he moves on out of town the happier everyone'll be.

Another half hour of leisurely cruising round, noting the Health Clinic, the Methodist Church and the First Church of Christ, the Agricultural Credit Union, the Extension Agent's shop front office, the towering gleaming white grain elevators of the Farmers Co-Operative. Among other homes, two near-mansions: one on North Washington and another on Lincoln.

– Those satellite dish antennae folk have out front on their lawns, they're the latest status symbol: lets everyone know you're someone with cable television. More than a hundred different channels you can choose from if you got one of those. The wives all say 'OK but so what do we need a hundred channels to pick from for?' Their husbands say 'To get all the sports channels honey, that's what.' What they mean is they want channel one seventy six, that's the one has all the late-night blue movies.

So well OK that's most the sights of our town for you. Give you a feel of the place? What say we head out west now and go to Garland? It's a nice morning, so if you fancy we could go north after that and take in Milton Reservoir, then turn around south and east and go see

Nicodemus where the negro settlement is, then come on back here. How's that sound as an itinerary for you?

– Fifty-five miles an hour, in Kansas and most other states that's the top speed you can drive anywhere, even here out on the open highway. That's not so in England? So what speed can you do then there? Seventy miles an hour? Well I'll be darned. If we caught you doing that here, you'd have a fine something in the region of 300 dollars.

– In area I'd say Auburn County is around 900 square miles. To cover it I've got five Assistant Sheriffs, the clerical staff in the office, and up to ten Deputy Sheriffs I can call on anytime there's a need. The principle of voluntary Deputies is to involve the whole community in law enforcement: gives them the feeling it's part of their everyday lives.

The Sheriff's Department's the supreme law-enforcement agency in the whole county: and then towns the size of Bird or more, they have their own Police Departments within their area limits. Then as well as them, there's the State Highway Patrol: that operates mostly in the outlying areas. Sure sounds complicated at first don't it? But we all work together: mostly we all get along pretty good. Say you see that brown bird there with a yellow breast on its front, perched on that wire fence? That's a meadowlark, along with the sunflower it's Kansas's state symbol.

What was I telling you, oh yeah three different law-enforcement agencies. Anyone ever trying to roll them all up into one, that'd have so many objections against it from so many different people it'd just be like the Civil War breaking out all over again. You might not believe this but it's true all right, I was there and I heard it: a couple of years back a State Senator from Topeka, he gave a speech at a dinner down in Gardner City and he said bringing all the different law-enforcement agencies under one centralised control, that'd be the first step along the road to communism. Those were his very words. Another meadowlark look, on that post there: start counting them to see how many you'll see in a day, you'd be up to a thousand in an hour you would.

A cloud of white dust pluming behind it like smoke, the Chevvy rolled on along the line-straight prairie road.

– 'Sheriff', it's kind of quaint we still use that word over here in the United States: it came here from England. Your counties, they were known as 'Shires', and the official who was responsible for one, he was known as a 'Reeve'. So he was the 'Shire Reeve': like the 'Shire Reeve' of Nottingham who always got such a bad press in the kids' books, for trying to catch that felon Robin Hood.

– I run my force whatever way I choose within the present budget. I'm elected, then after four years if I want to go on I have to submit myself for re-election. I run on the Democratic ticket, but it's not the political thing that counts for much: the County Attorney's a Republican, but that makes no difference to us working together. Before I was Sheriff I was six years in the City Police Department, then before that I was in law enforcement in California. When I was at college I took my degree in political science, right now I'm taking a correspondence degree in sociology, and I hope to end up with a Bachelor's in Police Administration. The whole subject area's my life, I love it. And being here, Sheriff of Auburn County and living in a town like Bird, with a little farm a few miles out east my wife and I've invested in for when I retire, I can't think of a better life for a man than that, no way. Fancy a cup of coffee, what say we stop off at Mickey's Diner that's coming up here?

It was clean, quiet, and not busy. Four middle-aged farm workers, dusty in check shirts and overalls and with their hats on sat at a corner table. A chorus of greetings: 'Hi Jim. Hi how are you Joe? Hi there Eldon, Dave. How're you doing Jim? Fine just fine. Say this is a friend of mine from England. Oh hi there, hi.' A woman with two children having ice-cream. Two bikers in fringed black leather jackets, and a large fat overweight man bulging inside a colourful Hawaiian shirt. A thin tired looking woman of about 40 with dark red hair came to the table, wiping it clean mechanically and unnecessarily, and straightening the arrangement of the ketchup bottle and salt and pepper.

– Hi Carrie, two coffees and two doughnuts uh? Real quick.

Out on the highway again, driving, the day getting hotter as the sun climbed in the sky.

– I guess my family originally must've come over from Scandinavia. I had a Swedish grandfather, he was homesteading somewhere near the Colorado border: he'd bought title to a public tract of land and lived and farmed on it. On my mother's side I believe there's some English and some Irish. I'm not like a lot of folk, I've never had the interest to go much into the detail of it. Prefer the present I guess. I know my family on both sides was primarily how you might say of agricultural descent: I was the first one ever took up with anything like law enforcement. And I never wanted to do anything but that, not since from way back when I was in college. I was mostly brought up in California, but I'd been born in Kansas so I've always felt this is where my roots are. I was in with the Los Angeles Police Department going on 18 years, but when the chance came up to come here, I took it: didn't have to think about it. Felt like coming home. I reckon I'm here now for good.

Garland. Silent and soporific in the pulsing heat: a cluster of low wooden houses grouped round a crossing of two rutted roads. He took the Chevvy slowly past some frontages that seemed deserted: at one a hand let a held-aside curtain close at the window.

– A lot of folk living here are what we call transients, itinerants looking for summer work on the farms till harvest, gradually moving northwards up the country. Others are drop-outs, what used to be hippies, people on welfare, women stuck on their own with small kids when their husband's left them, drifters, all sorts. Now and again we do a drug bust: we never turn up anything big, but it kind of reminds them we're around keeping our eyes open.

They say in the old days it was a much bigger place than now, with a store and a school and a post office. Some of the older folk'll tell you they still remember when it was like that. See that house back there, more of a shack really, the one with the broken down gable? Supposed to be an ex-hooker from El Paso lives there, she came last fall. Guess so long as she stays ex we won't have to bother, everyone's got to live somewhere don't they? That place there, the one with all the kids' toys out front: before the present folk moved in, they had an illegal liquor still there.

The down side of life around these parts, Garland is. If you live here you got problems usually. OK move on shall we, OK?

At Milton Reservoir the wide two-mile-long stretch of blue water glittered and sparkled in the sun, with a light breeze rippling patches of waves across it. At places round its tree-lined edges cove-like beaches had been created, with mooring piers for small speedboats and sailing yachts. In the woods behind them were landscaped standings for camper vans and mobile homes, with screened-off red-roofed toilet and washing facilities. A thoughtfully planned, scrupulously tidy and well-kept recreation area, spaciously natural and attractive. The whole of it was visible from up on the road viaduct crossing one end of it.

– This is where folk come weekends or summer evenings, get themselves away from their worries and cares. Good place to bring the kids out to too. One thing we're not short of in America is room. Go down one of the access roads over the west side there – that's always providing you can find where an access road is – and once you get down to the water you could go a whole day and night if you wanted, and never see another single living person all the time you're there. Definitely unrecommended in the winter though: get yourself off the highway and into a snowdrift, they could be looking for you weeks and not find you.

God's own country this must be for sure. I don't think lots of us know how lucky we are you know, do we? Well how say we go on now down to Nicodemus?

A 16-mile loop of the road, following round the edge of the reservoir.

– It's not like it was in California, crime's no big problem in these parts. The most important aspect to the job I'd say is deterrence, patrolling, letting yourself be seen. So folks get to think you could come round the corner any day, just when they're least expecting it. Back there at Garland, someone goes out on patrol there two or three times a week irregularly. No one knows exactly when we're coming.

Makes folk think before they do something illegal and maybe decide not to instead.

Crime around here's not much: a few drugs and some drunk driving, and that's about it. Break-ins we just don't have at all. It's not like the big cities: a place like this everybody knows everybody, who they are and where they live, if they're kids whose kids they are, where they should be at what time and when, everything like that. Folks go out and leave their doors unlocked, park their vehicles and leave the keys in the ignition and know they'll still be there when they come back. Everyone trusts everyone, everyone's trustworthy. We don't have all that many strangers passing through, we're not on the route from one big place to another big place somewhere else. If anyone's seen around and no one knows who they are, everyone soon knows about it and gets to find out. Crime in Auburn County: I'll tell you, someone once asked me, she said 'In Bird, what do we need a Sheriff *for*?' The guy with me, Joe Liddle of the First National Bank he said to her 'Every place needs a Sheriff, else who else could we blame if something real bad happened?' He'd got it about right I guess.

I suppose I'd say one of the areas we're most occupied in is what's called 'domestics', you know family quarrels between husbands and wives. They can be a bit well kind of tricky sometimes, specially if it's on one of the farms out at the edge of town or some place of that sort. You get a call, often you don't even know who it's from, one of the persons involved, one of their kids, maybe a neighbour. All they tell you's there's trouble at so-and-so's place. So you go out there, and you've no way you can tell what it is you're going to get yourself into. All you know is it's probably a situation that's volatile: when you get there tempers could be on the boil, drugs or alcohol might come into it, violence could have happened already, or be on the point of being. So there you go, it's your job to walk in and find out – and calm it all down, even though you don't know what it is needs calming down. And who you are is an intruder: and not infrequently the intruder's the one they all turn on and ask you what's it to do with you? To some folk, even worse is you're a uniformed intruder, you're an authority person walking in on them. On top of that they might even have a gun there some place: concealed on their person, in that table drawer they're walking towards. You don't know, and they're not going to tell you: so you're doubly disadvantaged in the situation.

All you can do is the best you can: cool, calm, very nice and slow, no threats or force or nothing: let's take our time here OK? We'll all sit down: first you sit down, then you sit down, now me. You know sometimes you think about it when it's all over and you think 'Well it worked, and I don't know how it worked or why it worked, but it did. And I wonder what I'll do about it when the day comes that it doesn't?'

After domestics I suppose the next most frequent things is traffic stops. Those I'll tell you, I do not like, I do not like those one bit at all. A routine one: someone runs a traffic light and so you go after them, behind them, flashing your lights till they pull over. And this is the thing they're always drilling into us right through all our training: there's no such thing as a traffic stop that's routine. Yes it could be a forgetful old lady on her way to the library. Only remember, it just too might be the very last stop you're ever going to make in your life. Because it might not be the old lady: it could be a fleeing felon from out of another state you haven't got to hear about yet over your radio. And only a few inches in front of him, right there in his glove compartment, is the weapon he's going to use on you if he gets the idea his freedom's about to be in jeopardy.

It sure puts a strain on you, you know, always having to think like that. It used to be the law you had the right to fire your weapon at a person if he was in the act of committing a felony. But it's not that way no more: now you can only draw and fire if you've good cause to believe your life or that of some other person's is threatened. Otherwise no, you let the felon escape. Well, maybe that's how it should be. The idea of the use of what we call deadly force, that can sure keep you awake at night thinking about it. But me, well I've so far been one of the real lucky ones: I've never used my weapon against a person, not once in my whole life. A warning shot maybe a time or two, but no more than that. This is Nicodemus coming up ahead of us, over there see on the right.

It stood a couple of hundred yards away from the road, facing in the opposite direction almost as though turning its back. It had only fifty single-storey panel and clapboard houses standing in two parallel lines: some of them had peeling paint. Beyond them was a large wooden spired church, and next to it a small square of recently built red brick little bungalows with a low-roofed community hall.

The slowly moving white car churned up the dust on the unmade up road. One or two people standing in their open doors in the shade out of the midday sun waved, and the Sheriff waved back.

– The folks here, they're all good, all friendly, we don't hardly ever have trouble. It's an all-black settlement, somewhere around one hundred people that's all: most of them are descendants of negro slaves who came into Kansas after the time of the Civil War. They used to call them Exodusters. On the way going back we'll stop by the roadside Historical Marker board, that tells you something about the place. But it'll only give you a little though, if you want to know more there's some books you could look at in the library, ask Mrs Oberlin to set them to one side for you. Say look it's coming up 12.30, just a short drive around and about then I reckon back on our way to Bird again heh?

– A lot of folk you know, they don't care for all this flat prairie everywhere, miles of it every direction whichever way you look. Only to me though, it's gotten a real hold on me now: the great flat land, the big blue sky. It makes you feel content with things, no one's hustling you, you've all the time and space you want in the world to eat and sleep and breathe. Everything's easygoing and friendly towards you, and all the people, pretty near, are exactly the same way. I don't know, neighbourly: it's hard to put it into words. I reckon fairly soon you'll get to know a lot of folk, and find them friendly and glad to talk. Some of our business folk, those in public positions, professional people, stay at home wives . . . Heh, listen at me telling you, you'd think it was me going to try and write a book.

3 *Two Lives* (1)

Having it hard: Mildred Davies

Her house on North Washington Street was one of the largest and most imposing in town: two storeyed, balconied, gabled and crenellated, it was set back from the road on an artificial hillock, surrounded by shrubs and rockeries and trimly-edged and pebbled pathways. 'My lovely home' she'd called it, and with reason: every room and corridor and stairway was spacious, softly carpeted, with elegant furnishings and cool-coloured décor all carefully chosen to blend.

A short energetic woman of 60, she had a blonded bouffant hairstyle and a rapidly cascading voice.

– Having it hard like I did so long, I guess I get carried away when I have folks here, I want to make sure they see absolutely everything. I just love to tell every little detail about every little thing: where it comes from and how we got the idea for it and why it means so much to me. Henry says I'm like a schoolkid with excitement about it all the time, and he's right, that's exactly the way I feel. Now isn't that ridiculous in a grown woman my age?

Let's sit in here, this is my very special favourite room. Now would you like to sit on that settee or this one here: or would you sooner the smaller one, or one of the armchairs? The French escritoire there, would you sooner be nearer that so's you can put your things on it? And I'll sit here I think, no tell you what I'll sit here nearer to you. Is the temperature OK, not too warm or too cool for you? Because if it is and you'd like it adjusted either way, please do say so, all I have to do's press this little button right here on the console and it automatically resets. Now where'll I start?

Oh but there's one thing you must promise me first. And that's if I start rambling and jumping around from one thing to another when I'm talking, you won't hesitate, you'll tell me straight away I'm way off track and pull me back into line. Folks do say that to me you know, I guess it must be true, they say I just never never stop talking. And Henry, he's such a one for teasing me, the other day he said to me 'Mildred' he said, 'Mildred you talk so much, not only other folk stop listening to you after a while, but I think you stop listening yourself to what you're saying!' Isn't that a wicked thing to say?

OK so that's a deal right, if you think it's necessary you'll tell me to stop. And you're sure this room is comfortable enough for you? Well thank you I'm glad you like it, it does have a nice ambience to it doesn't it? It's what Henry and I call our togetherness room, this is where we spend most of our time when we're relaxing, because we think it has a homey feeling even though it's so large. Henry has his own room in the basement as well, his private den for his studio equipment and things that he likes to play around with even if he has retired. I guess once an architect always an architect, only now he does it just for the enjoyment of it, he is, he's always planning and designing and drawing, thinking up new schemes for this that and the other.

Only my gosh what a bonus that was to us when we first took on this house, it surely was. Because it's meant over the years we've been able to design it ourselves, in exactly the way we've wanted it, as we've gone on. Henry drew out all the plans for every single room you know: every little nook and corner and detail, right down to the last screw in the air conditioning distributor vents. And if it was something that was my province, say the sewing room or the canning room, he'd set me down and tell me to describe to him what I wanted: and then he'd do the floor plans and the models of the equipment, and I'd move them around – and oh the fun we've had playing around like that, I just can't tell you. And most of all my wonderful kitchen that I've shown you, you know? All I had to do was say what my ideas were and what I wanted, and Henry then got down to it on his drawing boards and eventually there it was. I mean I don't think you'd see another kitchen like it anywhere in the whole world, everything so cleverly built on gliders like it is. That's because Henry's both an architect and an engineer, a truly talented man. I'd say working together on making our home has been Henry's and my biggest bonding together if you know what I mean: every one of the bedrooms and bathrooms, the dining room, the entertaining rooms, the pool, the extensions, the full-length basement, the outbuildings for the camper and the automobiles – there's not one part of it we haven't planned and designed ourselves.

Now you see, isn't this just exactly what I was saying to you? And you didn't stop me! I go telling you on and on about our home and how we love it, and what I'm supposed to be doing is giving you some detail of my early life and how it was when I first set out. Now I'm going to start over, and this time I am, I'm really going to try very very hard for you to stop jack-rabbiting about all over the place from one thing to another.

OK let me tell you now. Now I think the best place to begin is with the store. Loretta's Ladieswear, in the middle of Main on the southside, I guess you've seen it already? Well now in 1905 my grandfather bought it: in those days it was called Vernon's Store, and it was a general store that sold dry goods one side of it and a few groceries on the other. And my mother went to work in it right from school when she was still a girl: and she stayed working in it right up until when she was 87 years old. She always used to tell me I'd been born right there behind the counter, in between the times she was attending to customers.

Naturally there was never anything else I was going to do but go work in the store myself: so after I'd graduated from High School at 18, I went to college for two years to study merchandising and retailing, and then I came back home and went straight into the family business. And at the age of 21 I married a young man whose name was Roger, who was the son of another well-known family like ours in town.

Well from here on in, now I am going to do my very best to tell it straight and without any bitterness. Roger and his family you see – and I guess to be honest about it my family too – everyone thought it was a very good match, and as a wedding present Roger and I were given the whole of the footwear side of the store, to build it up into a proper business and run it for ourselves. Only that wasn't what happened: in just a few years it was showing a loss not a profit, there were family disagreements, and so in the end Roger and I left town and went to Minnesota to try and start over, and Roger became a travelling shoe salesman.

Let's just say he couldn't behave himself: I'll put it that way. He did a bit too much drinking too, and there was a lot of trouble and unhappiness between us. By then we'd been married 15 years and I had three children: one 14, one 11 and one not long born. And so I didn't know what to do. My mother, she was getting very badly crippled with arthritis, she was in a wheelchair and remained in one the rest of her life: so I came home to see her, and I said if I came back to Bird could I work again with her in the store? My father had died a year or two before that and it seemed it'd be the best idea all round, so we talked about it some more and she said Yes.

I moved home with the children and I settled in. What happened next hadn't been at all part of the game plan though, oh no. It was that Roger came back to Bird too. He'd gotten himself a transfer with his company which meant from then on the territory he'd have to travel was just the state of Kansas. And he said he wanted us to start over for the sake of the children, and he was going to try real hard to make a proper home for us all as a family. I wanted to do what was best by the kids also: so with a lot of reservations, I agreed to it.

To tell the truth to you, I honestly don't know what other words to use for it and I'll just have to leave it to your imagination. But the fact was he still couldn't behave himself, and in a very short time he was back to his drinking and other ladies and so forth. I put up with it for a while, but it was truly very very humiliating, and in our own home town at that. And one day I said to myself 'Mildred' I said, 'You've taken enough or more than anyone should be expected to take,' and I took steps to obtain first a permanent separation and then a divorce.

By then I was 38 years of age, and what followed was to put it to you truthfully five really terrible years. I can truly say I'd never have imagined if anyone'd told me beforehand that that was how it was going to be, I just couldn't have imagined it. My mother was almost totally paralysed, my father had died, the store was run down and showing a loss in every single department: and on top of all that, although Roger had faithfully promised me money for the children's support, and was legally supposed to pay it, from the very moment we separated he completely disappeared and I never had from him not one single dime.

All I did have, though I say it myself, was the drive and energy that'd once been in my mother. So I set myself to work: and hard. There was many a night I was alone in that store until after midnight, doing the stock checking and the ordering and the accounts control, to save money on employing someone to come in from outside to do clerical work. I had to feed and clothe my children, which I did, and look after my mother, which I did. But I can tell you, if I'd known what that was going to be like, how tiring and sheer exhausting it was going to be doing all those things, on and on and on – well there were many times I thought I had done wrong, I should not have separated from my husband Roger: instead I should have accepted his other women and his drinking, in order that my children should have some sort of a decent standard of living.

All told I was on my own for a period of seven years. And by then naturally I thought my life had finished in a ruin. A divorced woman in her middle forties, with three children, working 12 or 14 hours a day for almost seven days a week . . . I couldn't see a view of any kind of a future except working hard and getting what satisfaction I could out of that. Because at least very slowly the store began to turn around and if not show a profit, then anyway stop running at a loss.

That was how it was with me at that point in my life. But they always say you never can tell don't they? And certainly and for sure, in my case they're absolutely right.

There was this man, you see, that I used to catch sight of sometimes as he walked on Main along past the store. I didn't know who he was, and he was quite a little older than me: and I knew nothing about him, except what I'd been told from time to time by other folk. He was an architectural engineer, I think that's the term for it, and he was married, he'd been born in Bird and married a girl from Bird and then many years before they'd gone away because he'd had some high-powered job some place with a big company. And now they'd come back to town, because his wife was dying from cancer, and she wanted to end her life back where she'd come from, and with her own folk around her. I never spoke to him or anything, because why would he come in a ladieswear store? But everyone spoke very highly about him, and said he was by all accounts a very kind man who tended devotedly to his wife's every need.

It was two years later that she then eventually died: and like everyone else, I took it for granted he'd leave town again after that, and go start up a new life for himself some place else. And now let me tell you: do you know, I've never been able to find out why he didn't? Any time I've ever asked him, Henry'll only say it was because he used to see me in the store through the window, and hoped one day he'd find enough courage to come inside and try to get to know me. Oh he's such a tease you know is Henry! I mean can you imagine what a man would want to behave that way for?

So well time went on and time went on: and after a while he took to dropping by now and again. Then one morning he invited me to go along to Dorothy's Cafe for a cup of coffee: and in a while after that, to have lunch with him there. This was all set out in the public view and I guess it set a few tongues wagging for sure. And then, I know this sounds extraordinary when I tell it, and believe me I more than anyone at the time found it extraordinary too: he suddenly said to me one day would I consider marrying him. Oh my gosh well I can tell you, I didn't know in Heaven's name what to say! I said to him 'Henry Davies' I said, 'Have you gone clean out of your mind?' He said No he had not. And I said 'Well Henry' I said, 'before I answer such a question, I think you and I had better set down, later on some place else, not in public like this in Dorothy's Cafe, and have a talk about things.' So we did in due course: and I said to him 'Henry, now I want you to understand this straight. I've no money, I've three children to bring up, and I work very hard and very long hours. And what's more too' I said, 'you better understand that I've been doing it so long it's my life and I like working hard. So if you've got any idea of finding a woman who's going to stop home and look after you, then I suggest you look around elsewhere and see if you can't find yourself someone better.'

And you know what he said, just sitting there and grinning at me that great big grin of his that he's got? He said he'd already had a good look around every place he could think of, and he'd considered a whole lot of different women: but it still came around to the only one he wanted was me! Now for Heaven's sake what do you think of that?

Well, so we dated a little while just like we were a young couple: and we talked to the children about it, and they met Henry and liked him and told us it would be a good idea. And so after some months we then got married, and next spring it will be just 15 years ago that we did. Henry had no children of his own, but he sure became a very fine stepfather to mine, and I think if you were to ask them all three of them would go along with that. So you see, there it was: from that day on my life turned right around, it truly did.

We bought this house, and like I've told you over the years we've worked on it together until we've got it as you see it now. We wanted it to become a show place: that was our intention and our ambition, and we're so happy and proud now that it has. We love showing it to people, and we love entertaining in it: we once had 80 people here for a party, and for my son's wedding buffet we had 150 people, and there was room for many many more had we wanted them. We have three floors and together they comprise 4,000 square feet above ground and 2,500 square feet below ground: a total of 6,500 square feet of interior, which is truly a big house isn't it?

So I guess that's it, that's about my story, and there's only one thing more I'm going to add. Which is that just this year I've sold up at the store, and I'm now retiring. I truly didn't in all my life ever think I'd give up working, because I thought I couldn't live without it: I always had it in my mind, you know, that I'd be like my ma and go on at least until I was 80, or better 90 if I could. But Henry's 15 years older than I am, and one of things he's always wanted to do, so much, is travel. One of our schemes is to take our big camper on a long long winter trip, three months or more maybe, and go down south to Louisiana and Georgia and Florida and places like that, which we've always wanted to see. And then next year we're planning on we might go to Europe: say to UK for a week, followed by another two weeks for Belgium and Germany and France. So long as we keep our health there's a whole list of places we want to go: and the idea of travel is really beginning to appeal to me, it truly is.

When Henry and I married, you know, taking on me and my children was a very big responsibility for a man who'd never had no family of his own. And I wasn't sure of it myself whether it'd work out: after all I'd already had one husband who'd left me, didn't I? So we talked about it and I made an offer to him: he didn't ask it of me, I just made it to him myself. I said 'Henry, if you'll stay in the buggy with me until all three of the children are grown up and educated, I promise you that then I'll quit work and we'll go travelling anywhere in the world you want to, and as often as you like.' He'd made his commitment to me: and that was mine to him in return, and now I'm keeping it. Oh but Henry's such a tease, you know what he said to me one time? He said 'Mind you don't work as long as your ma, Mildred, because once I get past the hundred mark I'm not reckoning on doing much save setting at home here and watching the TV.' Wasn't that a thing to say?

Having it easy: Carrie Jones

She lived in a small wooden house that had once been painted white, at the south end of Hoover Street just where it petered out into a gravel track. Some of the veranda staves were missing, and she had to bang with the flat of her hand on the edge of the fly screen door to pull it open. In her forties, red-haired and thin, she wore old jeans and a faded black sweatshirt, and old red sandals. The afternoon temperature at three o'clock was 99°. There was no breeze, and inside the low-ceilinged sitting room she pulled the curtains half across the window to shut out some of the sun.

– Come on in, yeah. I'm sorry, right now the air conditioning's not working but I'll put this fan in the middle of the floor here, it should be OK. Have a chair, do you smoke? You mind if I do? I fixed it I've split my shift at the diner: I came home at two, I have to be back again to do the rest of it at five.

She sat at the table and smoked cigarettes slowly and intently one after the other, sometimes stubbing them out in the ashtray before they were half-way used up. While she talked in a low monotone she picked reflectively from time to time at loose threads in the dark brown chenille tablecloth.

– Waitressing at Mickey's Diner, well I guess you can't say much about it. Long hours, seven through four one week, noon up until nine at night the next. It's a job: and I have to have a job to keep myself and my daughter. There's not much work at all around these parts, specially not for an unskilled woman: even more specially not full time. Compared to some I'm having it easy. I can live on what they pay me just about: not in luxury but I feed and clothe Joanne and keep up with the rent. It'd be wrong to complain. Say that's a dumb thing to say.

Only you know what? When I talk that way that's just how my ma used to talk. The very same words: 'It's wrong to complain.' Guess your parents leave their mark on you for ever don't they?

Some ways I'm like her, some ways not. Not my pa though, least I hope I'm not like him. He had what they call a drink problem: he and Ma were always rowing, that's the main memory I have of my childhood. That, and having it told me by my ma once I was a late and unintended addition to the family: I'd two sisters and a brother all much older, and she said if it hadn't been for me she wouldn't have stayed around with Pa so long, she'd have left him years before.

My sisters and brother, I've not seen much of them in years now. In fact two of them I don't even know where they are. We kind of got split up when I was around ten, when my ma died. There were old enough to look after themselves but I wasn't, so Pa sent me to live with an aunt in Tucson Arizona. She was a kind woman, she wasn't never unkind to me or nothing of that sort. But she was always moving around, living first one place then another and never stopping anywhere very long. When I grew up and started to look back and think about it, I guess she had men trouble. Another thing I look back on's how I never got much in the way of a school education. I would have liked that, gone to college and improved myself, you know?

I can't say what next happened to me then was anyone's fault but my own. But what did I do when I was 16, I fell in love with a guy down the street who was much older than me. And oh boy when I say fell, did I fall. He only needed look at me and my head swam and my knees turned to water, he could do anything with me he wanted. So I got pregnant and we got married. And you know what, I was such a kid I thought then that was it, we were going to be happy ever after. I guess that lasted all of three months, maybe even four.

By the time I had my daughter – that's my first one, Loraine – he was running up debts everywhere: and then after that he was just running. We were living in a rented apartment one of my aunt's friends was letting us have cheap. This was in Phoenix Arizona, and he said there was no work for him there, he'd go to Vegas and find something: then he'd send back the money for us to go join him. What he found or didn't find I've no idea: the only thing for sure was he didn't send no money, so I had to go out and get work. I took anything I could find: baby-sitting, cleaning people's homes for them, doing the dishes in cafes, everything. And all the time I was just thinking and hoping and praying – you know what? That the guy would come back to me. That was how crazy I was.

It went on that way almost two years or more. And then what happens is he comes walking right in through the door one day with a big smile on his face, and he tells me he's got everything together. He's living in Boulder City, he's got a job and a place for us to live, and all he wants is for him and me to get back together again and go up there with Loraine and start over. I did, I cried and I cried and I cried – just from sheer happiness can you believe? I thought there really were miracles that happened, after all: all you need do was go on believing in them, and one day they'd come true. Was I dumb. Oh boy. To me it was off we go to Boulder City into the sunset together for a new life.

You know, it's taken me years before I've finally come around to admitting this to myself, and I'm not very proud of it. I thought it was true like he said, that he loved me and missed me and couldn't live without me. But what really happened was that he'd found out about something. My aunt had died just a few months before, and she'd left me some money. Not much, just a few thousand dollars that's all: but he'd got to hear of it and jumped to the conclusion it was more. That was all he'd got in his mind, that I'd had an inheritance and he wanted a share of it, or better still all of it. I was still so crazy about him he knew he could sweet talk me into believing anything: and he did.

Course when we got to Boulder City there wasn't no job he had, and no place to live either: they'd both gone, that's if they'd ever existed. All he had was debts and a woman friend he spent most of his time with. When he found out about my aunt's money, how little it'd been and how it'd pretty near all gone anyway on paying off things I owed, he made no more pretence about loving me and not being able to live without me, he just went straight back to his woman and lived with her. So there it was: I was in another two room apartment again with Loraine, and picking up any work at all that I could get. He did come around once in a while when he needed a bit of money. And what did I do about it when he did? I gave him money.

It took an awful long time before at last I'd finally gotten over my crazy feeling for him: almost a year I guess or more. A thing that helped me was there was this half-Mexican guy used to come around, by the name of Pete. He was another one quite a lot older than me, but nice and I liked him. He told me right off he had a wife but he couldn't get a divorce, the reason was something Catholic or something like that. But he was kind to me and showed me some respect, he didn't rob me and he was good to Loraine. So finally one day when he asked me, I packed all of my things in one suitcase and all of Loraine's in another, and the three of us took off in an old truck we bought and went on up into Utah. Pete was handy with truck repairs and stuff like that, and so for a while we made out pretty good.

And then, you know well this is just the story of my life, what happens again is that he disappears. Like that: just gone. No warnings, no reasons given in advance, no quarrelling, nothing. One night he doesn't come home to the tent we have by the side of the truck, and that's all there is to it. The only thing I could think of was there'd been a girl I'd seen him talking to a couple of days before on the street corner. Up till then I'd not even known he knew anyone in whatever the place was we were in. He didn't see me seeing him talking to her, and I didn't say anything about it. But there he was, one day he was with me and the next one he wasn't, and I've never seen so much as his shadow ever since. Of course again I kept hoping for him to come back: but I hadn't loved him so much as I had Brad before him, so I guess the hurt wasn't so bad as that.

So back to the familiar routine, looking for work. That time I think least there was more variety: clerk in a store, waitressing, tending gas at a filling station, a hop at a drive-in movie house taking out the orders to the customers. Anything and everything like usual, just to get a wage. Loraine'd be around ten at that time I think, and me I was 26. I can tell you, my life sure seemed like it was taking a long long time to get any place. Kind of funny, I used to think it was: only you know, funny but without a lot of laughs.

God it's so hot isn't it, I never knew thinking and talking could make you feel so tired about it. I have to have a shower and be back at the diner for five o'clock and I'd like to rest first awhile. Could we stop there today and talk some more again next week?

– A friend loaned me this bigger fan, I guess it might be better than before. It gets so hot in here though during the daytime. I don't like to have the windows open because of all the mosquitoes and things that get in.

Last time I was telling you all kinds of excuses for myself wasn't I, specially about men? I've been thinking though since then, it's not all their fault, I guess I'm just pretty dumb altogether where men're concerned. I fall for them too easy, and I fall for them too hard: and then when I get hurt over it I say it's their fault. I've been thinking you know maybe my parents didn't bring me up tough enough. I sure should be able to look after myself by now, and that's why I'm giving it a try living by myself without a man for a while. When I was divorced from my second husband two years ago I thought of that song, what does it say? 'Carrie not the sort of girl you marry, that's me.' I guess there's something in that.

I didn't get that far before though did I no. OK let me tell you. My second husband was a guy I met around when I was 30. After Mexican Pete had left me I told myself I'd had enough of men. But it's always the same way, one starts being nice around me and I always after a while get to imagining things and being romantic. I didn't have much time for relationships that were very deep because I was usually always working so hard. But then one day at this laundromat where I was this guy comes in: and I'm helping him fold his shirts and stuff, and we get to talking. He tells me he's living on his own because his wife's taken off with their kids and left him for another guy. Well if there's one thing I'm good at it's providing the shoulder to cry on: only to be fair about it I think all or most he told me was true. Anyway one thing leads to another like it does, and we start regular dating, and then after a while he moves in with me and we live together. Same pattern as always only this time with a difference, it's him wants to marry me.

And so Mike and I got married. What do you know, he really has a job and everything, with an office equipment firm where he's a salesman. Then I got pregnant: and that was when I had Joanne. Well by that time Loraine's 15: and she and Mike, it was sad but they just didn't get along together, not one little bit. I mean I don't blame her, she'd had a tough time all around since she was a kid. I think she'd kind of liked it best when there was just her and me together: and now it was all going to be broken up with Mike and Joanne coming along and everything, and she didn't want to be there no more. She showed me some letters she'd had written to her by the parents of a friend of hers from school, back from the time when we were in Boulder City. They'd wrote that any time she wanted some place to go for a change or a break or something, there'd always be a place with them there. So she was moving out she said.

You can't blame her I guess. And me, well I was so set on making a new life for myself with Mike, and then Joanne: so I thought well maybe it was best to let her go, and then if things turned out right in a year or two I could offer her a stable home and ask her would she like to come back again. I didn't exactly what you might say try very hard to persuade her to stay. Instead I said OK, but let's keep on writing to each other and see how it goes. But while I on my side I did write to her, I had no replies and no word from her any more ever again. That'd be 12 years ago now, she'll be coming up to twenty-seven November this year. I'd like to hear from her, how she's making out and stuff: only now I don't suppose she knows where I am even.

Well from there it went on like it always does: me getting to be crazier and crazier about Mike, and him after a couple of years starting to be restless and looking around. I don't know, maybe men just don't want a woman being devoted and like a slave to them all the time. I think that they did's an idea I picked up from my ma when I was little That's sure how she was with Pa, for all their rowing and stuff: no matter how drunk he behaved in the home, he was always still the lord and master there, his word had to be obeyed.

Or maybe, I dunno, maybe it's the sex side of things I'm not good at. Every guy I've ever had, one thing's for sure, he's always after a while gone looking for it some place else. I just can't work it out somehow. You'd think after all the things have happened to me I'd see trouble coming way way ahead, but I never do, I just go on getting hurt and feeling all sorry for myself. What it comes down to is I'm a bad failure in life that's all.

So Mike and I, in the end we divorce too. There you go. That's the way it's always going to be for me I guess. You see all these pieces in women's magazines don't you: they're always giving it out this is the age of the liberated woman, raising women's consciousness, all that stuff? When I read it it makes me feel just I'm right out of date. If I was 20 and could start over, maybe I could try and you know shape my life differently. But I don't see how I can start now, not the way I am. I'm not ever going to have a proper hold on my life, I'm just going to be the one stands there and waits till she's told what to do.

And I don't like it either, that's the funny thing. Not waiting or being a waitress or any of that, not being a proper person in my own right. Know what I mean? At the diner I don't like it at all that the customers are my pay check and I have to be polite and friendly to them all. They can say what they like to me: but not me, I can't say what I like to them. You get the guy comes in with his buddies and they all order their hamburgers or pancakes or whatever, and they think that gives them a licence. 'Heh you're a pretty lady, how about coming out with me tonight, what time'll you be through?' But you can't spit in their eye, oh no: you've got to take it, play it back to them you think they're cute. Because if someone once says to the manager you haven't been what he thinks is polite and friendly enough to him, that's your job gone and you're finished, and there's ten more right behind you waiting to take over.

Anyway, like I told you: my ma said it's wrong to complain. I should look at it I'm having it easy, right? God this heat sure is something isn't it? You know sometimes I look at Joanne and I think well right now she's 12, how long'll it be before she ups and goes? When she's 16 like I was, 15 like Loraine? Seems like it's a pattern. But what to do about it, well that's something else again isn't it?

4 *Some of our business folk*

Gerry Meister, *Gover's Supermarket*

In his office at the end of the warehouse behind the store he flicked off the telephone switch to prevent interruptions. He sat at his desk with one foot up on it, hands clasped behind his head, talking quietly and swinging his swivel chair gently from side to side.

– I'm 25 so I guess that's how I came to be elected the Chamber of Commerce's President for this year, to kind of try and give the town a younger image. I don't suppose I can do a lot of damage in one year, so at the end of it, if they want to they can put back in someone more respectable again.

I'm manager and proprietor here, or should I say more accurately part-proprietor with my brother. It's a family business, founded by Lester Gover way back in I'm not sure exactly when, and I'm his grandson on my mother's side. She died when I was four, so it was our grandparents who brought me and my brother up: and as long as I can ever remember, that was always the idea, we were going to come into the business and take the supermarket over from Lester when he decided he'd had enough and wanted to retire.

When I graduated from High School I went to college in Baxter to study business management. I really only horsed around there, I wasn't greatly interested. All I wanted to do was get back here and start work. From 13 or 14 I'd spent darn near every Saturday working here and all through all the school vacations too, so I'd had plenty of experience and knew most of how it operated. Grandpa Lester he used to put me to work emptying the trash cans and sweeping the floors. He said 'That's so when anyone asks you how you started, you can tell them from down at the bottom.' He paid me only very small wages too: he said that way I'd learn what it was like if I was going to employ folk and not pay them enough, I'd have a taste of what it meant. Quite a character, Lester.

I don't think I regret it too much that I didn't consider anything else as a career. Except just the once while I was at Baxter, I never entertained anything else. Very briefly I had the idea I might try and do something different which was be an architect: I got into doing drawing and plans of things for my own amusement, and I remember talking about it one day with Henry Davies who lives on North Washington. But apart from math, there was nothing much else I was strong on and I don't think I'd have gotten through with it. A lot of training and a lot of hard work and books and studying, I don't think I was cut out for that. Oh yeah and once too I had the idea of being a veterinarian: that was because of a girl I was interested in at the time, that was what she was going to be.

Sometimes but not often I regret it a little I never had more of an education. But I'm happy enough in the business here and I've plans for expanding it. You see I'm lucky I guess: it's one of the drawbacks of Bird there's not a big future here for young people. If they want to get on after college they have to go some place else where there are opportunities. Not many folk have got a family business to step into like I did.

What else can I tell you? Well just a couple of years back I bought myself a little home of my own on Monroe south of Main. That's my chief interest outside of here. I'm redesigning and rebuilding the interior of it to get it the way I want it: a patio in back of it, a shower room downstairs, that kind of thing. I live on my own and I'm not married: I guess right around the time I've gotten the house exactly how I want it, some girl'll come along and we'll marry, and she'll have me alter it all around back again because that's how she wants it. I don't have no one in view at the moment though: I've friends but I like to keep myself loose, well for the time being. In around ten years maybe, something like that.

I've ambitions to try and develop the business into something like a small chain: say another branch in Deerfield which is 12 miles south of here, and perhaps another at Conway City 19 miles east. But nothing like East West Hardware, not on that scale: I like the feel of Gover's as a family business still, and I'd like to preserve that.

I'm happy living and working in Bird and this is my home town, I belong here: most folks know me and I know them, and I like it that it's that way. It's a good community to live in: if like I said, always providing you're one of the fortunate ones who can make a living out of it. It's got its drawbacks though, I guess all small communities have. There's not much here for kids, teenagers in particular: if they want entertainment, movies and discos and arcades and the rest, they have to go forty miles to Baxter. But in a kind of way that has its advantages for them: it's altogether bigger, a population ten times ours, around 20,000 or so. That means if they're having fun they're not so conspicuous about it. In Bird everyone knows you: they mayn't exactly be keeping an eye on you all the time, but whatever it is you're doing pretty soon everyone gets to hear about it.

And like other small places too I guess, it's a little conventional in its attitudes. There's a fairly strong code of behaviour for instance where morality's concerned: they frown on anything even a little out of line. Out at Garland for example there's some couples who for reasons of their own are living together but not married. That'd cause real shock waves here if people did it openly, and Garland gets talked about like it was some kind of Sin City. It isn't: I go there often to see friends and it's just a place like any other. Maybe it gives folk here a what do they call it, a vicarious thrill to think there's a place like that only seven miles away to the west along the highway.

One of the reasons, I think, is we have a higher proportion of older people live here. This is one thing I've never been able to figure out yet, you know? These older people, they were all younger people themselves once: and when they were, did the older generation to them think *they* were all wild and irresponsible? What age is it at, that all of a sudden you turn around and forget how you were yourself? I guess I'm coming up to it myself maybe. Stop by in ten years time, come and see me and see if I am.

Sandy Carlton, *Beautician*

A little over five feet tall, slender, with short cropped dark hair, almond-shaped brown eyes, small delicate hands, and a serious manner.

– I bought this beauty parlour five years back now, it's always been something I wanted, to have a business of my own. I'm 47 and I've three grown-up children: my eldest son is 27 and he's in Europe with one of the big oil companies there, then I've a daughter married and lives in Illinois, and my youngest daughter is at college training in business studies.

I've lived here in Bird since I bought this business, but I'm not from Kansas, I'm from Colorado. I was born and raised there, and went to High School in Denver. While I was in my Freshman year, that's like your first year at senior school when you're around 14 or 15, I started to do some modelling for Junior Miss type clothing at one of the big stores. I liked it, I was the right size and figure measurements and everything, so after I graduated from High School I went into it professionally. I married at 18, had my son when I was 20, then my daughter: and when I was 23 the marriage broke up and my husband went off and we divorced. I didn't have much of a tough time, in modelling you can choose assignments and hours that fits with homemaking and bringing up children, so it was OK.

After a couple of years or so I remarried. My second husband came from Clinton Bend here in Auburn County. We had a daughter, then that marriage broke up also. I was still doing modelling work, but when there was a vacancy in the local Sheriff's office I applied for that and became the Despatcher: that's the person who takes the telephone, handles calls and gives instructions via the radio to the men out on patrol. I liked that so much that I took training and became a full-time Deputy, qualified in weapons use and unarmed combat and the rest, as well as all the book knowledge you need.

I was the first woman in that part of the world ever, to go out on patrol on her own. The usual reactions of people when a Deputy Sheriff appeared who was a woman who was five foot one and weighing in at around a hundred pounds, as a rule it was to crack up with laughing. But as soon as they got the message I was for real and I wasn't laughing even if they were, then there wasn't any trouble. I never had a man fight me, or threaten to: if you look them straight in the eye and tell them you'll go right as far as is necessary, and you're trained to do it, that's all that's needed. You don't back down: if you tell someone you're going to take them in you take them in, and word pretty soon gets around afterwards about it and helps to build your reputation.

I guess sometimes my kids were a bit feared for my safety: now and again it'd come up and they'd say they were. I promised them the first time I was ever in a situation that scared me I'd quit. But one never did, whatever it was I always knew I could handle it. I guess though when I finally handed in my badge and put my capital into a quiet little business like this, they were happier. I'd had some knowledge of the basics of the beauty world from my modelling experience, and I did courses to bring me up to accepted professional standard.

You know, just visiting with you about it like this, do you know what? It brings all my old feelings back to me, it really does: how the time I was a Deputy was the best time I ever had in the whole of my life. In England do you have that show, the one about the two women detectives with the New York Police Department, what are they called Cagney and Lacey? Well now I'll tell you: that's just what it wasn't like. That's the most ridiculous television programme I've ever seen: kicking down doors, drawing their weapons at every opportunity, chasing people up and down stairs. I just can't watch it. Everything they ever do is what you're all the time trained not to do, and if you behaved that way you'd end up dead in five minutes flat. It's not the excitement and it's not the glamour or anything: it's just the feeling you're doing a good job and a necessary job, and one which makes you important. Only not self-important, you mustn't ever get that way about it or you're doing it wrong.

I guess I'm getting too old now to think about getting back into it: I can't consider it, not seriously. But I still keep myself fit and trim: I've recently started early morning jogging, and I keep my tan up with a turn on one of our sunbeds once in a while after we've closed up at night. I haven't thought much yet about the future, but I guess in time all the children will have children themselves. Age doesn't scare me, and I'll do my best to get all the enjoyment I can out of being a grandmother. One thing's for sure, I shan't marry again: twice is enough for anyone.

About the only other thing I'm certain of is in a few years' time I'll sell up here and go back to Colorado where there's mountains and scenery and things. Kansas can't compare with it, I loathe it: it's a big boring desert of miles of endless prairie. The truest thing I ever heard said about it was in one of the James Bond movies, I forget which one it was. But the villain had invented a laser machine which could wipe out just everything, so he said he was going to demonstrate its power to the world by obliterating Kansas. This other guy said to him there wouldn't be any point in that, no one would notice the difference. My sentiments exactly.

Percy Doberen, *Auctioneer*

– I'm going on into my fifties now, and my wife and me, we've lived in our little place out beyond the north side of town almost 30 years, so I guess it suits us. Wouldn't like to live no place else, before here we were around Topeka way but the folks there are more big city types, or think they are. Thing about Bird is, most of us we're not payroll people. We don't work for the big companies, everyone pushing in to the parking lot all together in the morning at the same time, then going home the end of the day the same time too. Here most folks you'll find work for theirselves: small farms, small businesses, individual operations where everyone stands on their own feet. Some folk like myself are into two or three different things to make their living by. We like it like that, and the result's you've got a good community spirit, everyone more or less at the same level. No one very poor and no one very rich: leaving out Harold Albert of course, he's the richest man there is. But you wouldn't know it, it don't make no difference to the way he lives, or to the way he treats people nor the way they treat him. Far as we're concerned and he's concerned, he's just another guy lives in Bird.

So what can I tell you Tony, what'd you like to know about? So long as it's not too libellous or slanderous, whichever's the correct word for it.

A small man with a weathered face and blue eyes and a baseball cap on the back of his head, he chewed on a toothpick while he talked. He wore an open-necked short-sleeved check shirt and leaned forward resting his bare forearms on his desk from time to time to emphasise his words.

– I went to High School in Lawrence, Kansas, then to college in Topeka which is where I met the lady who became my wife. She was training to be a teacher: me, I wasn't sure what I was doing except I wanted to finish up in business or accountancy or something of that sort, quiet and peaceful and just plodding along. So after college I went into a bank. It was quiet and peaceful OK, in fact it was too much that way. I reckon if I'd stayed there I'd have been an old old man by the time I was 25. Alva and me we weren't married then: she was teaching school in Topeka there, and then she was offered a good post in Baxter which is the big town you may know 40 miles north and west from here. But it was 200 miles or more from Topeka and that was a long way, it meant she'd have to move to live. I didn't like that idea and nor'd she: so I decided to make an honest woman of her and marry her and go along with her. It'd been my hope maybe I could stay in banking or something of that sort: meantime I started studying some, thinking maybe it'd be useful to know about things like the real estate business, oil land prices and so forth.

I spent a year or so bumming around and not getting anywhere much, then I got the chance with a man who was a cousin of sorts to go into partnership in auctioneering around here. I took it and we moved here from Baxter and we've been here from that day to this. We'd started a family and Alva wasn't working no more, so financially it became a little what you might call precarious, specially when my partner told me one day he wanted out. He was having some domestic difficulties and went to live some place else, up north west, Wyoming someplace I think. So here I was, kind of on the edge like that, trying to figure if I shouldn't find me some kind of a regular occupation which would give me security, or carry on and try to make it on my own. I'd hung my shingle up and I didn't want to take it down without making a fight of it. So that's what I did: and that wasn't easy neither, not with three children which we'd had come along by then. But Alva supported me in it, both in what you might call spiritual encouragement, and also now and again when she could by doing a little teaching here and there, filling in for someone who was temporarily off sick or that sort of thing.

Couldn't have done it without her: what we had was a real partnership. All these things you hear about these days, only just last week I was reading in the paper where it said in America today one in every two marriages ends in divorce. Well ours was the other kind, the one that didn't. A bit of give and take, sickness and in wealth, good times and the bad: that was always the way we both looked at it, and it brought its rewards. Three fine grown-up children, two grandchildren so far and another one on the way. We'd like it if they was all a bit nearer us, but we see them regular so that's OK.

I'm not rich but I make my living. No, correction, let me put it to you a different way. I make my living and I'm rich: not in money market terms but in the quality of my life that I have. Because I work for myself and strictly on a commission basis, therefore I don't have to maintain regular hours. If the weather's good and I feel like a day's hunting or fishing, Alva and I we just pack up a picnic and go on out to Milton Reservoir or somewhere in the shooting waggon. And we're answerable to no one but ourselves for where we go or how long we stay.

Pretty good life I'd say all round. Bird's a nice place with nice people live here, not like out at Garland where everyone's on welfare and they have hookers and drug problems and all stuff like that. We're not what you might call great socialisers, me and Alva, don't do a lot of entertaining: but we got friends if we want them, neighbours who don't become intruders let's say.

You're welcome. Been a pleasure visiting with you Tony.

Fran Webber, *Art and stuff*

A small plump ebullient woman of 40 with curly brown hair, wearing bright red trousers and a tartan-patterned blouse with a high-necked frill.

– My I felt so awful about it afterwards, I felt you must think I was such a big dumb schnook you couldn't believe! I told my friend Dolly about it when I saw her in Dorothy's next day, and she said 'Oh Fran you didn't really say that to him afterwards, not really did you? But Fran that's the English sense of humour, he knows there aren't any lighthouses in Kansas you mutton head, he was saying it for a joke!' I wanted to run out the cafe right then and there and call you up and explain and apologise, I felt so bad about it I can't tell you. Well I'm glad we've got it straight now though. And next time if you see me looking at you kind of funny when you say a thing you mean as a joke, remember I need time to think some first, will you?

Now, to tell you about myself, well the first thing is I'm a local girl and always have been. Well isn't that ridiculous, what's the matter with me? The first thing I say, and it's not true. I was an army child: I was born in Wisconsin, and I lived in Iowa and Minnesota and Oklahoma and several other places too. Around the time I was born my mom became very ill and went into a hospital for people with nervous disorders, I guess you'd call it a mental hospital, and she was never afterwards well enough to live outside it ever again. She and my dad had a divorce, then he remarried when I was four: I was his only child and I don't remember much about my stepmother except that she already had a child of her own when Dad married her. Then he died, my dad: I don't know what of and he was pretty young I guess, and my stepmother gave me to an aunt and uncle of his to bring me up.

They lived here in Bird, so that was when I came here, when I was five or six. They didn't treat me bad or anything, and I don't know why it was but I remember I was always very lonely as a kid. I always thought people were talking about me you know? My aunt and uncle, they'd no other kids, and it wasn't covered up from me or anyone else I wasn't really their daughter. I think that's right, I think that's how it should be: but kids are funny people, and I think I thought around the time it was happening that it should be covered up and I'd be happier if people didn't know.

I was treated fine at school, all the teachers kind and sympathetic to me and all that. When I got upset about something and cried about it like kids do, they'd always say 'Poor Fran' and put their arms round me. I know it must sound kind of a funny thing to say, but I always felt they should have been tougher with me instead of like they were. I felt I had a label round my neck that said 'Poor Fran' on it, and I wanted to be ordinary and like the other kids instead.

I didn't graduate from High School, I left the year before, when I was 17. I think I had some kind of a crazy notion that I wanted to be out in the world, independent and earning a living and being a proper person in my own right, though I don't think I could have told you if you asked me what I meant by that. I went to work at Deerfield 12 miles south of here, at a home for old people as what you'd call a sort of live-in general hand. It sure wasn't the greatest job in the world and I was even more unhappy and lonely. I suppose that's why I then did something even crazier, which was to get married and become pregnant and have a child. The boy I married wasn't much older than me.

By the time I was aged 25 I'd had four children. Two of them died at a very young age, and two of them are still alive now and with me. I guess it was no surprise the marriage didn't work out: it wasn't my fault and it wasn't his, and we'd both been very young when we married. He was an agricultural machinery maintenance worker which took him away a lot of times: so I took to living with my kids at my parents' home or rather my aunt and uncle's, who I regarded as my parents.

He and I, we hadn't had fights or anything. One day he said I could have the children, but he wanted out, and so that's how it was and we divorced. Everyone was very kind to me: there was still a lot of that 'Poor Fran' business, but I guess because I was older it didn't bug me so much. It's kind of a strange thing to have to say, but the only place there was any hostility to me over the divorce was at the church I went to. It wasn't the Catholic one, where because of their beliefs you'd expect it, but one of the others. I taught Sunday School there: and some of the older members of the congregation got together and said it wasn't right a divorced person should, and so I was asked to resign. I've stayed pretty bitter about that ever since and I've never again from that day on set foot inside that or any other church. I don't reckon people who call themselves Christians had a lot of Christian feelings towards me, I really don't.

I had a few years which were hard and depressing for me with the kids growing up, but then something nice happened and I met the man who's now my second husband. He'd been divorced himself but he didn't have children, and he'd come to join his brother who had a farm at Hammond, just north of here. He used to come into town to eat which is how I met him one day. When he suggested we got married I was a bit scared because we'd not known each other too long: and all those feelings I was telling you about, about being lonely and a loner, I was having those come back pretty strong and thinking that was how it was always going to be for me.

But that was 12 years ago now, and things have worked out pretty good. He gets on with my son and my daughter, and they liked him so things are OK there, in fact things have worked out fine for all of us.

Then just last year some premises came empty up near the east end of Main, and Lloyd and I talked it over and we decided we'd invest in a little business venture of our own. He's still with his brother on the farm, but with the kids growing up and maybe in a year or two both of them going to college, it's something for me to put my energies into and see if I can't build it up. It took us a while to decide just what sort of a business exactly: we looked around the town to see what there wasn't and what might be something there was a need for, and we went to Baxter and Conway City both, to look at the kind of small individually-run type stores there were there.

What we finally came up on is our shop that we have here now which sells art and stuff. Picture reproductions, prints for people to have on their walls, ceramics and novelties suitable for gifts: and also if you like painting yourself, which a lot of people do these days, we keep a good stock of different kinds of paints and brushes and papers and all the rest of the other things you need. I've a friend lives out at Garland, Anne Wheater who's a very good painter herself, almost up to professional standard, and I have one or two of her originals for sale. I don't do a lot of that kind of thing yet but I'm hoping to build up on it.

This is something where Bird people are very good, they come and buy things from me whenever they possibly can, say when they want to give a gift to someone. Or they'll buy painting materials for their kids, or ask me do I have suitable art books which I don't, not yet at least. It all kind of makes you feel people want to help you and support you and they want you to do well. I don't think it's too much of a feeling either of 'Poor Fran' any more either. Because it suren't needn't be, I'm a grown-up lady standing on my own feet now.

Betty Holt, *Retail Liquor Store*

A small thin woman in her thirties, with glasses and long fair hair: she talked slowly and sadly, in a low quiet voice.

– I'm not a person does a lot of talking, specially about myself these days, but I'll do my best for you only you have to forgive me if I'm nervous. There's not a lot about me to say.

The first thing I ought to start with I guess is that I have a ten-year-old son, and I live with my ma on North Truman. You'd think really that when I also tell you I've been divorced two times I must be some kind of a what's called a *femme fatale* or something, but I'm not. I'm just an ordinary girl who's not made a great success out of her life that's all.

I was born at a place in Orlando County, that's the next county north and west of here. I was an only child and my pa died when I was very young, so my ma came with me here to Bird to live because she had relatives here. After I graduated from High School at eighteen I went to Baxter University and did two years of general courses: but college was a lot harder than High School, book work didn't come easy to me there. I had the idea to be a home economics teacher but I couldn't get the necessary grades. The only thing college did do for me though was it helped me grow up: my ma had always been very protective and so I learned how to get along on my own, budget my money and things like that.

I was a serious girl, not one for dances or having fun a lot, and very shy. Then I met a boy and it's the usual story I guess, I decided I wasn't going to do anything brilliant at college and I'd sooner be married instead. So I got married, and it turned out so fast it wasn't going to work out you wouldn't believe. I mean in like only a few months I knew it and so did he: and it was something less than two years before it was all over and'd ended in divorce. I didn't have enough money to even consider going back to college and starting over: instead I went to work as a clerk in a store at Deerfield.

You have to put me down as an impetuous person, because it wasn't long before a boy there started dating me, and then there I was into marriage again. This time I did better, it lasted 11 years, and I had my son Emerson who's now ten years of age and coming up going to High School. My second husband, I did really think he was the right guy for me and that my life was going to look up. But it didn't, at least not as far as the personal level was concerned unfortunately.

Nobody who thinks divorce is easy can have gone through it. It's always very very hard, and it hurts you a lot because you've been such a failure. And I mean to have it happen to you two times, I think that's terrible. I start to think sometimes there must really be something the matter with me. But I've made my son the centre of my life, to look after him and to bring him up. I guess it's going to mean heartbreak ahead when he grows up and goes to college and maybe gets married himself, but I'm not thinking too far ahead about that, I'm just enjoying him while I have him. The way I kind of look at it he's my responsibility until he's 18 and graduated, but that don't mean he's then got to be responsible for me because it's his own life he's got to lead. It would be nice though if we could still be friends together, but we'll have to wait and see.

Apart from Emerson I don't have much else interest in life. The store's open until nine o'clock of an evening so I'm pretty tired at the end of the day. Once in a while my Ma comes down and looks after it for a morning while I take a break and go to Baxter or Conway City and take a look around. There's not much in the stores there I can afford to buy, but I sure do enjoy looking at all the pretty dresses and things and maybe treating myself to an ice-cream.

We bought into this business a few years back now, my ma and me. It's not a greatly interesting thing because you're selling the same items over and over, and you have very strict regulations that control you. Kansas as you'll know is a dry state, you can't have alcohol to drink with a meal in a public restaurant, you can't take a bottle of wine with you if you want to go on a picnic, you can't have an open bottle or beer can in your automobile. People can come in and buy liquor for consumption in their own homes that's all. In a small town like this there's quite a few people who're hypocritical about it, they don't want people even to know they buy liquor so they go some place else like Baxter and buy it there. No one under the age of 21 can buy alcohol either, and if like me you have a liquor store then it's your responsibility as proprietor to make sure no one does, otherwise you'll lose your licence and they'll close you down.

The side of it I like, well which makes me smile a bit, is one or two of the folk who come in kind of regular. There's one guy, he's in most every day, quite elderly: I don't know his name because he never says anything at all except just the one word 'Bourbon'. He takes his money out of his pocket like that and puts it down in front of me and says 'Bourbon'. So I give him his Bourbon in a brown paper sack and I take the money and he goes straight on out again. Some days what he's given me is not enough, other days it's over the top. But he never waits to find out. I reckon it works out about even. Then there's another guy, he's always snockered whatever time of day it is, and he comes in every day of the week and has a half a pint of Scotch. Once or twice I've said to him why doesn't he buy the larger bottle, the pint size, because that way he gets more for his money. He tells me no, the doctor's said to him he must control his drinking, so buying it the way he does is controlling it. He's another nice old guy, never gives me no trouble.

Nor does anyone give me any trouble, not ever really. That's the nice thing about a town like Bird, you don't get folk who are passing through very much, so you don't have to worry about holdups or that sort of thing. I don't like it when it's dark being in the store on my own of an evening, you read these stories in the newspapers and sometimes you get to feel kind of scary. But you always know somewhere not far away there's a police patrol car on the look out: sometimes one of them sets for a while on the corner opposite, and gives me a signal by flashing his lights to let me know he's there. So I don't really ever get to feel somebody's going to come in and rob me or try and kidnap me or something like that. I mean I'm not saying I'd be bodily any great prize for anyone, but you never know there might not be someone who had something on his mind that I wasn't willing to fulfil.

Well if you'd asked me you know, I'd never have thought I'd have had that much to say about things, I really wouldn't. I've surprised myself, I sure have.

Larry Manders, *East West Hardware*

A small bald-headed man with wire-frame spectacles and a nervous manner. His office was a tiny alcove with a low ceiling behind a screen at the far end of the store: a desk and a telephone, some shelving crammed with files and piles of papers, and while he talked he kept frowning fretfully at the disarray.

– Well I'll tell ya, so far things ain't turned out too good: with my wife I've been here three years this fall and it's not been how we hoped it would at all. We come from North Dakota, least that's where we were before we were here: but my family, well we come from Oregon and my wife, she was born in Washington State. We have one child, my wife's from her first marriage, a boy who's 16 and he's at the High School here and doing pretty good. He likes it and he's got friends, so for his sake we want it to work out. But the way it's looking right now, well I have to say I don't know. Business is bad because the farm economy's bad. And when the farm economy's bad, people like us we can't do nothing to affect it, so we just have to set and see.

It's a franchise, and you buy it like you would a franchise for anything else. There's a chain of stores right across this state and the next one: and depending on the size of the business and the turnover, you can buy according to how much money you got plus how much the company will lend you. They supply you with the store and the site and the fittings and the stock and everything else: then you reorder your stock according as to how much you want and think you can sell, but you have to order it from the company and nowhere else, because they bulk purchase buy. You pay them back out of your profits to pay off the loan they gave you less your deposit: and that way you reckon say in ten years or about that you'll have recouped your original investment and start showing your profit to yourself.

That's the theory of it, that's what their brochures tell you when you're considering being a franchise. I have a brother-in-law and he has a franchise in a different kind of operation where he is, which is Denver Colorado. Now in his case he's doing pretty good, paying off his loan without any trouble. So naturally when you hear that, you wonder if you shouldn't ought to have given it more thought yourself, and maybe gone into that particular line instead of the one you chose. He's in perishable foodstuffs, and that always seemed kind of risky to me. I looked at it if you'd got a trashcan for example on your shelf, it wasn't going to matter too much whether you sold it this month or this year, there was no way it was going to deteriorate its value. Guess what I didn't sufficiently take account of was there was going to be five six other stores in Bird also selling trashcans, and maybe four of them at a less price because they've got so many other kinds of goods they're selling too, to make their profit on. Sometimes you get to wondering 'Heh what's going on here? Are these folk into something between themselves to try and close me out?' You know, like maybe they don't like a stranger coming in to their town.

And my wife, she notices things that happen too. Everyone told us what a friendly place it is, but we've not found it that, least not so far. For instance there's all these organisations the ladies of the town have, what they call the sororities which is a word means sisterhoods: Phi Beta Kappa, Alpha Gamma Omega and all those other fancy Greek names they give them: or PEO, that's another one. Well all of them, you get to be a member by invitation see, someone says 'Come along to one of our evenings, we'd like to have you join us.' Only my wife – she's the clerk on the till out in the store there, so you ask her this yourself if you don't believe me – I don't think once in three years has anyone said that to her yet.

We're neither of us church-going people, so maybe that has something to do with it. But I don't think so. Most of the townsfolk don't go to one church or another. Those who do make a lot of noise about it, but they're not a majority. And like most everyone else around here I'm a Republican, so that can't be the cause of it either. Just something about Kansas people generally I guess, they don't take to strangers.

Don't get me wrong though, I'm not saying there's ever been anyone downright rude or hostile or anything of that sort. The Chief of Police gave me a ticket last year for running that red stop light there on Main. He was in the right and I was in the wrong, so I don't claim he was harassing me or anything: but I've no criminal record else. Just don't belong in Bird, I guess.

5 *Stay at home wives*

Nicki Russburg, 621 North Lincoln

She sat on the floor in a pink track-suit with a red cord belt, her elbow on the dark blue velvet upholstery of the four-seater settee, propping her head on her hand. A long way down the room the big ceiling fan revolved slowly and silently, gently stirring the air.

– Oh I'd say I was pretty ordinary I guess, average, a typical American homemaker, 25 going on 30, who looks after her husband, has two small kids, keeps a nice home and is happy at it. Fairly good-looking: I don't think it's wrong to say that, anyway Jack's always telling me I am. Not rich, but getting that way. I don't know that I can say much else, it's not easy to describe yourself. Not much different from lots of other young American wives.

In my life my first priority's my husband and my kids, as it should be. Jack and I met at High School here, both our parents live here: after I graduated I went to college for a while with the idea of studying to be a nurse, and Jack was going to study law and then go on and join his uncle's law firm in Bakersfield. We didn't like being separated so we decided to get married, which we did, and then lived with Jack's mother's sister while he went on with his studies. I took a job as a receptionist at another law firm near there: we didn't have a home of our own, but we were happy because being together was the most important thing there was for us.

In time Jack joined his uncle's firm as junior partner. He's always been a very hard working person and he's done very well. A few years back we'd saved enough money to buy ourselves this nice home north of Main, with some help towards it from our parents. And we now have our two lovely children, Dana's who's four and William two years three months. So there you are that's it I guess, that's us: like I said, ordinary.

To be a homemaker, I think it's the most fulfilling thing there can be in a woman's life. You hear of problems and worries other people have and you get very thankful, least I do, that so far nothing very serious or disturbing's happened to you. There's always the possibility, because you don't know what's around the next corner, so I think you should enjoy what you have while you have it and be thankful for the position you're in. Does that make me sound some ways a sort of superficial person? I hope it doesn't because I don't think I am: I'm more a sort of person who knows what she wants, and when she's got it is grateful for the opportunities and happiness.

Marriage and divorce that you hear so much about, I mean everyone seems to do it, sometimes I think even in a small place like this almost everyone's had two marriages, to hear them talk. I can only truthfully say Jack and I seem to be ideally suited to each other: we look at things the same way, we never have quarrels or anything. He leaves home every morning and drives the fifty miles to Bakersfield, when he comes home at the end of the day around seven he's not a person who wants to go out again, he likes to eat the meal I've cooked for him, play with the kids a little, and then settles down for the evening with a couple of beers in front of the TV. He likes that and I like it that he likes it, and to me that's what happiness is.

I think it makes me what's called a truly liberated woman. Not in the way those crazy people you hear about mean in burning their bras and all that sort of thing, that's not liberation. The way I mean it is I'm not like my mother who all the times acts like she's someone not as good as her husband. All I've ever had from her all my life when I've asked her her opinion of something is 'I agree with your father.' Jack and I, we talk on every subject under the sun either when we're on our own at home or if we go out to friends' places for an evening: and my opinion's as good as his, and is listened to. I sometimes don't think my mother ever had a life of her own. My father doesn't help around the house, and he never did at any time, not that I can remember. But Saturdays and Sundays Jack takes his full share of the domestic chores: he does cleaning and cooking, baths the kids, washing dishes, everything.

I guess the only one thing I'm at all unhappy about in my life is our money. Or maybe unhappy's not the word, now and again uneasy would be more the right thing to say. I do sometimes frankly think that it limits us in the friendships we have. Our closest friends of anywhere near our own age are John and Magda Stone, he's an attorney with his office on Main, I don't know if you've met him yet. He and Jack have a lot in common to talk about naturally, both of them being in law: and John's another one who's always worked hard and done well. We both have our nice homes and cars and pools and camper homes and boats and so on, and sometimes we take vacations together like in Florida one time or the year before last in Hawaii. What I'm saying is that financial-wise, we're on about the same level. But most of the other young women my age, and a lot of them are people I went to school with here in Bird, well their husbands maybe haven't got on quite so far yet. I don't mean we're any better than they are, what I'm exactly saying is just that, that we're not.

But to be honest about it, I do think some of them are a little bit jealous or perhaps I ought to say envious. I've got a lot of very nice clothes Jack's bought me, and some good jewellery: and I do have to say that I feel bad about wearing a lot of the things I've got, well here in Bird I do. Once in a while we leave the kids with their grandparents and we take off for a weekend in Chicago or Las Vegas or someplace: I like the good life and the bright lights, and I like putting on beautiful things. And Jack likes me to. I mean it was his work that bought them for me. But I can't dress like that or behave like that in Bird too often, because people wouldn't like it, you've always got to behave like you're a small town girl the same as everyone else. Which I am of course, and I do want to stay well liked in the community. I don't want to move away from here, this is my home town and I'm happy with it.

I guess that's my only problem, nothing else. With the kids you don't start worrying till they're older, and already we've provided them with a financially secure base for their future, education wise and health wise and everything else. So all round, I guess that's me for you: happy, ordinary, fortunate, secure. Yeah.

Karen Ostler, 14 South Jefferson

Thin, dark haired, blue eyed, in frayed jeans and a sleeveless navy woollen sweater, she sat upright in a rocking chair, keeping her feet firmly on the floor to prevent it moving.

– I'm 28, and the most important thing in my life is my religion. I am a Christian, I go every Sunday without fail with my husband and children to the First Church of Christ on Harding Street and we take an active part in church worship. We also pray together every evening, to thank God for the blessings we have. We may not have very much money, our home is simply furnished as you can see: but we have our home and our happy family based on the firm foundation of our Christian marriage, and so long as you have that then it's my opinion that other things will follow if God wishes you to have them. If they don't, then that's God's will also and he will give you your happiness in other ways.

I have two children, my son James who is nine and my daughter Ruth who is five. My husband's name is Andrew, and we have been married for three years. My first marriage ended in divorce, which is something I regret very much because as a Christian I don't believe in divorce, I believe that it's sinful. I've no objection at all to talking about it because my mind is very clear now about the subject, but at the time when it happened it was a very distressful situation. There are still times when I wonder if I ought not to have remained in my marriage with my first husband Blake. But I think if God had intended that to happen there would have been some kind of sign to me, rather than what actually happened which was a sign to go in the opposite direction.

I've lived in Bird all my life, I was born and raised on a small farm a little way out of town south and west. I was the eldest of three girls. Pa died when I was aged 15 and at school: he was a deeply religious man and he'd always wanted that I should attend theological college, and had provided in his will for me to. So after I graduated I went to the College of Mary and John in south east Kansas, and it was while I was there that I met Blake who was studying to be ordained. After knowing each other for more than one year we married, but shortly after that

Blake began to be ill with a form of mental illness, and for some months he was hospitalised. This interfered with his study programme and we'd little money, so after talking about it with my mother we came to live with her here. Blake took a series of casual jobs but he still suffered greatly with his illness: he had both drug treatment and electrical treatment, and he had periods when he seemed in normal good health, but other times when he was severely depressed. I did what work I could, but by that time my son James had been born so I was handicapped in that respect. For a while it seemed Blake had hope of recovering sufficiently to go back to college, which is what we both hoped.

I have to accept, I guess, that that wasn't part of God's plan. Blake didn't get better, he got worse and worse. He was morbid and he was violent to me personally and he started saying things like all his troubles were my fault, we'd be better off if we were all dead and things like that. He had a gun in the house and ammunition, and I became very frightened of what he might do to me personally, and especially to the children. He never offered them any violence, but he did talk an awful lot about ending all our lives. He was very sick in his mind. It seemed to me it was my Christian duty to stay with him and if necessary accept a certain amount of the physical violence he inflicted on me: but I did have to have regard for the children. At that time we had a small temporary home in a house we rented on South Garfield Street, but I was so frightened that one day when he wasn't there I took the children to my mother's home, and had a court order made that he wasn't to come there.

I went to see the minister of our church, and he gave me counselling. He pressed me to accept that divorce would be in God's eyes a lesser sin than endangering the lives of the children. And many members of our church too, they gave me their love and made me feel their arms were around me. So at last in the end with their help, and through prayer, I found the strength from God to take divorce proceedings. Which I did, and so my first marriage came to an end four years ago. Blake has been to some degree permanently in hospital since that time: but I sometimes wonder how I'd feel if I heard he'd completely recovered and was able to live a proper life again without endangering people. I ask myself if I'd feel I should have stayed with him until that came about, you know whether it was a test God had set for me and that I'd failed it.

But then I think of the great happiness I've found in my second marriage and the closeness with Andrew that's come into being between him and my children, and the religious bond we all four have as a family unit. I feel God's saying to me that no, this isn't wrong, he's giving me a second chance of happiness and showing his understanding and kindness.

Everyone in our church, everyone I know in Bird and have known since I was a child, they've all shown me their love and understanding, and no one's ever said to me one word of reproof. I do find that a very lovely thing that people are like that, just as I'm sure for example the three girls at the High School did. To know that your place in the community's secure is a great blessing and source of strength: and if you can be secure in your faith too I don't think there's anything much more that you can want in life. I thank God every day for it.

Irene Finney, 110 South Washington

– Hi, welcome, come right in. You wanna know what a goofball I am? Let me tell you where I was ten minutes ago, Dorothy's cafe that's where. I'm having a cup of coffee with Fran Webber and Enid Osterman, and Fran's saying she's been talking with you, and I say 'I'm going to talk with him too' and Fran says when am I, and I say 'Oh . . .' and then I look at my watch and I holler 'Oh my God, now!' So I just made it back about one minute before you got here. I didn't get to finish my coffee so I'm making more, you'd like some?

Small, energetic, big pink-framed glasses, short brown curly hair. One wall of the room had a great arch of a rainbow curving over it, red, orange, yellow, green, blue, painted on a light grey ground. She sat on the settee, sipping at her coffee mug and lighting up a cigarette.

– That, oh I did it a few months back to amuse the kids. We'd been last year to see their grandma in Colorado Springs and she took them to the movie of *The Wizard of Oz*. When she found out they'd never even heard of it, and they didn't know it was supposed to be Kansas it happened in, *and* we hadn't taught them to sing 'Somewhere Over the

Rainbow' either – well that really settled it for her, then she *knew* Bart and I weren't bringing them up right, just like she'd thought all along. So at least now I tell her well I've painted a rainbow on the wall for them and we all live underneath it, and I keep telling them if they look down behind that chair there at the end of it, one day they'll find a pot of gold. So I tell her next time she comes to stay with us, not to forget to bring it else they'll be disappointed.

Well I guess you don't want to hear about my ma though. I could talk to you all day about her, she's my Number One problem in life just now. You know what she does? This is a recent thing: she doesn't sleep too good since Pa died, so she calls up on the 'phone for a chat because she's feeling lonely. That's what I told her to do, I said 'Any time you're feeling down Ma': so she does. Only I didn't mean at five o'clock in the morning. And you know what she says? When the 'phone goes I know it's her, I mean who else'll call us up at five in the morning? So when I answer, I say 'Hello Ma.' And she says 'Oh Irene, you can't sleep too huh?' I say 'Yes Ma, I can sleep Ma, and I was sleeping Ma.' Only that's not what she wants to hear, so she says 'No I couldn't sleep either.'

Look, now I promise, that's it, no more about my mother, finish. Do other people have the same problem with their mothers? No don't answer that, no more about mothers, not mine or anybody else's. End of mothers: end.

Well now me, I've been thinking about it, about what to say. Did you ever see a movie called I think it was *The Stepford Wives*? All the men in this little town, they'd found a way of recycling their womenfolk turning them into like obedient little dolls who dressed smart and looked perfect and hadn't any minds of their own. The other day, Friday, I was in Gover's and there was about six of us there all getting our provisions for the week. And I suddenly thought 'Oh my God, we're just like those Stepford Wives.' Only not as good-looking. Least I thought maybe we'd look that way to an outsider, even if we're not. I mean what do we do all day? We look after our homes and our families, two mornings a week we're all girls together in Dorothy's, we join our sororities, we bake cakes and make cookies, we have our charity activities, at weekends we go out to the Reservoir. But what do we *do*? We follow a pattern, we do what everyone else does. And that's our life.

I mean don't get me wrong, I'm not saying I'm unhappy with it or anything. But then I think sometimes well maybe I should be unhappy with it. I remember an English teacher when I was a senior at High School, he read us a passage in class once, I think was from Tolstoy's *War and Peace*. I don't exactly recall it word for word, but it was something about every individual had in them something that was different from every other individual. Only you know if you said to me now 'So Irene OK what's individually different about you?' I'd have to tell you I didn't know, I couldn't come up with any real answer. I mean no way: and that's a kind of scary thing to think, you know?

My husband, well he's got something outside of himself, he's got his job. He's in farm insurance with a company in Baxter: each day he goes to his office, he goes out and meets people, he likes what he's doing, least he says he does and he seems a happy enough person. My kids, they go to school, one at Junior High the other at High. They have friends, activities, sports, my daughter plays band. You know what I think I am? I think I'm a kind of background for their lives, the person who runs the home and makes sure it's here for them to come back to. I guess that sounds an awful thing to say huh, that you're a background to three other people's lives? No, correction, four, I've got to bring my mother into it too.

Wow, I'm kind of getting in deep here talking like this. Not unhappy, not unhappy at all: and I'd say not even discontented with my life in any way. Just kind of generally wondering about it. Somewhere at the end of the rainbow there isn't a crock of gold, I know that: I'm not wishing for one or searching for one. Sometimes I think maybe now the kids are growing up a little I should try and get me a job. But I don't know what as. I could see Gerry Meister and see if he'd hire me, I guess. I could tell him I spend so much time in his store just looking, I already know the price of every item in there and which shelf it belongs.

Heh this coffee's real cold now, how's yours, you want I should freshen it up?

Linda Burns, 290 North Harding

– We've been here 14 months now, prior to this we lived in Seattle: we're both natives of Washington State, in fact we're both big city people, so a place like Bird's taking us time to adjust to. My husband is an agronomist with a company in Baxter and he drives to and fro there each day. It's a 40-mile journey each way and that's not ideal for sure, as we discovered last winter: maybe we'll move nearer to his base, but Baxter's not a place either of us likes much so it could be we end up some place else. I don't know where, we're going through an unsettled period: before he joined his present company he worked for the Government and I think he may go back to that. I'm 34, he's 36, and we have two children both at High School here and they both like it: maybe we'll wait for them to graduate before we move, we don't think it's a good idea to keep on unrooting children and asking they should make an adjustment at a time like this in their lives.

As far as that goes though, I think it's me who's so far the one who's having the biggest problem. This is a much much smaller community to any I've ever lived in, and I kind of feel I wouldn't say hemmed in, but somehow as though I'm expected to live my life more in public view somehow. I was surprised to find this, that I was disturbed by it and to a degree resented it. I don't know if it was pushed on me too fast for me to take, maybe I'm getting old and less adaptable: I don't know what it is.

The kind of thing I mean is, well an example would be this. We'd been here a few weeks and everyone was kind and friendly and helpful, whatever we needed we only had to say and so on: and then one person, someone around my own age, she asked me to go have coffee with her one morning. We chewed the fat a bit, I told her about my husband Walter, his job, all about my kids, and something but not too much about myself: about how before I'd married I'd been a teacher working with autistic children, that I was interested in civil rights, that I'd been told there was the negro township, Nicodemus, not far away and how I'd be interested to try to get to know some of the people there. Nothing very much, a sort of mild radicalism she could have picked up on if she'd wanted to. Then I said to her I'd be interested to know something about her. Well, did she surprise me: she told me how she'd been divorced on account of she and her husband had had difficulties with their sex life, exactly what those difficulties were, how they'd been to a clinic in Kansas City for sex therapy sessions but it hadn't helped. And on like that for about a whole half hour. I don't think of myself as prudish and it wasn't what she was saying that disturbed me, it was more that she was telling it all to me on a first meeting. I wouldn't talk in intimate detail about myself like that except to a really close friend who I'd known a long time.

And what went with it you see as well, was a sort of clear suggestion I ought to reciprocate immediately and talk about things in the same way, give her back confidences about myself. She didn't exactly ask me outright how things were in my marriage, but it was getting that way.

That's only an example, but I've felt the same way about other things people have said sometimes, about say their financial situation: great detail they go into, exactly how much their debts are and what for. I can only use a slang expression for it, 'up frontedness'. Or they'll tell you the problems they're having with their teenage daughter, how she's sleeping with her boyfriend but she's not using any contraception and it's a big worry. I don't have a teenage daughter, not yet: but when I do I won't talk that way about her in front of six or seven other people. I think it's inconsiderate to the girl herself for one. You could say you're being a very honest person to talk that way in public about your worries about your daughter, but I don't see it like that.

A thing I do find strange though is that alongside with that goes the fact that they don't gossip about others. The three High School girls last year that all had babies, you don't have people whispering and shaking their heads about it, it's in the open and no one tries to hide it or anything: they don't condone but they don't condemn, which I think is surprisingly liberal and unusual for a small town community.

Yet on a number of other things I think they have rather closed minds. An example of that is how much emphasis they put on being independent, standing on their own feet and working for themselves. The farmers for instance, most of them work very hard: and when you say you come from Seattle, they tell you how they wouldn't want to live in a big city and work on a factory production line. When you tell them hundreds of thousands of people live there in Seattle without working on factory production lines, you can tell from the way they look at you they don't believe it, or can't let themselves believe it. It's like they all saw Charlie Chaplin's *Modern Times* and you can't tell them it isn't little guys swallowed up by big machines, because it is, they know because they've seen it.

All this must be sounding like my view of Bird is a totally negative one. But it's not. I like the generosity of people, their open-heartedness towards strangers coming in and the big effort they make to help them feel at home. When we moved in, in the first week we had visits from people from five different churches inviting us to go along on Sunday to their church. I know the churches like to keep a high profile and are keen to recruit, but I felt it was more than that, it was a genuine welcoming. And the honesty in the way people live, not locking their doors and so on, that really amazed me when we came, after Seattle. I met a neighbour one time just a few days after we arrived, she'd said ask her if I needed anything, so I saw her on Main and asked her could she loan me a casserole dish, mine was somewhere I didn't know where in our packing? Sure she said, I knew where her house was, all her cooking pots were in the cupboard by the cooker, go on back and help myself. Well I mean in Seattle that just couldn't happen: no way.

One other final thing that's different too is I notice here everything's much slower and more easygoing than the city. It can be kind of insidious though, that's a danger. Before, I nearly always worked, even if it was only part-time, even when the kids were a whole lot younger than they are now. I worked A because I liked working and B because I always kind of felt I should work, I should be doing something even if it was voluntary work or political activity. Everybody did, everybody worked at something or other. But since coming here I've gotten to be what I'd have called before a lazy slob. All I do's sit around all day, listen to the stereo, read books from the library, wait for the kids to come home from school, cook an evening meal for the time my husband gets home. I'm getting to be the typical American homemaker and that's terrible. And what's even more terrible still is that I like it.

I think only for a while though. Before long other bits of me'll start pushing through, I'll get restless and want to involve myself in something. In Seattle I was a member of a women's group, mothers protesting nuclear weapons, handing out leaflets and organising discussion evenings, that sort of thing. I've not seen too much evidence of that kind of activity around here: about somewhere short of zero I'd say. But who knows, maybe one day I'll meet one other person who feels the same way and because there's two of us, we'll give each other the courage to try and start something up. But not yet, I'm too much of a newcomer in town, I'm not going to show my head above the parapet yet. The bad thing would be if I got too satisfied with staying home though, and decided not to think any more.

6 *The happiest days*

Dan Forgan, *Teacher*

In the classroom after afternoon lessons, he sat on the edge of a desk. A big fair-haired man in an open-necked check shirt and jeans, aged 35.

– I don't myself come from Bird, I'm not even a Kansan. Originally I'm from Nebraska, I came ten years ago with my wife, she's a Kansas girl from Wichita. Where we first met each other was at a college in St Louis: I was studying English, her subject was history. The two of us were both members of a campus drama group, so that was how we came to meet. I'd always had the intention to be a teacher, but Ruth had wanted to do research work. Before we met each other she'd had in mind trying to get herself a scholarship to go to Europe. Her family originated in Germany and she's German-speaking: what she wanted to do was research into the effects of Nazi indoctrination on children who'd grown up, whether when it had been instilled into them at an early age it'd had a permanent and lasting effect on them.

We met and we fell in love, and we wanted to get married, which we did. Ruth gave up the idea of going to Germany for a year or two, and we decided we'd move back to her home at Wichita even though neither of us had finished our college studies. The reason for this was Ruth's mother had been diagnosed with having cancer: Ruth was the only child, so she felt she should go back home and be with her ma. Her father worked in an aviation plant there and he didn't bring home a lot of money: so if I could get me a temporary teaching job then Ruth could stay home and take care of her mother. That seemed like it was the best idea all around.

Ruth's ma was a real tough old lady, and she went on living for another two years. I took a job teaching history in Junior High School: it wasn't my subject, but Ruth gave me help and most times I got through, even if it meant sometimes I was preparing a lesson just the night before the day I was due to give it. We'd have liked to start a family of our own, but it didn't seem too good an idea financially at that point.

It's always a shock when someone dies even when you've known it was going to happen for a while: however much you think you've gotten used to the idea, it still hits you. And when Ruth's mother did die, her father took it real hard. He seemed to go kind of completely to pieces and started to drink, and it got to be a real problem because it affected his job. Like he took to stopping home and drinking instead of going to work. Well no one's going to put up with that for long, so the result was in about six months maybe less, he was out of work. Ruth had spent two years looking after her ma: now it looked like she was still going to be chained down, having no independence and no money. All we'd got was my salary for the three of us to live on, and her pa drinking away more than one third of it. So as anyone'd guess, this started to put a strain on our married relationship and things weren't too good all round.

Then one day I was turning the pages of an educational magazine and I happened across this advertisement for an English teacher in a place called Bird. We knew nothing about it so we got out an atlas to find out where it was, that's how much we knew. It seemed to Ruth and it seemed to me we either had to do something of that sort, go to a new place and start over, or else we had to draw a line under our marriage. Ruth's pa said he was all for it, he'd be able to look after himself and get back to work: but we said no to that, he had to come with us else we weren't going. He had all his drinking buddies there in Wichita, guys he sat around all day and played cards with or went to the races: and he took a deal of persuading, I can tell you that. But at the finish we persuaded him, and so we came.

What we had in mind was maybe Ruth would be able to get a teaching job someplace not too far away, and if she did we could start getting ourselves more together financially. We neither of us knew how we'd make out moving from a big place like Wichita with a population way over a quarter of a million people, to some place like this. But like a lot of these things that happen, the problems you imagine don't turn out to be problems: instead you get new ones take their place that you hadn't thought of.

The first one for us was no sooner we'd arrived than Ruth was pregnant. And the second one wasn't a new problem, it was just the old one in a new setting: that her father went back to his drinking, only more so, and before long had to be hospitalised for it. But against that, what we had been worried about didn't happen at all: all the neighbours, all the townsfolk almost without exception, they all immediately welcomed us and made us feel part of their community. I think maybe this had something to do with the fact I'd come to a job at the school. I was going to teach their kids at least in some cases, and they feel towards you in a different way to how they'd feel if you'd just come to set up a store and take their money.

Either way, everyone was really great to us and so that made that side of things easy. Only a few months on from when we came, Ruth's father took very ill with something else on top of his drinking, and then it was only a few weeks more and he died. However difficult your life's been with a person, however difficult that person's made your life for you, it's always sad and it's always a shock: and for Ruth it was specially hard, being six or seven months pregnant as well like she was.

But once more you know, I have to say it: the people of Bird showed to us all the kindness and help anyone could ever want. In a kind of a way, death and birth both, they sort of bring you closer to the folk around you: you seem to get to know them quicker, and them you. That's how it was then at that time for us: we made some real good friends and quickly, and we still have those same friends now. Our little boy he's now nine, and we have our daughter who's four: so I think we're really integrated here, and neither of us ever thinks now of moving on. It's funny how your life can change: I'm 40, Ruth's 41, and ten years ago when we didn't have children, we really were seriously considering we might divorce and go our separate ways. We were both of us young enough to have a fresh start. But now today, well I guess you'd say we're approaching middle age: and any such thought would be unthinkable. We've plans that when the kids are a little older we might go on a trip to Europe: that'd chiefly be for Ruth's benefit for her to see whether she wants to pick up her studies again. If not, she'll maybe decide to do some teaching again: but that's for her to find out herself what she wants to do. The one thing though we're both happy to contemplate now for sure is living out the rest of our lives here in Bird. This is home.

Jean Eagleton, *School Counsellor*

A big soft-voiced woman with a cheerful manner, in her fifties.

– My husband and I've been married 33 years, and we've three grown-up married daughters. I was born on a small farm about four miles out of town here, and I'd say I've lived here most of my life except my husband's career's been in the United States Air Force: when he had a posting some place where he was going to be for any length of time, I always went and joined him. So in that sense I've not lived all my life here, only part of it: but Bird's always home. He's now retired and from now on we reckon we're here for good.

School Counsellor is my principal activity, but I do some career education classes also. My responsibility is to try and teach children moral values, right up through the school. I'm in contact with every child all through their school career, year in year out, right from when they come here to when they graduate and leave at 17 or 18. Mostly I work with small groups, or individuals one at a time. Hopefully they bring me their problems or worries or difficulties themselves: but if I do get to hear, either from teachers or other pupils, that a particular pupil is having a hard time – it could be at home or here at school in either work or relationships -- then I will make an approach myself, and offer to help if I can in talking the matter through.

Every pupil in the school knows that I keep utter and absolute confidentiality. If they didn't know that, really know it for a solid fact, then I'd have no base to my work. If any one boy or girl could ever say I'd broken a confidence, all the others would get to hear of it and that'd be the end of anyone talking with me ever again. So that's point number one. Number two's that I never make fun of anybody: whatever a problem is, and however trivial it might seem to me, as it sometimes does, I keep it in my mind that it's serious to them. At least at the beginning: we may get around to seeing it together that it's not all that serious after all, but we start off that it's serious. And I suppose the third thing is that I do believe deep down in my heart that your education is one of the most important things that ever happens to you in your whole life, its effect on you lasts all through your whole life, and therefore it's not something you should lightly give up. In fact the opposite: what you should do is fight to hang on to it and to extend it, and never just put it aside as not of great importance like a sports game or something. It's something shapes you as a person for the whole of your future.

You'll have heard maybe by now about the time a year or so back when we had three of our senior girls all became pregnant. This was when I really had to make a fight about what I've just been telling you. What made it different and difficult was there was three all together at the same time: people were saying 'Heh what goes on at Bird High School, three girls pregnant all at once, what sort of a den of promiscuity is it up there?' Of course, a schoolgirl getting pregnant, that's nothing new: it's not the first time it's happened here, and I wouldn't imagine it was something never happened in your country, or in any other country in the world either. But three all at the same time: well that was something caused a stir all right.

We rode that OK: and then the next problem was what to do about it. Three girls, and from three very different families. One of them, they wanted her to go away, have the baby, give it for adoption and then come back and forget all about it and pretend it hadn't happened. Another, they wanted a shotgun wedding: the girl and the boy concerned, they'd better get married pretty damn quick before the baby was born. Only the third one, one family out of the three that is, were straight away ready to face the implications of the situation and ask the girl herself what she wanted to do.

It seemed to me then, and it still seems to me now looking back on it, that the right thing was first of all that it should all be out in the open, it was something that ought to be talked about and no one – not the girls, or their families, nor the school itself – should pretend it wasn't happening. And the second right thing to do was that given the circumstances that there were three babies coming along, if it was at all possible these girls ought to be able to feel this wasn't the end of the line for them educationally: whatever their choices about what they individually did, their education was still here for them to continue with: and that what's more, we all of us wanted them back here when they could come.

In all of the cases, it was a tough decision those girls had to make. The one where the parents were insisting the boy who was the father should marry their daughter, I had the mother up here and to put it bluntly she raised hell because I'd said to the girl I didn't think it was a good basis for a marriage, to marry someone because your parents said you had to. I thought it was better she and the boy should hold off a while, and so far that's what they've done, they haven't married. The parents of the girl who'd wanted her to have her baby adopted, what happened there was pretty much what you'd expect: the moment the baby was born there was no more talk of adoption at all, she's now living back home with the baby and her parents and they're devoted to it. And in the third situation, like I said it was no real problem all along.

The thing is now that all three of those girls had their babies, and they then came back to school and resumed their studies. They were made to feel welcome, not like they were outcasts or that they had to hide something. No one treated them like they were heroes, I'm sorry I mean heroines: but no one turned their backs on them either.

I reckon this was a pretty good reflection on our community all round, and I was glad the school had been able to play a part in it, because that's what I think any school is for: to help kids face up to life as it really is, to make judgements about the best way to handle situations, but not to pass judgement on people and then think it's got no more to do with you.

There's maybe one important thing though I think we haven't come to grips with yet here, and that's the subject of colour. Just along the road down at Nicodemus there's an all-black settlement, where the people are descendants of negro slaves. OK they keep themselves to themselves a lot: you don't see many of them coming into town here to do their shopping and so on, and very few of their kids either. We don't have a single black child in our High School for example. I think the people of Bird are happy to let it go along like that, as though Nicodemus wasn't anything to do with us: I'd go further and say as though black people altogether weren't anything to do with us, even if they are only just a few miles away. This worries me, this situation where people seem to pretend Nicodemus doesn't exist, and if we don't think about it perhaps it'll go away. I had a parent only the other day, to all extent otherwise a reasonably intelligent well-educated person, who told me quite seriously 'Do you know, in all my life I've never met a black person and I wouldn't want to. Not because I'm colour prejudiced or anything, because I'm not: it's just I don't like black people, that's all.' And I'm sorry to say this but I think it's true: I think what she said's true of a lot of people here.

Bernard Westerman, *High School Principal*

We talked in his cool shady office: a tall man, quietly-spoken, studious in manner, wearing a suit.

– What we have here at this High School is around 150 pupils, in Grades nine through 12, ages from 14 to 17 or in a few cases 18. Mixed boys and girls, usually in a proportion around about 50 per cent. Next door's the Junior High, where kids go first, from 6 through 13. We teach a general range of subjects, something like 50 in total: that's not as big a range as I'd like, but we're only a small school. I'd say our strengths are the basic subjects: English, Math, History and Geography. Our biggest weakness as I see it is the only foreign language we offer is Spanish. We don't touch French or German and I'd like it if we did. But nobody asks us for it, and right now we don't have anyone could teach it.

As a general rule in the whole United States, education's free up to High School graduation level. After that if it comes to college or university, it has to be paid for. It seems to be an increasing habit nowadays, by the way, that we use those words interchangeably. Most often people use college and university to mean the same thing. Like I say further education has to be paid for: but we have a huge number of scholarships to help. Some are federal, some business sponsored, some established by individuals in memory of someone, and some were set up way back in time nobody seems to know how. One way and another we like to think that here, even in a small place like Bird, if a boy or girl has really made up their mind on further education, the necessary money can be got together. If their family can afford to help that makes it easier, if they're prepared to contribute themselves to the cost of their education by taking a job while they're at college that's another help, and finally there's a system of state or federal loans they can take advantage of. So if you really mean it, you can build a package that'll take you through.

Other differences we have between our system and yours, least from what little reading I've done about it, is that for one we don't have religious teaching as part of our curriculum. It's forbidden by law, and I guess the reason for it is we've so many different religious groups in America, the only way to handle it is to exclude them all so there's no controversy. We have a local church pastor who comes and gives the address each year at the annual graduation ceremony: and who it should be's voted on by the pupils themselves, and the custom is they work on a rota system.

The other difference is our semesters, which I think you call 'terms', are on a different basis: we have just the two, one in the fall and the other in the spring up until May. Then we have our vacation all in one lump, from the end of May through August. This allows the students to get themselves summer vacation work, and in that time save up money towards the time they eventually go on to college.

One particular thing this school like most others puts great emphasis on is extracurricular activities. Sport, music, photography, drama: these feature in the curriculum but they also extend a long way outside the school. I don't think it's too much to claim that in a whole lot of ways the school itself is the most important social feature in the whole town: not just for the kids but for their parents too, because of all the functions and activities there are for them to attend. There's something, some school function, taking place most every night of the week except Wednesdays: by custom that night's left free for other organisations such as churches or sororities to have their functions.

Like all schools, I guess, we have our problems from time to time. Whatever they are, we try to handle them by bringing them out in the open and never covering up anything: the line we follow is we don't have secrets from the pupils. I expect you'll know already of the time last year when three of our girls had babies. I think as a school we were very fortunate that we had Mrs Eagleton on our staff as Counsellor, and the line she followed was one we all went along with.

Sometimes just by talking about things as problems, that very fact of doing that makes them sound worse, or bigger or more important than they are. Bearing that in mind, I'd say that as of now our two main ones are drink and drugs, but I want to keep them in proper perspective, because neither of them's all that serious. Out of our school population of 150, I'd say no more than three at very most take drugs to any extent. And maybe 12 or 15 are regular attenders at drinks parties, either in their homes or maybe sometimes out at Milton Reservoir. And when we're talking about drinking, we're talking about drinking just the mild beer that's the only thing kids can buy. It's so little alcohol in it you'd have to sink about 12 cans before it could have much of an effect on you.

In a small town like this where everybody knows everybody, most kids behave themselves I think for two reasons. One is the example they get from their parents, which is a good, solid, decent and law-abiding example: and the other is that the kids themselves want to behave well, and be liked by their own group who are mostly all good behavers. Nobody sets up gangs who steal or terrorise, or things like that that you get in cities: and if they tried to, it's most likely they'd get very few other kids wanting to join. The ideal is conformity. That has advantages and disadvantages, but I'd say on balance it makes for a good kind of life.

Returning to the problem subject for a moment, there is one other aspect's just crossed my mind. It's what the kids do after they've graduated and been through college. There's next to nothing here in Bird for them unless they're one of the few who have family trades or businesses to step into. This really is a problem, and not one I think we've properly addressed ourselves to so far. Inevitably it means our youngsters, and especially the brightest among them, drifting away from the town. We've plenty of the older folk who'll reminisce for you about how things were, and be happy to do it. Sitting down and looking back, that's no great difficulty: but if you're a young person trying to see forward, well that's something else again, and I don't envy many of them. But it's my philosophy as an educator to give pupils a good basic grounding to go forward from if they wish: and most of all to try and foster that wish in them, so they grow up regarding their education not as some kind of suffering process they can't escape from, but as a tool for living and growing with. I want, I know all my staff want, that kids here enjoy being here and enjoy being educated: I hope they'll look back at their times in school as the happiest days.

I would be very happy for you to come into the school and talk with the pupils, either individually or in groups, whenever you wish. I'll leave it to them and you to schedule visits to match in with their timetables: and feel yourself free to visit as often as you like.

7 *In public positions*

Gordon Osterman, *Town Manager*

Medium height, dark-haired, business-suited, 35. He sat in one of the high-backed chairs along the side of the big polished table in the Meeting Chamber, under portraits of three generations of town dignitaries in rows behind him on the panelled wall.

– Well the Town Manager, he's like the Number One top guy around the place. When he walks by, folks draw aside on the sidewalk and hope he won't pick on them for throwing shadows: everyone's in fear and trembling of him, what he says goes and no one dares cross him. Least that's what I'd read when I applied, only somehow it doesn't work out that way.

I'm an employee of the Town Commissioners, I look after day-to-day activities and am responsible for financial management, and I hire and fire personnel such as those who work for the highways, the fire brigade and ambulance, and the cemetery.

I came three years ago from Missouri where I'd been doing a similar job. When I applied my wife and I looked around the town and liked it: and the Commissioners looked at us and I guess they thought we'do, so that was it. We'd expect to be here a few years and then move on to a bigger place and go on up the career ladder. I don't ever see myself being an administrator in a city: I enjoy civic administration which I have a degree in, but so long as where we live is a nice environment and our kids get good schooling, we're happy being your ordinary American family. My wife teaches part-time at the High School here, which she enjoys and I think that's helped us integrate. Bird's a good community to live in so long as you're not looking for the bright lights and razzmatazz. Everyone drives slowly and carefully, keeping an eye out for kids: you don't get a lot of rough characters hanging round or passing through, so it's a pleasant little haven to live in, nice and quiet and easy.

This atmosphere reaches out into work too. The best way I could put it is to say no one bears down on you. Among other things, my job involves liaising with such people as the Chief of Police and the Co-op elevator manager and pretty near everyone else: and I find that all the business and professional people of the town are the same, nobody comes after you to bawl you out or tell you this is wrong and that's a disgrace and you're not doing your job. If something wants attention they mention it kind of offhand: 'Say Gordon, could you have a look at that fence runs along the back of the woodyard and maybe check it please?' That kind of approach. So you go down there and have a look, and you make the same kind of approach to whoever's responsibility it is to repair it. In turn, you know that if they don't do it today they'll do it tomorrow: or if not tomorrow, then for sure next week. What they won't do, and you can bet one hundred per cent certain on this, is not do it. That makes for a real nice working life.

There's lots of differences between St Louis Missouri and here: the one I notice most is that folk here are more what they call 'independent' and I call something else. Sure I can give you an example: the Kansas state legislature has recently passed a law saying people have got to wear seat belts driving their cars. And oh boy, let me tell you, I find the reaction of folks here to this mighty strange, I sure do. The first thing is the local law-enforcement guys tell you even if it is the law, for the first year nothing's gonna happen if they catch you not obeying it. All they'll do is tell you you should. Then the time after that, if they catch you still not obeying, they're going to bring out the big hammer and fine you ten dollars. Can you imagine? If you try to tell folk you think it's a good idea safety-wise, you know what they say to you? They say, I'm quoting actual words that have been used to me: 'Well maybe it's a good safety precaution and maybe it isn't. But I'm going to decide that for myself, I'm not having those jackasses on Capitol Hill telling me what's good for me and what ain't', and they go on to you about state interference into the liberty of the individual. So like I said, 'independence' would be one word for it, but I can think of others. No I'll not say, you want me to lose my job?

If I'd a serious criticism of the place, it'd have to be that conformity is all: tradition should have preference over change, least that's the way most local folk see it. They won't encourage new businesses or offer inducements for small factories or things of that sort. I think this is short-sighted, because the greatest need for the place to survive and have a future is if it can offer something to its young people when they've finished their educations. The way it is now they've no alternative in most cases to going away and living some place else where there's work.

They could do with creating more leisure facilities in the town to attract visitors, and certainly more eating and entertainment places. Say that to the older folk though and they tell you No thanks, they don't want pinball arcades and the Golden Arches, they like their town to retain its character. So a discussion never even begins: that's not what you're talking about, those things, but they're convinced you either are, or you're going the long way round to get to them. But they'll all tell you at the same time how they're worried about the future and who's going to take over, and how the young folk just don't seem to care anymore. The Chamber of Commerce has made what it thinks is a start this year by electing a young man, for the first time, as Chairman. But that's about exhausted their imaginations, and they're so overwhelmed with how bold they've been doing that, they sure don't want any more revolutionary innovations for a long long time.

I notice this more, coming from around a big city: and of course it's easy to make fun. If I were going to live here the rest of my life I'd maybe want to try and improve things a little, specially having growing-up kids myself. The way things are I don't have to let it concern me too much: but I still reckon in maybe ten years' time or before, there's going to have to be some pretty solid rethinking by people who live here what direction they want their town to go in.

Melvin Penn, *Postmaster*

The Post Office was a small glass-fronted single-storey building at the corner of Jefferson and Main, with an exterior lobby for the banks of rented mailboxes round its walls.

– Melvin said to tell you he's sorry, he's had to go playing, said the counter clerk. He says go around his home at one ten South Garfield this evening instead, OK?

A small, chirpy, bright-eyed man, middle-aged, with wire-rimmed spectacles. We sat at the kitchen table, drinking coffee.

– No I ain't in no rock and roll group, no sir that's for sure: not that kind of playing. I'm a Sheriff's Deputy, and we got a call this guy escaped from Leavenworth Penitentiary and was holed up in a barn out at Silver Lake and had a gun. So five of us went out there with Jim Arnoldsen who called us out: when the Sheriff wants you, you have to go. We couldn't find him in the barn, we walked through the woods with dogs and that, but he'd been gone a good while before we arrived I reckon. So no fun for us and even less for the felon. Kansas is one big state to be on the run in: he'll need food and water, so I guess he'll turn himself in anyway before long like they mostly do.

There's two kinds of Deputy: one has authority only when he's called on, the other has full powers all the time like me. I'm only paid when I'm called, but if I see something like a traffic violation it's my duty to take action. I can carry a weapon at any time, and I'm authorised to use it up to and including deadly force if necessary to protect life or property. When I first took my weapon training, I came home and hung my gun up and asked myself whatever did I think I was getting into: but that was 15 years ago and I've never fired anything other than a practice round. I hope I never have to too, I can tell you.

I've been Bird's Postmaster how long, let's see. Well working for the US Mail, coming up now towards 30 years. If that sounds like a long time, it's because it is. I was 17 years old when I started, right here at the Post Office straight from school. It offered security, that was the big attraction: my family wasn't poor but we sure weren't rich either. There were four kids and I was the next oldest: from the age of 13 on, I did odd jobs most the time so's I could help out with the financial situation at home. Pump hand at the local gasoline station for a couple of hours before school, stuff like that.

When I was 23 I had to do my two years in the Army on the draft. Something sensational happened. You hear these stories about what the Army does, like if you're a mechanic putting you to cook, or if you're a chef getting you to camouflage tanks? Well you know what they did with me, a post office clerk? They put me on the window in an Army Post Office. Guess that must be about the only time in history something like that's happened. When I came back from the draft I moved up to supervisor, I suppose that'd be ten years ago: then I moved up again, and became Postmaster.

I guess I'd say what I like best about the job is everybody knows me and I know them. Walk down the street, every second person says 'Hi'. You wouldn't get that in a big city, people look at you like they've never seen you before and walk on by like they're never going to see you again. While here, well in lots of ways you're a kind of an important figure in folks' lives. Folks tell you things about themselves: guy'll come in asking if there's a letter for him and when there isn't next day he's back again. The third day, you can bet money on it, more often than not if there's still no letter he'll tell you what he's anxious about. 'The wife's sister in Detroit, she's ill, it's sure beginning to worry us we ain't heard nothing from her son.' Or someone starts getting bills from some place followed up by letters, and after a while out it comes: 'Those folks up in Detroit, Melvin, they sure are hounding us for money we owe them.' They feel a worry shared's a worry halved, is that what the phrase is?

We have the system that a lot of folk rent a mailbox in the outside lobby, so they can stop by any time and pick up their mail. It's an extra little facility that specially the business people are happy to pay for: we've only one mail man and he doesn't go out on his round until a lot later on in the day. And quite often you know from sorting the mail and putting it in folks' boxes, you know how things are going in their lives. I know this'll sound crazy, but when someone's waiting for a letter and it comes, I get I can hold it in my hand, and most times have a feeling whether it's good news or bad. And you'll see the person a couple of days after and when they say to you 'Heh Melvin, you know that letter came for me from Detroit, it was good news,' you feel you wanna say 'Yes I thought it was.' I hope it don't sound like spying on folks' business, because it ain't. But it sure gives you a kind of feeling you're connected with what happens to people.

I'd sum me up for you as a man who likes his job, likes his life and doesn't want to change, and isn't going to either. For me to get any further on in the job, promotion could only mean one thing which would be to apply to take charge some place else in a larger town. Well the way I look at it, and my wife, and our two kids, we all think there's more to life than more money. To sell our home and buy a higher priced one, move to a different school, new neighbours, different friends: we none of us want to do that, we're happy enough where we are.

Those two years when I was in the Army, I went to Germany, Spain, Alaska and lots of other places. By then I was married: and the first night I was home after I got out, I walked around the town holding hands with my wife and I told her that of all the places in the world I'd been, there wasn't one of them I liked as much as Bird. That was true then, and it still sure is, only even more so now.

Clare Oberlin, *Librarian*

– I've lived here nearly all my life and wouldn't want to live nowhere else, that's the first thing. My parents came to a small farm just outside of town when I was in my school sophomore year. I was an only child, and big and awkward and ungainly and bulky, even then like now. I was left-handed too, so at school I always felt an outsider and a loner because I was made fun of. My only real friends who never laughed at me were books, and that's where my love affair with them began. I got married as soon as I left school: my husband was in the armed services and we moved around a lot, then we came back here 28 years ago so's he could work on the farm with my folks.

Almost straight away a vacancy came up for an assistant in the old library and that's how I came to work here: first as assistant, then taking over from the Senior Librarian when she retired. I'd say working in a library is Heaven: you meet folks, when they bring books back they've loaned you talk about them, get to know what they like and what they don't, their news and views and everything. I like being part of all that, I think there's nothing luckier than to spend my life working among books.

Two years ago, this beautiful big modern library that we have here was built for us. And you'd have to go a long way through Kansas or outside of it to find one as fine as this one. Everyone agrees on that, and it sure was a really very remarkable thing that one of the townsfolk should give his home town a brand new library to remember him by. That Harold Albert, he sure is a lovely man, and everyone likes and respects him. Only thing is he's very very shy: but if you could ever get him to talk to you, that really would be something. Usually though he turns round and runs if folk approach him.

I guess you've heard about by now what happened is that oil was found on his land. A great lot of oil: and Harold and his wife Louie, they suddenly found themselves with more money than they'd ever been able to dream of. Someone said more money than they'd ever been able to imagine there was, and I'd say that was near how it was. The little old Carnegie Library we had next door, it was real small and dark and old: I reckon it'd have put more people off books than it inspired them for. And well it's a joke in the town: but everyone'll tell you they're the person who first put the idea of building a new library into Harold Albert's mind. I don't suppose anyone'll ever know the truth of it, and it doesn't matter who it was: the fact is we've got this lovely big building that's the finest feature of our town. Mr Albert called in different architects from Deerfield, Baxter and Bakersfield, and he asked them to design something that would match up in colour and outward appearance to the old one next door. But inside he wanted it to be a welcoming place where folks would want to go. Well that's now just exactly what we have, and we keep the old building as an extension for meetings and exhibitions.

At the old library we had 600 users a month, here in the new one at the last count we had more than 2,000 a month and growing. As well as the loan section there's the big reference section there, then behind the partition a copier, typewriters, cameras and a microfilm unit, all for free use. We have a magazine and newspaper loan section, and for the kids we're setting up a toy library. A lot of folk donate us things such as equipment or people give us a subscription to the *National Geographic*, *Reader's Digest*, the *Wall Street Journal* and things like that. I guess what we've got here is what you could call something like a Community Centre of the printed word.

Supervisorily, there's a Library Board of people appointed by the Town Commissioners: it's their responsibility to oversee what we have on the shelves, and how the library's run. They don't interfere, not in any way: they leave all the choice of books to me. We get our basic stock through the Kansas Central Library system, and I work on the basis that if I think a book might interest readers, I get it. I choose things which I hope people will read, or which I think they ought to read, plus anything that anyone's asked for to read. On the whole I think that system works pretty good. Since the time I've been in charge, I can recall only two complaints. One time a person complained about one of Judy Blume's books: and another time, it was the same person, they said we shouldn't have a book about Rock Hudson telling how he had AIDS. I paid no attention: the way I see it is what folks read is their own affair, and if it's kids then it's for their parents to say what they should or shouldn't read, not me. I think kids themselves are sensible about things: I'd sooner they read books they wanted to, and most of all I want them to read read read.

In the old building, the children's section there in the old library was the most depressing place you could imagine. Dark, serious, you mustn't make any kind of noise, like it was some sort of religious sepulchre you were in. Now that's all changed: you can sit on the floor with piles of books all around you, you can meet other kids here and talk to them and play with them, and not even look at books at all if you don't want to. About the only rule there is, though it's not written up anywhere, is if you're a kid you're not allowed to run around and chase one another up and down the aisles. But we tell them it's the same for grown-ups, we don't let them do that either.

For young people and old ones too, I think a library should be a fun place and one that people look forward to going to, and really enjoy when they're there. That's what we try our best to make it here.

– Oh and you wanted some books about Nicodemus right? I've a few here I've kept aside for you.

Nell Irvin Painter, *Exodusters: Black Migration to Kansas after Reconstruction.*
Charles E. Robert, *Negro Civilisation in the South.*
Glen Schwendemann, *Nicodemus: Negro Haven on the Solomon River.*
Myrtle D. Fesler, *Pioneers of Western Kansas.*
National Geographic Magazine: article about *Nicodemus.*

Shirley Cookson, *Extension Agent*

– When Alan and I came here from south east Kansas fifteen years ago, it took us a while to assimilate: in a small town outsiders stay outsiders for quite a time. We came because we were newly married after we'd both been divorced and we were having a new start: Alan had a job with the school, and I got this post with Extension, both at the same time.

Extension means an extension of Kansas University: there are one hundred five Extension Officers throughout the state, offering programmes to both adults and children. In my particular sphere I deal with Home Economics, which is a very wide field: it covers just about everything – cookery, health, furniture restoring and upholstering, canning, buying equipment and furniture, child care, you name it. If there's a need and a demand, we try and meet it.

It's our aim to provide something like a college education for adults who didn't have the opportunity when they were younger to learn the sort of things they need to know about now. Particularly we're concerned with food production and distribution because naturally in this part of the state it's what most folks are concerned with. Then the other side of our work is we do things *for* the state: surveys into farm accidents is an example, and we put on exhibitions on subjects like cattle management, bull selection, pasture control and forest production. A third area we work in is child health information: immunisation and diet and so on.

I have two grown-up sons, one at college and the other working in hotel management in Colorado, so I find now that I can devote more and more of my time and energy to my job, and I love it. In my spare time – no don't laugh it's true, I do have spare time and I like to use it – I like to do mostly the same things that I do in my job, because that's what I enjoy. I guess I'm a very organisational lady and a very organised one too, I run at full speed ahead most of the time. I walk fast, I talk fast and I really do have a hard time sitting still. Alan laughs at me lots of times: I guess I do sometimes wonder how he puts up with living with me, specially seeing me doing my lists.

Well, those are things I have two sorts of. One list I make every night for the things I'm going to do the following day: people I have to write to, call up on the telephone, check out arrangements with for classes or exhibitions or whatever, as well as personal things like buy stamps, get a greetings card for someone, go see if Gover's have gotten that fresh delivery of pimentos Gerry was saying about. And then there's the big list as I call it, which I do January 1 each year, of the things I want to accomplish in home, job and life generally by the end of that year. That one could include anything from reupholstering a particular armchair to reading up and learning about some new subject or foreign country I don't know enough about. The year list'll have a total of I'd say 50 different items on it, and as I do them I tick them off. Then at the end of the year if I haven't gotten around to any I carry them forward to the next year: they then become my priorities for that one, because I don't like it if I have things hanging around more than a year that I haven't done.

Do I sound like one terrible lady? I'm sure I must, but I don't see myself changing much now I guess, not at 46. All my life I've been this way: at college I was a very serious student and determined to get my Bachelor of Science degree. Clever a bit I guess, and with this same desire to organise everything, myself and other people too. That's one thing can be a bit of hazard and I'm aware of it, and I do have to struggle sometimes to hold it in check. I like fixing things and putting them as they should be. But I know it's not always appreciated, because I can't say I'm always that tactful about things. I go in a friend's house and see something isn't the way it should be, well of course they don't always jump up and down with gratitude if I tell them. Even worse is when you say, like I have to admit now and again I do, 'Look OK, leave it to me, I'll fix it for you.' Many's the time Alan's saved a situation of that sort by making a joke out of it and telling me to keep quiet and sit still. I need to have him around me when we go to people's homes, that's for sure.

Another aspect of my life I enjoy a lot now I have the opportunity is travel. For these last few years Alan and I have been connected with an organisation called the American Institute for Foreign Study: it runs trips to foreign countries for school kids, on a programme with the title 'People to People'. Last year we went with 16 kids from South Carolina and Kansas to Europe: England, France and Holland. This sure was as much a great experience for us grown-ups who were in charge as it was for the kids: and we all of us learned a lot from it. Most of all we found out, I think this applies to everyone who went, that because ours in such a big country and on the whole people don't travel a lot outside it, I think Americans in general and specially those in small places, they tend to have what can only be described as a very limited outlook. We think our way of life and our customs and our viewpoint, they're the only ones there are: and it comes as one big shock to us that other people in other countries don't necessarily think and act the same as we do.

The tour was an educationally based one, the kids had formal lessons as we went along: where we were, what the country's set-up was governmentally, and so on, and we had projects about cooking and eating, daily customs, newspapers, and how their ways differed from ours. The thing that came up very strangely in the discussions was the conclusion Americans must seem very ignorant and arrogant. Kids in shops for instance, when they found people couldn't understand them the first thing they felt was they must be dumb: it only gradually came around to maybe it was us who were dumb because we hadn't taken the trouble to learn their language. And when they found a lot of European people could speak maybe five or six different languages, that really did, it blew their minds. I suppose the place that gave us the rudest awakening of all was France: the French made it pretty clear to us they didn't think we were teaching them about civilisation, rather the other way around: if we wanted to become civilised we'd better start trying to be like them. For school kids of 15 or 16 you know, that was quite an experience, as well it was too for all of us grown-ups.

Lester Gover, *Mayor*

A big old man, sitting deeply sunk in the middle of a big old settee in the sitting room of his comfortable home. His wife was busy in the kitchen through an archway off at the side.

– Heh Babe give us some iced cinnamon tea here will ya? If you've never tasted Babe's iced cinnamon tea you've missed one of the real great things of life. You like brown sugar in it? No, no brown sugar for him Babe.

Well OK now I'll tell ya, my ambition in life's to go on living long enough to say I'm the oldest inhabitant of Bird. So far I'm up to 84, and I reckon if I can stay around another 20 years or so that'll take some beating. I was born in Oklahoma where my father was a cotton farmer: he wasn't doing too good there so he moved on to Missoura, and that wasn't too good either so then he came to Kansas and did odd jobs. There was just him and my Ma and me and my sister, and we wasn't what you might call rich or educated people, so we all did odd jobs: farm work, soil work, clerking in stores, anything we could find. Then I went as a hand in a grocery store in Elgin, Columbus County, and by the time I was 19 I was the manager of it. The man who owned it was in poor health and he left the running of it to me, so what I had there was a pretty good grounding in how to run a business. Another couple of years and I'd saved up a little money and me and Babe married. Then we saw in the newspaper one day there was going to be a new grocery store opening up here in Bird, and there was a vacancy for a manager for it. More than 60 years ago that was, and that's how we came.

That was in the thirties, and those were what they called the Depression Years. Me and Babe could see what was going to happen, so we saved up our money as hard as we could. And sure enough it happened, the company that'd bought the store decided they didn't want to keep it no more, they wanted out. So me and Babe stepped in, we bought it for ourselves, and we put our whole lives into it and every penny profit went back into the business. It was hard but we were fortunate that we didn't have no competition: after the original company pulled out, none of the big chains wanted to risk coming back in, and they still haven't. They've gone to Baxter and they've gone to Conway City where there are larger populations, but up to now they've left Bird alone.

OK thanks Babe, oh and cookies too. Say if you've not eaten some of Babe's cookies, that's another of life's great experiences, she makes the greatest cookies anywhere between Colorado in the west and Missoura in the east.

I can't answer that question, can you Babe? I don't know why some folks say 'Missoura' and others say 'Missouri'. What do I say, I say

'Missoura' do I? What do you say Babe? There you are, she says 'Missouri'. Now what d'you know, I'd never noticed we said it different.

Well now, back to the store and that stuff. I have five children and 16 grandchildren and 13 great-grandchildren. All of our own children, they went off to college and got themselves educations, and that was the way it was with the grandchildren too. Only Gerry and his brother, they were the only ones wanted to be in the grocery business: so they went into financial partnership and bought in. Gerry looks after the store side and he's a fine young man, and he's carrying on the family business just the way I hoped it'd be.

Babe was always telling me four years ago when I retired that I wasn't going to know what to do with myself. But I've kept pretty busy, and it wasn't no effort to do it, things just come to me. I've had a year President of the Chamber of Commerce and another year as secretary, I'm a member of the School Board and the Library Board, an Elder of the church and in the Rotary Club. So those are just a few things for me to do.

And the busiest of the lot I guess is I'm a Town Commissioner, I've been elected in for three years. There's three of us and we appoint and supervise the Town Manager. We're lucky we have such a good one right now with that young man Gordon Osterman, he's a pleasure to work with.

It's a nice feeling to have, when you're a Commissioner, that you have a part of the handling of your own home town. This year because it's my last year of my term, they've made me the Town Mayor too. It's mostly just an honour, you sign documents and things on behalf of the town, and you're the kind of honorary head of the township. You don't have robes or insignia or none of that stuff, but you'd maybe end up with your picture on the wall of the town meeting chamber down there.

Bird, well I'd say it was pretty near as good as any other place you could think of in the world. Babe and me, we've been to Venezuela to visit one of our daughters where her husband works: we've been on vacation trips to Spain, North Africa and Egypt, and we've been to Europe, to Switzerland and England and France and those kind of places. It was sure all very interesting to us, but mostly we seemed to keep finding ourselves in big cities like London England and Paris

France. I mean that's what you'd expect if you take one of them packaged tours right? But well you know I guess now at my time of life, I'm a feller likes wide open spaces where you can see the wild turkey go by, and a little town where everything is kind of all together, everybody knows everybody and that sort of thing. Just last year I met an old friend come back here from New York where he'd been working on something up there in an advisory capacity to do with agriculture. And when I asked him how it'd been, you know what he said? 'Lester, can you believe, I was there a whole year and I never went to a single funeral? All those people dying there every day, and I never got invited 'cos I didn't know a single one of them.' Well here ya know, everybody goes to everybody's funeral.

Sometimes when we've been travelling around, folks have asked us where we're from and when we've told them Bird, they look at us like we've said the moon or something, because it's not one of your famous places or well known or anything like that. You won't find Bird in no guidebooks – but then you won't find Kansas either, least not in some guidebooks I've seen. That don't stop it being a neat little place to live and die in though.

8 *Professional people*

Robert Lubin, *Doctor*

A soft-voiced man, dark-haired, man with heavy spectacles and a gentle smile.

– I'm 53 years of age, and my parents were farmers: they had a place 50 miles north and east of here, and I went to High School at Conway City. I'd two brothers and a sister, and they still farm there: but I never fancied the life, I was studious and I enjoyed studying. When I was 18 my pa asked me what I wanted to do, and I told him I wanted to be either a doctor or a lawyer. He said he'd back me financially through medical school but if I went to law school he wouldn't give me a cent. His exact words to me were 'To be a good lawyer you have to learn to lie, and the better you lie the better you do. I don't want to see no son of mine making his life out of lying.' He had great bitterness in him, because him and his brother, they'd been involved in a long legal battle over the ownership of some land one of their uncles had left as his inheritance. It'd cost them both a big lot of money, and my pa was the one in the end who'd lost.

It took me almost ten years to qualify including a spell in the Navy: and at 29 when I'd been married three years, I wanted to settle down somewhere in Kansas that wasn't a big city, and maybe start up in practice on my own. Most times you have to buy into one that's already in existence, but I was lucky: I heard of another doctor who was looking for someone to join him starting here, where they were building a new clinic for the town. I made an appointment to go see the Chamber of Commerce, and they offered me and the other doctor this:

it was then a brand new custom built medical centre, and that's how we're here.

I make daily calls at the hospitals in Baxter and Hammond, then come here around 10.30 and see patients until five in the afternoon. It's fairly leisurely, today for example I've seen only 14 patients, and I like it like that because it gives me time to chat with folk and sit and listen to them if what they mostly want to do is talk. A visit's $18, that'd be around £10 I guess in your currency, right: that's for the consultation, then on top of that you pay for your drugs, medicines, bandages and anything else you need.

In America yes, money comes into medicine a lot, in fact all the time, and everyone has to carry a lot of insurance. If you have a serious illness, especially one that requires hospitalisation, you can find yourself having a hard time after a while, because it often happens the insurance covers only part of the cost, or the cost for a limited period. As you get older and more liable, your premiums increase on that score too: or if you've a medical history, that's another reason.

Yes I think that does mean there are people who don't seek attention when they should, especially in the cities where there are people who are poor: they suspect they're ill with something which is going to put them in for big hospital bills, they leave it to see if it'll go away, and sometimes leave it too long. In a small place like this we try to encourage our people not to do that. Anyone who's come to us and said they don't know when they can pay for the treatment they need from us, in all the time we've been here we've never ever turned a single person away. In that kind of case we don't send a bill, or we hold it back until things are easier for them: I'd say at a guess we've maybe ten per cent of our patients we have that sort of thing happen with.

The other side of where money comes in, and it's an increasing thing these days, is where patients sue doctors for wrong diagnosis or misdiagnosis. This is really getting to be on the up and up: one of our medical journals only just last month had an account of a lady who'd been around a total of 23 doctors over a period of three years and sued every one of them. These are extreme cases of course, and again they occur most times in the cities. We've had nothing like that so far ever in my time here in Bird: but there's always a first time and it's worrying. All doctors now carry very heavy insurance against being sued: in my case it's 16 per cent of my income per year. A good lawyer can make a real good story out of how much pain and inconvenience and mental anguish someone was caused by their doctor telling them they'd got something they hadn't, or hadn't got something they had. I guess talking like this takes me back to my father and how he instilled in me deep distrust for lawyers.

One thing I've never gotten used to in all my time is folks being killed in road accidents, I've never been able to get hardened to seeing people all mangled up. In some ways and in most instances there's a degree of dignity in dying, but not when life's been suddenly crushed out of you and you weren't prepared for it. I'm glad to say that since the state decreed a 55 mile an hour speed limit on our roads everywhere, the number of accidents on the road, and death or serious injuries resulting, has dropped very dramatically indeed: and I mean really dramatically, we haven't had that kind of call out in maybe all of four years now anywhere around here, while before we used to have regularly maybe four five a year.

In this kind of a practice where you know pretty near everyone in town and they know you, you can't avoid it that you get involved with patients on a personal level. You come to know a lot of them as personal friends: and however much you say it's all a part of the pattern of life and death, you've got feelings that can really upset you when someone you know and like is dying. My partner and I have an understanding that we see each other's friends if it looks like it's going to be something terminal, unless that patient specially asks for you to tell him the truth of the situation. Some folks prefer not to know of course, and you have to respect that. My own wife who passed away last year very suddenly, she had cancer: I suspect she knew the symptoms when they occurred, but she never told me about them or asked for medical treatment anywhere.

This was to me a time when instead of me being the community's doctor, they gave me help and comfort, and it was something I was very glad to have. Before she died I'd been thinking I might retire and maybe go on a trip, but there seems no point to that now. I'd sooner stay here and go on with my job.

John Stone, *Attorney-at-law*

– An Attorney-at-law is a lawyer who's qualified and licensed to act in court and to prosecute or defend criminal cases. Most of my work's defending, and I enjoy that more than prosecuting: I don't have a great sense of mission or zeal, I don't fancy myself as Clarence Darrow, but I think it's often just that bit more difficult and challenging.

Most often when someone's accused of an offence of a minor nature such as a traffic violation or a small amount of drugs possession, which can be handled at local court level, they're guilty: and all you're saying on a Not Guilty plea is that the prosecution has to prove it though, and do it properly and above board. It wouldn't be too good a system if someone could be accused of something, and it was all left in the hands of the law-enforcement people both to prosecute and to give the verdict. There's also times now and again when you feel well hell, sure the guy's guilty but he's more dumb than dangerous, and there's other folk doing the same thing and getting away with it because they've more brains or more money to buy themselves a good lawyer. It's all a question really of seeing things from a prosecution or defence point of view and operating accordingly. We have a good County Attorney and a good Magistrate Judge: both of them very fair-minded people, and I find it a pleasure to be in court.

I came three years ago with my wife and our two daughters from Daneville just over the county line in Orlando County, about 55 miles north and west of here. I'd been in practice there with another person, just a small town firm: but the partnership wasn't a happy one and we brought it to an end. The guy was a nice guy, but we didn't have the same way of looking at things. It was kind of sad because we'd built the practice up together for 12 years. He had a certain amount of domestic problems also, and he drank a little as well, so the whole thing was generally unsatisfactory, let's put it that way.

We like it here, we have a nice house on North Truman Street, and our daughters like their school. I think you know our eldest, Jody: she's 15 and then we have Bobbie who's ten. They're ours by adoption, and we've had them both since they were just a few weeks. I think things have been harder for my wife: her mother died not long after we moved from Daneville, and it made her feel guilty like it often does in cases where something like that happens.

It's taken us a little time also to feel we fully belong in the community: we've not reached that stage yet 100 per cent, but you can't be too pushy, you have to wait for folk to come towards you. A difficulty is that if you're a professional person such as an attorney, people are just a little bit reticent in approaching you. It's hard to explain, but I'd say it was like at times they didn't feel they were quite at the same social and educational level as you. You don't want them to feel that, and you don't feel yourself that you're some kind of superior being. But it is a fact there's a division, and up to now the Russburgs are about the only friends we have, which is maybe because he's a lawyer also.

Another factor that affects us is we've no farming background in our family, so again this is something which limits both contacts and conversation. What you might call the middle class, most of the law work to do with them is land work, the buying and transferring of property and matters of that sort: and if people are involved in that, naturally enough they'll go to lawyers who've handled family business for them before. It takes time for a comparative newcomer to build up that side of the work.

The other area too is divorce, but again it's not a straightforward thing. Someone just the other day who was a neighbour of ours, he told me he and his wife were divorcing and they'd got it in the hands of a firm in Baxter. When I said to him well I could have handled it without an 80 mile round trip for him every time, he said he and his wife had done it that way because they didn't want local people to get to hear of it until it was all sewn up. Anyway he said, they looked on Magda and me as friends, and they hadn't wanted to bother us with their affairs. Folk sure can be strange in their ideas: I think if it was me I'd want to have something like that handled by someone I knew rather than a stranger.

But I don't want to tell you things that are only on the negative side, because like I said, we feel even if it's slow and it takes time, we gradually could get settled very nicely here. It's a clean tidy town and that's something that counts for a lot, to feel you live in a place that's got a certain pride in its appearance, but without being too formal about it. I think we'd like it if there were one or two more eating places to go to, and the girls complain sometimes there's not much here for the kids. But I seem to remember that was one of my own complaints when I was a kid too.

Do I see myself still being here in ten years' time? Well it's a funny thing you should ask me that: we were talking about it at home only just last week one evening. Magda was saying how when she was younger she'd had some accountancy training, and how maybe in a year or two she might go back to college for a while and get her proper qualifications. Jody asked her what for, what'd she do if she did, so Magda said well then maybe she'd set up here in a little business of her own as an accountant for local businesses, tax advice and stuff like that. Jody looked real surprised, she said 'You mean you wouldn't want to move on to a city or somewhere?' Magda said No she wouldn't, that was absolutely for sure. And you know what? Jody gave one great big sigh of relief and that really surprised me it did, that living here should mean such a lot to her after only this short time.

Bev Daniel, *Veterinarian*

Most mornings around 8.30 she rode leisurely along South Jefferson on her big dapple-grey horse, with a smile and a wave as she went by. A dark-haired slightly built woman in her thirties.

– I was born here, I grew up here, I went to High School here, and then I went to Kansas State University to train and qualify. My dad has been the veterinarian in Bird most of his life, and ever since from when I was a little girl he took me on calls with him, to sales and breeding tests on cattle, and let me watch him do surgery at his clinics. I was the gopher, I stood where he told me to stand, carried his bag for him and picked things up when he dropped them. I'd two sisters, one older and one younger: neither was interested in veterinary work, but for me from as long as I can remember it was all I ever wanted to do. I'm now in partnership in practice here with him: I like it, it's my life and we share the work equally. About one quarter of it is domestic animals and horses, and the rest is cattle: he has a fine reputation around the area, and it's my ambition to be as good as him or better. Sometimes if it's strangers I get a funny look because I'm a woman and small, and there aren't many women in the job of any size: but when they see I can do it, that satisfies them.

It takes something over seven years' study to qualify and get all your necessary certificates. First of all you have to have a year's experience before they'll even accept you at veterinary school, but I was well placed for that. It's still a pretty tough training though: but I knew what I wanted to do, I was determined I was going to do it, and I did.

While I was at college I met my first husband: he was studying to be a veterinarian too, and we got married at Christmas of our second year. In college, the first and second years are all classroom work and they don't let you touch living animals: then you have to combine studies and working in clinics, and it was hard for us to get jobs close to each other in the vacations. What was even harder though was after we graduated when we were trying to find permanent work: a practice'll maybe have a vacancy for one but not often for two together.

What we managed though was to get jobs fairly near one another: and then after a while we hit real lucky and got the chance to set up a practice together in a small town in Wyoming, just about the size of this one. It was a hard struggle to build it up, but we were very happy doing it: we had two children, our two little girls, and after around five years or so it looked like we were going to make it, and we were, we were very happy.

This is something I've not talked about for a while and I'll do the best I can: but I hope you'll excuse me when it gets a bit difficult. My husband you see, well our plans ended because he got killed. One of our daughters was four years of age and the other was two years of age, and it was in the evening when he was in the paddock riding a colt. They were sitting on the fence watching him, and I was watching from the window of the kitchen where I was fixing supper. I guess the animal put its foot in a hole or something and it tripped, it flipped over on top of him and he was killed instantly. It was a completely freakish thing, a total accident, and it's not something you can ever forget if you've seen something like that, or the girls either, I'm sure they won't too. Excuse me, it's so very kind of hard talking about it. No no we'll go on talking, I'm OK. Yes really.

Well my mom and dad came over and helped me with the girls a while, but of course Dad had his work here and had to come back. I decided I'd sell up the practice and come back here too, but in a small place it takes a time to arrange things, there aren't all that many buyers around waiting. My relatives weren't near nor were any of my husband's family, so I decided all I could do was keep working and get someone to come in during the daytime and take care of the children. But then there was the problem of night calls. You have to take them, you can't tell people to find someone else in a small place that's no other veterinarians within 100 miles, so I ended by having someone live in. It's not easy either to find the the right sort of person: I thought the woman I had was OK if a bit religious-minded. But I then discovered one day she'd told the kids that the Devil lived inside of the television set, and if they switched it on he'd come out. They'd been living in fear every time they'd heard me with it on, and I'd not known anything about it.

So she had to go, and there was a period when if I went on night calls I took the children along with me in the truck. But that was no sort of deal for them or for me. Eventually though in the end I did manage to sell the practice: but not the house up there, that's still on the market. I came back here last year after I'd sold the practice and came in with Dad: then a few months ago I met the man who's now my second husband, we were married just a few weeks back. I thought life was finished when my husband was killed: but Clive's a sweet man and a very kind man, he's formed a good relationship with the girls and we think if we work at it we can build a successful family. One step forward is I've forced myself to start to ride horses again, mainly for the children's sake: I don't want them to grow up with it in their minds they're dangerous animals.

Life's been a little kind of hard to me in some ways I think, and since I've come back here I seem to feel somehow that a lot of my contemporaries, girls particularly that I was at school with, they haven't sort of grown up as much as I have in a lot of ways. I'm not very outgoing so it's not easy for me to pick up old friendships again. One of the things I do find really hard is that it's a basic in the American way of life that you're somehow not supposed to be unhappy. If anyone enquires, the standard response they want to hear from you is 'I'm just fine.' You might feel like hell inside but you've got to not let it show. It makes me laugh a little talking to you about it, because it's what we always say about the English, you put up a front and you have a phrase, 'keeping a stiff upper lip' is it? I guess there ought to be one for Americans, about how important to them it is they should always show 'a stiff upper smile' or something like that.

But I don't want to sound too critical about this as far as other folks are concerned. I do have one big advantage that a lot of women my age don't, which is my professional qualification. I've married my second husband out of love and because I wanted to, not because I had to for economic reasons for the kids. An awful lot of people wouldn't have that freedom of choice that I did, so in that way I'm a fortunate person.

Leonard Demarr, *Mortician*

– It's the question folks most often ask me that is, do I like my work, do I enjoy it? It's difficult to give a straight answer. There's no simple yes or no to it. If you say yes folk think you must be some kind of ghoul or something: if you say no, then they come right back and ask you why do you go on doing it? I suppose the simplest answer is the mortician is a central figure in the community: and if you're the only one there is, like I am, however much folk'd sooner not think about it, you're a social necessity. Death and dying, they're very sad things but they happen to everyone. You get your satisfaction afterwards when people tell you they've appreciated what you did for them, how much help and comfort you gave them in their sorrow and loss.

Because it's such a profound experience for them, many folk don't know how they're supposed to behave, how they're supposed to feel even, when they have a member of their family die or be killed. You can sense sometimes, say if it's the end of a long illness or something, there's a degree of relief, both on behalf of the person that's died and for the relatives themselves. There's nothing wrong with that, it's a perfectly natural understandable feeling. If you can convey that to them, and that you're someone who understands and doesn't criticise it, I think you're helping them. Or if the one who's died's a young person say, and their relatives are so stunned they don't seem to be able to react in any way: you can help them by getting on with performing the practical duties necessary for the funeral arrangements, things which at a time like that are beyond them altogether. You try and guess in every situation, whether the relatives want you to do pretty near everything, or whether they want to do things themselves. That's another thing takes folks different ways: and it's only your experience'll help you sense which way they want it to be.

We sat at the table by the big picture windows which stretched the length of one wall of the sitting room of his house on North Adams Street, looking out over the view to the distant prairie. He was a small man with a tanned face and bright blue eyes, with a friendly smile: he spoke slowly and precisely.

– I was born here 79 years ago, and my grandfather and father owned what was then a furniture store on Main. The funeral business went along with the furniture business because cabinet makers were the people who made coffins. It wasn't until the 1930s that the two businesses were separated, and around that time I went to a special college for a year, to learn embalming and become licensed as a funeral director. My father and grandfather trained me in what you might call the people side of things: to both of them it was a first principle that people should know they could rely on you absolutely and in every way. That included they should know you'd never take advantage of someone's grief, encourage them to spend more money than they should, or enter into heavy financial outlay which they couldn't afford. I've carried on that family tradition after them, which I guess is why folks still come to us.

The biggest change I've seen over the years, I think, is in the increase in mobility in society, and what that entails. People move around all over the country much more than they used to: so of course they don't always die in the most convenient place. If you've already bought your burial plot in the cemetery here, as many people have, and left it in their wills that they want to be buried here, and then you go and die in Alaska or California, that's giving your relatives a lot of expense in bringing your body home. And naturally of course they're going to carry out your wishes: if that's where you've said you wanted to be buried, that's where they'll bury you.

With that thought in mind, some folk leave it in their wills they want to be cremated if they die some place else a long way away, and just have only their ashes sent back to be buried here. So that creates different problems. It's not always what the children want: they feel the chance to have a proper funeral's denied to them, they wanted to perform the last functions as a mark of their love and respect. Or out of the best possible motives, people sometimes make all the arrangements for their own deaths themselves: they pay for their own funerals ahead while they're alive, so they'll be putting no burden on their family. But understandably some people feel they didn't want to be excluded that way: they wanted the responsibility, it's a way to show their sorrow. So my advice always to folks in general is to tell them not to lay down hard and fast requests in their will. As much as someone should only says is 'If it's possible I would like': but the final decisions about place of burial and so on, they should be left to the family.

I've no desire to retire, but I am easing up a little now. Someone else will be taking over the business. None of our grown-up now married children is in it, but I'm sure the person carrying it on will keep up the tradition of service to the community. What my wife and I would like to do before we get too old is travel. We've been to stay short periods with our children in Oregon and New Hampshire, and we went once also to Europe to visit our daughter and son-in-law in Germany with the United States Services.

We took the opportunity then of making a short visit to England, which we liked very much. We particularly admired the way you've preserved your history in places like Stratford-upon-Avon, and some of your great cathedrals which we visited. This is a heritage which we don't of course in America have, and we're very envious. To us something 100 years old is of great antiquity: so when we see something 1,000 years old, that's very very awe-inspiring.

I'd like to go again to England and visit more with people in their homes: but they're not as openly friendly, I don't think, as American folk. I think this is due to a certain reserve, almost shyness: I guess English people would say in return Americans are too noisy and attract too much attention to themselves. I sure hope one day to go and see if we can find a way around it.

Joe Liddle, *Bank President*

A large cool modern open-plan office, ceiling fans, glass partitions, piped music. His staff call him 'Joe'. A burly gravelly voiced man in his fifties, in an open-necked shirt.

– Well, I normally come in here around eight in the morning, then I work through till around five or six in the evening. Sure, I enjoy it very much: we have a nice atmosphere here, I think those who work for me are happy and friendly with each other and with our customers, and we like to keep a relaxed atmosphere around the place. We don't have anything at all in the way of counter security, anyone can walk right on in and through to here in my office if they wanted to. That's because we don't have no need of it: there's not much in the way of bank robberies goes on in central Kansas rural areas, least not so far as I've heard of. We keep Kitty on that desk there nearest the door because she's the prettiest: if anyone wanted to take a hostage, she'd be the one. Then we'd all do just exactly what the felon said, so's we could get her back again.

We have only the one bank branch and this is it. It's a private family business. My dad and my uncle both, they first of all had the bank in Bakersfield: then they sold that one and bought this one. I went to university and majored in finance and business administration, and then as a family we all bought into here 28 years ago. I have two fine sons who work with me here, when the time comes I'll step down to make room for them: but while I've got health and enjoy working I shall keep on going.

If you have the town's bank, that puts you in pretty much a central position in the community. The bank and the school, they've got to be the two most important institutions there are. You're on personal terms with most every single person in town, you know a whole lot about them, not just how their finances are. People like to come in and talk with you if they've got money to invest or they need a loan: they tell you things about themselves, about their pasts and their hopes for the future, about their family and property situations and everything: it's a nice feeling you have that you're a confidant to people. You can drive along a street, and most every house you pass you know pretty well who lives there and how they're doing.

One of the things we go big on is getting kids to look after their money and handle it sensibly. Most folk go along with that's a good idea. Our youngest customer is 11 years old: he has his pocket money paid him every month by his parents, and he brings it along here and puts it into his account. He puts a proportion of it into a savings account where it earns him interest, and the rest stays in his checking account. He has a check book which he uses if he wants to buy something or make a cash drawing. He's our youngest customer, but there's several only a little older than he is. The youngest person we've ever made a loan to was 14: he came to see me one day, his pa had sent him along to consult with me to see if I'd loan him five hundred dollars to buy some hogs, so's he could fatten them up and sell them off at a profit to earn himself some money for later on when he goes to college. He didn't have no collateral to offer me, but I told him I knew his father so I'd take a risk on him, which I did: and then just last month he sold the hogs and paid me back the loan and put his profit in his savings account. His father could have lent him five hundred bucks himself, but he wanted him to get the feeling of a business deal with a bank.

In an agricultural community, we work in with farmers and along with the credit unions and such, and we make some pretty big loans. But this is a family business and always has been: we want to keep it that way, so we make a feature out of small loans to individuals too. See, let me show you a page in this list here: you can see right there in the loans column how we've made folk loans of quite small sums. Nine hundred fifty dollars to that person: seven fifty there, three hundred dollars each to those two, one there for one hundred dollars. If a person comes for that sort of a loan and they're one of our townsfolk, there's no way I'm going to turn them down. They know that: and we know what sort of people they are. In many cases we've known them since they were kids at school: so we can keep it informal and on a personal basis. Just yesterday someone called me up, he said 'Heh Joe I need a thousand dollars for a few weeks.' I didn't even ask him what for or to come in and sign forms or anything, I just said 'OK Tommy that'll be fine.'

This isn't to tell you folks are so rich around here there's no problems. That's for sure, they're not. But what they are is honest: if a guy can't see how he's going to pay you back, he tells you it when he comes to discuss it with you. Then it's up to you to make the decision whether to help him or not. That's the business you're in as a banker, helping folk out: you discuss a man's problems with him, and if you can, if it's going to be viable, you help him. But it's no way of helping him if you can see it'll end putting him in a worse position than he already is now. If that's how it looks, you tell it to him straight: you're not in the risk business of trying to make a few bucks out of him because he's so desperate he'll agree to anything.

One of the things that's affected quite a lot of folk here was the oil boom we had started six or seven years back. At the peak of it there was something around 200 oil wells drilling in Bird, and it went to some folks' heads. They thought it would continue that way for ever: they went out and bought themselves new houses, new automobiles and everything else. Then when the oil dropped off again, they'd gotten themselves used to a standard of living they found hard to give up. The most sensible man, you'll know him I guess, was Harold Albert. There was more oil found, for longer, on his land than anyone else's in town: but Harold and his wife Louie, they didn't let it make not one piece of difference to the way they lived. They just went on exactly as they'd always been: same house, same automobile, same way of dressing and eating, same way of talking to folk, nothing changed at all. Harold invested his money wisely: and he was very philanthropic to the town also with the library. There's one or two folk, I sure can tell you, would have been wise if they'd followed his example and not started giving themselves fancy ideas.

Well Tony, I sure have enjoyed visiting with you. You know what's one of the things that I've liked the best? It's listening to your English accent, that sure does bring back memories for me. When I was a young man in the Air Force in the war, I was in your country. Our base was in a part which I think was known as East Anglia, would that be right? I flew 33 bombing missions before the war was over and I was sent back here to Kansas. While I was in England I had two or three short leaves and I went to London, and to the city of Chester which I remember had some very historic black and white structures. I also went to a town, I think it was called Peterborrow. I liked the countryside around there, it was very green and trim. But I sure was lonesome, I remember that: we didn't have the chance to meet many people because we was flying so much.

I heard a few years back the place where I'd been, our aerodrome, it'd been taken over and was now a turkey factory, owned by somebody by the name of Mr Matthews is it? So least it's a consolation to me to know it's still got something to do with flying.

9 *Law and Order*

Ralph Hacker, *Chief of Police*

A short man with close-cropped grizzle-grey hair, he sat in an old swivel chair at his desk which had nothing on it but a pen stand, an ashtray, a personal radio contact phone with its volume turned down low, and his revolver in its holster.

– I've ordered no crime in the town the next couple of hours while I'm talking to you OK? It's some rough place you know is Bird: and I can honestly say to you with my hand on my heart if I never get to go anywhere tougher than here, that'll suit me just fine. If it gets no worse than it's been in my 17 years so far, praise the Lord and pass me my pension.

When I joined the Police Department I started as patrolman, and after eight years went up on the Chief's retirement into his position. I've three full-time men under me, one part-time and five reserves I can call on: my area's everything inside the town limits, and outside of that it's looked after by the Sheriff's Department and the State Highway Patrol. I don't have a secretary, which means I have to do my own book work: and I don't like doing it, I'd sooner clear my desk first thing every morning and then get out on patrol. Because I'm the community's Chief of Police, that means I get calls at home and nights even when I'm off duty: mostly it's not anything very criminal, it's advice. About once a week I'll get a call at gone midnight from some guy or other, like 'Say Ralph we're having an argument here, what's the maximum number of wheels you can run on the sidewalk before you get a ticket for it?' I'm the authority they turn to when the beer's drunk and the card game's over.

The worst thing in my time here was we had a rape a few years back: apart from that it's the odd drunk now and again, or a traffic stop. I don't like those, no law-enforcement officer does: every time you go for freshen-up training they keep telling you and telling you, never take anything for granted. People go crazy, remember that: the guy you were having a soda with yesterday in Dorothy's, when you stop him today he might have gone noodles overnight in his head, filled himself up with drugs and liquor and taken his gun for a ride, looking for someone to blow away. It could happen to you even from your own brother: he's forgotten who he is and he's forgotten who you are. So be very very careful, that's what they're always preaching at us: put the handcuffs on your own grandmother and then apologise to her afterwards, if you've got the slightest sense there's anything unusual about the situation at all.

Most stops though, they're – well we don't call them routine, that's how we've one hundred per cent not got to think of them. But we do have a routine procedure say, for speeding. I flash my light at you from behind to pull over, then I get out and walk up behind you and invite you to come back to my vehicle and look at the locked-in radar I have, which shows what speed I've a reading of for you. If it's within hours and you're from out of town, I take you along to the Post Office. There you buy a bond and an envelope and a stamp from Melvin the Postmaster, and you post it there and then in the mailbox to Judge Hertzog, together with the ticket I've written for you. If the Post Office is closed, I ask you for proof of identity such as your driver's licence, and ask you to sign the ticket: then I take you along to the Sheriff's office, and we ask the despatcher to check with the Police Department at where you're from, so we know you're who you say you are. On no account are we ever allowed to take the money from you ourselves: and if you don't send it to us by the time you've said, we have a reciprocal arrangement with other states that they take your licence away from you.

That's an English driver's licence? May I examine it please? Yes well now the first thing I'd ask you is how come it don't have your picture on it, where's the authenticated photograph? Yeah, I see: well now if this were a real situation we were in and you showed me this, I'd first of all sincerely apologise to you about the delay that was now going to be caused, and all the trouble and inconvenience I was going to put you to, having you having to sit around here for the so many hours it was now going to take to check out you're who you've said. I would be genuinely apologetic about it: and I wouldn't say it, but I'd hope it'd teach you a lesson never to commit no more traffic violations in Bird.

I like living here, and me and my wife have a happy family home. That's something very important for a person in law enforcement, to have a stable domestic background. We've been married 32 years, and to be able to say that is more valuable than anything else there is. A policeman's job is very stressful, and in all your training and so on, keeping up the high level of watchfulness I was telling you about, it's almost as if the need is to keep it stressful. No one'll deny to you, or they shouldn't deny to you anyway, that among police officers in general there's higher than average level of personal problems, drink, marital breakdown and the rest. And someone who's gotten in one of those kind of situations, he doesn't make a very good police officer either: because he's likely to carry his troubles out into his job with him. In one of our police magazines not long ago, I read an article where it said statistical studies have shown the greatest danger to law-enforcement officers is themselves. On the national average, five kill themselves to every one that gets killed in the line of duty. Most times the cause of it's family stress. A man and his wife aren't getting along, or he drinks too much, or he's got financial worries: and yet he's the guy supposed to be the real good citizen who wears the uniform that mustn't bear a stain. Well at all times, everywhere he goes, he's got his gun: so one day it's too much, he can't take any more of it, and he blows himself away. There was this poor lady in the article they were writing about, she was in the kitchen fixing breakfast and she called up to her husband if he didn't hurry up he was going to be late for work. And the reply she heard was the shot. Terrible, a terrible thing: I've never felt that way myself, but it sure didn't surprise me to read about it, not from some guys I've known or heard about.

So there you are, I guess that's about it. Except to say to you please remember while you're here, if you want assistance at any time our police force is as much at your service as it is to anyone else in the community here. Only say, just in case, get yourself some less troublesome ID than that funny old piece of paper you got there for a driving licence, OK?

Marvin Taylor, *Highway Patrolman*

We sat on wooden chairs at the small table in the kitchenette of his small house in South Truman Street. Children's brightly coloured crayon drawings and paintings covered the walls. The worktops were full of cereal packets, jars of fruit and opened cartons: the sink was full of unwashed dishes. He was a tall man in shirt sleeves: sallow skinned, 40, thin and seeming tired.

– Well sir the exact correct title of what I am is Kansas State Highway Patrolman, and it's what I've wanted to be ever since I was a kid. I was born and brought up in Alton, Tipton County, which is around 115 miles due south of here: I went to High School there, then I went on to college to learn law enforcement. I took a degree in law enforcement and sociology, so it was straight down the track all the way.

My family was poor and I had to work my own way through college. I did odd jobs, anything I could get: in my final year I was working 11 at night through seven in the morning at a filling station, then catching a few hours sleep and going into college around two in the afternoon. One night it was raining, and the most beautiful girl I'd ever seen in my life drove in, in this real old heap of an automobile. It had the headlight out on one side, and she asked me if I could fix it for her. I made a big play about it, told her that it was very difficult, only a really very skilled person could do it. I made it last about three times as long as it ought, just so's I could keep talking with her. When it was done she asked me what the cost was, and I told her no, that was OK. She was so grateful, so I took a chance, I asked her would she give me a date instead. And she said Yes: and that was it and we went on from there. That was Shelley who's my wife, we have three kids and I still think she's the most beautiful girl I've ever seen. I guess she must love me a lot, because in all the time we've been married, 16 years now, she's never asked me to do some other job. It's not the greatest pay in the world, we've had some hard times: but she knows I'm happy doing this and nothing else, and she's never complained of the hours or nothing.

We work to our own times: you do 24 hours a day for four days out of seven, but you can spread them how you like within the period. It's pretty varied stuff: accident investigation, vehicle inspection, traffic incidents and patrols, and you can go near anywhere you like within your designated area. I like the freedom this gives you. I enjoy the weapon training they give you too. For us in the State Patrol, it's pretty intensive: I don't know if I'm supposed to say this, but we train members of both the Sheriff's Department and the Police Department. Our weapon training is the highest level below only two other organisations in the United States. Which I know I'm not supposed to name, so maybe we'd better stop there on that.

A place like Auburn County here, we don't get a lot of crime: there's the Interstate Highway up north goes through, where you might get someone passing by and be given radio information to watch out for them. But I've been lucky and had mostly a quiet life. I've drawn my gun a time or two but nothing worse than that. The worst moment of all I ever had, well I'll tell you: that was a couple of years back when I stopped a little old lady. I guess she was coming up to 70 years of age, grey hair and glasses and a little hat. I flashed at her for speeding and she pulled over, and I got out of my vehicle behind hers in the regulation manner, and walked towards her. I'd gotten just level with her car door when she whipped round with a pistol in her hand pointing it at me. Then she burst out laughing and showed me it was a plastic toy one. She told me she was taking it for her grandson as a present. I can tell you, I was already into stage two, which is cold and ready to fire. When I got my voice back and my heart started beating again, I said to her 'Lady' I said, 'Please don't ever do that again, not ever, not to no one. Otherwise you could find yourself a very sweet old lady who's very very dead.'

I had a funny one only a few months back when I stopped a guy for speeding. He had sitting next to him his very pregnant wife who they said was in labour, and he was rushing her to hospital. So I told him that was OK, I'd escort him: which I did, all of 40 miles to Baxter and right up to the door of the maternity unit. They got out and they were both so grateful, what was my name and they'd name the baby after me. I can tell you it was a real tear-jerker. So in they went inside. Only I'd noticed something, see: so I just set there in my vehicle and waited for them to come out, which they did in about three minutes. What I'd noticed was they didn't have no suitcase or anything for him to bring her clothes back out: oh yes she was pregnant, but maybe not more than seven months yet. We all had a big laugh about it together, specially me while I was writing out his speeding ticket for him.

So those are the only incidents I've had that I can think to tell you about, that might be of interest for you. That certificate over there on the wall? Well sure yes, if you want to, you can read out what it says if it's of interest. 'Presented to Patrolman Marvin Taylor by Kansas Highway Patrol in recognition of your outstanding efforts on 10 May 1985, when at high personal risk you alerted the citizens of Elgin in Auburn County, Kansas, to a huge tornado that was threatening their community.'

I don't know there's all that much to tell about it, except to say there's not many folk been so real close up to a tornado. In my case, I was out on patrol about four o'clock one afternoon, and I saw it in the distance: I went closer to see if I could see how bad it was, and which direction it was going. They later estimated its base was a little over a mile wide, which is pretty big. I got up to it about as near as a quarter of a mile. It looked to me like it was coming right on top of me, and the thing I'll least forget was the total silence of it, like being in a cathedral. This enormous rotating black wall right ahead of you, the sky gone very dark, no wind and everything completely still: except this thing going on coming quietly towards you steadily at maybe 15 miles an hour. That's very slow for a tornado, which was lucky for me. Everything very cold, the temperature dropped right down: my ears started popping like I was in an aeroplane.

A real weird aspect about it later is I was talking to the despatcher on the radio, I was telling her exactly where it was and which way it was going. And afterwards she told me she kept telling me 'Speak up Marvin, I can't hear you, speak up, shout!' I couldn't hear no noise myself: but what it was, was the rattling of the hail on the roof of my automobile, which she said sounded like some one was spraying it with machine-gun fire.

I don't go to church myself, but that was a time when at first all I could think to do was say a prayer. It was just like this thing had spotted me and was coming closer to look at me. As far as I could tell its general direction of movement was west towards Elgin: that's only a tiny little sort of a place, and I knew they'd no public warning system there. So I turned around my vehicle and headed in that direction at a fair rate, faster than that old twister was going I can tell you. There's two things I know about tornadoes, that for years I'd been saying in talks I'd given in schools to the kids once in a while. Number One is if you're in an automobile, and you see one coming, get out and get under it: inside it is the most dangerous place you can be, because a big twister'll pick it up and throw it a mile. And Number Two is never, but never, try to outrun it by driving, because it's usually going much much faster than you can get up to. So there I was: breaking both of them, Rule Number One and Rule Number Two.

When I get to Elgin I drove around the streets there with my outside speakers on, announcing the thing was coming, and that people should take cover in their basements or in the centre of the ground floor of their houses or whatever. Talking calmer than I felt, that's for sure.

So but that's all there was to it. Just about a few hundred yards before it reached the town, it veered off and went away over the countryside and disappeared from view. So there we were, no harm was done. Before that I'd only ever seen pictures of tornadoes in books, and I can tell you it was sure an experience to be as close up as that to a real one. And I can tell another thing too, I only want to see pictures again, that's all, for sure.

Say look at me sitting here and talking and I've not offered you nothing. You'd like a cold beer or something? I'm not a well organised guy at the moment, my wife's been three weeks in hospital in Baxter, I have to go each night and bring the kids home for the night from their grandma's in Conway City. But let's have a beer or something first before I go huh?

Annabel Braun, *County Attorney*

Long brown hair, softly waved: brown eyes and high-cheekboned face. She wore a neatly tailored two-piece maroon suit and a frilled white blouse. We talked in her big office in the courthouse.

– I come from a family where it's always been stressed you get yourself educated, you go to university and get a qualification. When she was the age I am now, 28, my mother was widowed and had seven children: so she made all of us, me and my brothers and sisters, get educated and go into professions. When I was at Junior High School Bobby Kennedy was assassinated: it was that more than anything made me want to go into law, he was such a big hero of mine. After I graduated from High School here I went to university and took Bachelor of Arts and Political Science, then I went on to Washington and took my law degree. I met the man there who's now my husband: he's in law practice in Baxter now and we have two children: our son who's three, and then two weeks ago we adopted an eleven-month old baby girl.

As County Attorney I have to stand for re-election every four years: but if I'm lucky when that's due I don't think anyone will stand against me unless I fall down on the job really badly. It's not a high enough paid job to arouse strong ambitions in someone else, they can make more money in private practice. But you never know, there might be some youngster coming up behind I'm not even aware of yet.

All the felonies and misdemeanours come up through this office. Those we can deal with here, we do: those we can't, either for the seriousness of the offence or because a heavy enough sentence can't be passed, those go on to the District Court. In the cases we handle, mostly traffics and worthless checks, as County Prosecutor I have absolute discretion what to do. I can prosecute in court, or I can decide on a diversion. You don't have that? Well what it is, is that if it's not too serious an offence and the person is say a first offender, in the case of a bad check I can tell them to make restitution and behave themselves for six months: if they do that, then I don't prosecute. Yes that does mean to some extent I'm acting as judge as well. But I think it's a good system, in a lot of cases it's giving someone a second chance, making them stop and think, which is maybe all they need to change their ways.

It wouldn't happen in a serious case. Fortunately we don't have too many of that sort here: when we do it's mostly someone from out of town. It's funny how it seems to go in kind of phases: within four months of when I first started, I had a rape, an attempted rape, a kidnapping and a molestation. Since then, in over a year now, I've had nothing of that sort at all. It was a heavy start for me though: cases like that I have to take all the way up to the state capital.

Mostly in Bird we've a pretty crime-free area: we don't have that many big cases. Traffic violations are the most frequent: if people haven't paid their ticket on the spot or mailed in the fine, mostly by the time the hearing comes up they've decided to plead guilty. I don't have the exact figures, but I'd say people passing worthless checks are second most frequent. They're a real pain because of all the paper work involved and for usually only small sums. That doesn't mean to say it's not important, both to the person they've laid the check on, and to the community in general: nearly all your life's based on that you believe other people are honest and trustworthy, so it creates havoc when you get those who don't have those values. Most often in any store along Main, you could go in to make a purchase and you could say 'I don't have my money on me' or 'I didn't know I was going to buy this, I don't have my check book.' And most often, eight times out of ten, nine times even, the store keeper'll say to you 'That's OK, take it and drop by with the payment for it next time you're in town.' That's how it should be, that's one of the things that makes it nice about living here. But when people go out of their way to deceive somebody into giving them goods by taking trouble and writing out a false document, I think that's a pretty mean thing to do.

Then what next do we have, drunk drivers I suppose: we go pretty hard on them, I won't often give a diversion there. And also not common but not uncommon, we have domestic assaults. The complainant lays a charge: and I've found in my experience with those, it's a wise idea for me to do nothing in most cases for 48 hours and let it cool off. That's the period of time most people seem to need to decide whether they're going to go ahead or let the charge drop: which is what in most cases as a rule they do.

I'd say in our criminal set-up generally, I don't know if it's the same in England, but I think our main problem is people getting off on technicalities. They know they're guilty and you know they're guilty, but there'll be some funny thing in the law somewhere that you can't clinch it. It's frustrating, specially when it's a case you know otherwise you could make stick. On the other side we don't have too many cases, least I hope we don't, where an innocent person gets convicted: I never file for prosecution unless I'm absolutely certain of guilty. If there's even the slightest doubt at all in my mind, I don't go ahead with it. I must have no doubt I'm going to prove it. I may not always get the conviction: but I can say honestly, in my time so far, I don't think I've ever seen anyone get a wrong conviction.

An average normal day for me is I get up around seven and make breakfast: Steve goes off to Baxter and at nine o'clock I take the kids to the baby-sitter. I come in here and go through the mail, discuss any points that need it with the judge, then usually three mornings a week I'm in court here. At noon I go get the kids and take them home, and make us something to eat: then I take them back to the baby-sitter and I'm in here again around 1.30. Afternoon it's mostly office work and preparations until five, then pick up the kids once more and take them home. Play with them a while indoors or out in the yard, depending on how the weather is, or take them to the lake: then home for supper. If Steve's back by then he'll maybe have started in on doing it himself. More play with the kids, and in the evenings friends, visiting, or on our own watching TV. My favourite programme is *Night Court*, where you have that zany judge and those crazy attorneys all getting themselves into ridiculous situations with the folks they have to deal with: it has me near crying with laughing sometimes, because I don't mean it ever happens here but it sure reminds me now and again of us.

I like the job. The first time or two I had to go in front of a judge at the Capitol and stand up and say 'Your Honour, I represent the State of Kansas', I was pretty scared. But not now: it means I represent the people, and that's good, I like it.

Diana Hertzog, *Judge*

A soft-voiced small fair-haired woman in her thirties, I'd seen her often, shopping in Govers. Her office in the courthouse was cramped, its walls lined with shelves crammed with law books.

– This is my sixth year in office here. My jurisdiction's over Auburn County and there's just the one of me. Above me is the District Judge: he's responsible for several counties, and I pass on up to him cases that by law I can't try because of their nature or because of sentencing limit. I can fine someone up to 2,000 dollars, give them up to one year in the county jail here, or place them on probation for two years. If the offence's an indictment that carries more than that on a guilty finding, then it's for the District Judge, and on beyond him if necessary to the Capitol at Topeka.

I deal with something around a hundred criminal cases a year: my area also includes probate of wills, applications for guardianship of children, legal requests for letters of administration and such. On top of that I have adoption proceedings, care of children orders, and juvenile offenders between the ages of ten and 18. And above all, traffic tickets: last year they were something like a thousand on up.

I enjoy it all, there's not a single day I don't look forward to. Whether it's civil or criminal work, you wouldn't believe the variety of people appear: most you're never seen before and probably you're never going to again, but every single one of them's interesting, and you have to remember each one's unique to himself or herself. The only thing's a strain about it to me is that it's a lonely profession: I don't discuss cases with anyone except my District Judge. I can ask about points of law from the County Attorney or the Sheriff's or Police Department, but primarily I'm on my own and responsible for decisions I take.

I'm not like Annabel Braun: I've no legal training or background at all. I just saw the job advertised in the local paper one day, that there was a vacancy for Judge, and put in for it. I'd been working with mentally handicapped children and we'd opened a small shop on Main to sell things that patients in a hospital where I was also working had made. I'm married with three children and I like to be busy and active and I enjoyed doing that. But I was feeling it wasn't enough for me somehow, the children were growing up, and I was ready for full-time employment that would really stretch me. So like I say, there was this job vacancy advertisement, and I thought it sounded really good.

It could have been for some other completely different job, and I could have gone in some totally other direction, sure. Other people applied for it too, I don't know how many and who they were: but I was the one was appointed. Then I had to take a nine-month course of instruction: that was a real lot of study and book work before I took the certification tests, and it was only when I'd passed those I was allowed to hear cases. I still have to read my books pretty good to keep up with changes in legislation, and I rely a lot on my District Judge for advice. I can't give you a specific example because I can't discuss specific cases. Except perhaps one, OK: when you asked me could you come and interview me, I asked *him* if I could, and when he said go ahead then I was in the clear.

We have this system here where our judicial appointments are subject to the electorate. This means two things: the first is that you have to get responsible sponsorship to be accepted to run on a party ticket, even though you're not expected to behave, and you don't behave, politically in any way. The other thing is that if you're not good at your job, or people get the idea you're doing favours or leaning too much one way or the other, well then at the next election somebody can run against you and turn you out. I think it works pretty good, or seems to as far as most people are concerned. If you're fair and honest, they're not going to throw you out at the end of four years just because you're a Republican or a Democrat as the case may be. But you always know in your mind you've no divine right to your appointment, you're there on behalf of the people: all of the people, so you better try and show them you're aware of that.

I don't know now that there's any other job I'd like to do: it'd have to be something pretty good to tempt me away, because it has such a high interest content and you feel what you're doing's worthwhile. It's a little embarrassing for me to try and answer for you what the most important qualities are to be a Judge, but I guess I'd say I think you have to try and be calm and sensible in the courtroom where often people are under a lot of stress, you have to be level-headed about things and not have too much sense of your own importance: and most, I think, you have to be as fair as you can to everyone, and let them see that you're trying to be fair. Maybe you ought to talk with someone I've had to come down hard on, see if they thought even if I was hard I was fair.

And perhaps another aspect too that's important is what you represent, which you might call the ordinary person. He or she, I think they need to feel they have a part to play in the legal system: it's their legal system after all, it's important they should feel it's got something to do with them. And if it's got ordinary people like me in it, I guess that might be a plus for it.

There's no one in Bird feels, least I hope there's no one in Bird feels, that I'm all that separate from them or in any way above them. I have my family relatives living in the town, my kids at the school, my home which is the same size as most everyone else's, my husband who goes out to work like other folks do, and I'm no different from anyone else. I belong to some of the women's clubs and organisations, which is a good way of getting to know a wide circle of people and meeting them on a regular basis, and seeing folks regularly and developing friendships. I don't go along with the idea of living here in the courthouse in some kind of an ivory tower. Anyone can walk in and consult with me anytime they want, so long as I'm free. If I've got the knowledge and information they need, I'm happy to give it them: if I haven't I'll pretty soon find out who has and point them in that direction.

That's part of my job. Hearing cases and passing sentence is part of my job also: but outside of here, I'm just another woman and a member of the community.

Jed McClusky, *Probation Officer*

A tall man of 60 with big hands and his hair cropped short, he wore a light blue suit and a flamboyant floral tie. His basement office was windowless, and harshly lit with an overhead fluorescent tube. He had a loud chuckle, deep and frequent, which seemed to echo round the walls.

– I'm what they call the Adult Felony Probation Officer, right? I have four counties: Auburn, Hudson, Joplin and Vernon. That gives me an area something like well my God I've never totted it up: guess if we said 36,000 square miles, that'd be about it. Right, 36,000: three six, zero zero zero. If I had one felon for each square mile, that'd be one hell of a lot of felons wouldn't it? But I don't: Kansas is the peacefullest, the least criminalest state of the USA. You know why? Because it's me that keeps it that way, they'd sooner steer well clear of crime than have old Jed McClusky on their backs. I give 'em hell, a term of probation with me's worst than being in one of them old chain gangs.

I'm a Kansan, my folks are Kansan. I've been Probation Officer for this part of the State of Kansas for 23 years. Before that I was in the Army, involved in criminal investigation work. Nowadays to be a Probation Officer you have to do a four-year degree in criminal justice, sociology and psychology. You didn't have any of that when I started. These times the young ones who have it, I feel it gives them one big advantage over me, that they use better English than I do in writing out reports.

Only you know, if I'd had 50 years of schooling I still don't reckon I'd have known all the things I'd have needed to have experience of. I'm a mental health worker, a marriage guidance counsellor, a finance counsellor, a moral adviser, a psychologist, a law enforcer, a teacher, a father figure, a judge, a prosecutor. I could give you a list stretched from here to here and it'd still not include all the things. I don't see how any kind of schooling is going to have given you all that. I reckon you need to know one thing and only one thing, which is when you're out of your depth and can't handle something, that's all. If you can recognise that, and know who or where to pass it on to, I'd say that's the main thing you need. Maybe what's wrong with teaching these days is it gives some kids ideas they can handle everything, and if they can't they're failures. I don't see it that way: you've got so much specialist help these days, the best you can do is get the person to go seek it, or leastways give it a try. You've got some feller's got a drink problem, I don't see it's much help to him if you sit talking with him for hours about whether his father had a drink problem, and his grandfather, and his Aunt Cissy in Missoura: you want to get him to sign himself up for a detox programme, and let them sort all that out.

Don't get me wrong though: what I'm saying to you is not what a wise old bird I am but the exact opposite of that – I'm a dumb old bird who knows nothing, but knows he knows nothing. Over the years I've had so many cases I can't recall, when I wouldn't have given you a plug nickel for someone's chances of keeping themselves out of trouble, but somehow they've survived. Then the next one, you'd put your last dollar on it they'd seen the folly of their ways and would stay straight: and the next you know, they're back in court in even worse and deeper trouble. Well, you don't take it home with you, you don't go crying and ask yourself where you went wrong. If it gets into the area you think you're a personal failure that's bad: you should just look at your work and see if there was anything wrong with that, not look at yourself.

I don't have that many statutory powers, and where I can I try not to use them unless I have to. In the system we have, the Judge can put someone on probation without conditions, which means they don't have to report to me: or the Judge can make it that they do. So then they come along to me, and we write out a written contract between us that they've got to abide by. The first condition would be they mustn't violate the law in any way at all, not from a traffic violation right up to a felony. The next is to report to me here, or have me visit them where they live, as often as we decide. Then, pay any fines have been given within a specific time, and finally any special conditions like going to Alcoholics Anonymous or a drug treatment unit. Sometimes you get a funny situation: maybe someone wants to go to California where his uncle's promised him work, so he comes in here and shows me the letter. I say to him OK, does he want to be transferred for supervision to a Probation Officer in California, or will he stay under me and do it by mail? If he elects to do that, then I'll let him supervise himself, and so long as he writes his report to me every month, we go along like that. If he misses one though, just one monthly report that's all, and his supervision's transferred.

A main difficulty I'd say is we get a drifter picked up on the Interstate or somewhere, he's passing through and he's in possession of drugs or something. We don't know who he is, where he's from or where he's heading, and he won't tell us. The Judge wants a report, so's he'll know what he's dealing with: we check with the FBI and they can't tell us anything because maybe the guy's given us a false name and address. So we just keep him in jail till he changes his mind and gives us the information.

But we don't have too many of those: I'd say we don't have too much crime of any kind around these parts. There's no one I have on probation at all right now in Bird: there's one or two out at Garland, but that's the place where you've a number of people with problems and troubles anyway. It seems like they tend to congregate in that area. Baxter, because it's altogether a bigger place, I've a few there too.

It's been a good life for me and I've enjoyed my time. Shortly now I'll be taking retirement: our two children are grown up and married, and my wife and me, we feel we want to do a little travelling. Nowhere special, just get to know a little more about our own country than we do, we've no big plans for any long trips or anything. The thing I like is fishing: and I'll be happy to take the good weather days out by Lake Morrow or Milton Reservoir, those are both favourite places of ours.

We don't plan on moving far from these parts though, we're Kansas people. The folks around us are good, we've many kindly friends and neighbours so we couldn't ask for more. I feel the job I've had all these years now, it's had a lot of satisfactions, I've always felt it was basically something useful to be doing.

Say, there was a Judge the other day, did you read it in the paper? In Kansas City it was, Kansas City Kansas: he said he was putting this guy on probation, but it had to be in Kansas City Missoura over the river, he'd no faith in the Kansas Probation Service. What about that? You know what it didn't say in the paper though? That that Judge, he was a Missoura Judge, that's what it didn't say. How'd you think about a guy saying something like that eh?

10 *Two Lives (2)*

Harold Albert, the richest man in the world,
and Louie, his wife

Their house was one of the smallest and plainest, halfway down South Adams Street. Outside it stood an ordinary Buick pickup truck: last year's model or the year before's.

He was tall, long-legged and wiry: he wore a check shirt and blue twill overalls, the legs tucked into the tops of cowboy-style calf-length boots. She was short, in a plain brown blouse and a shapeless navy skirt. Her grey hair was cut in a schoolgirl fringe. She had bare legs, and white canvas tennis shoes on her feet. A big table in the sitting room was piled with newspapers and magazines, and there were three chairs and an old settee. Several cardboard boxes were scattered around on the floor, full of files and papers. Under a side window a large extractor fan in the wall was motionless, not working: instead a rattling fan swung noisily from side to side at the far end of the room.

HAROLD: This here's Louie my wife. She ain't feeling too good today, she's got trouble with some bad teeth. She'll just set there and listen to us, but she doesn't feel up to talking much.

LOUIE: I'll say something if I want.

HAROLD: You bet.

LOUIE: If you say something wrong or I don't agree with.

HAROLD: Shouldn't be all that long before you start speaking then. I didn't know after when I met you in the library that day whether you'd come around visiting with us or not. I've not had an education and I don't talk all that good but I'll tell you anything you think's interesting you want to know. About our early life and everything, you said?

LOUIE: How'd you know that?

HAROLD: He told me it one time last week when I saw him on Main.

LOUIE: You didn't tell me you saw him on Main.

HAROLD: Oh, him and me we've met a time or two. Once when him and the Sheriff were drinking coffee with Lester, and one time when you came into Dorothy's with that woman right?

LOUIE: That's something to say, that's no way to speak about his wife.

HAROLD: It wasn't his wife, it was a lady he maybe doesn't want folk to know about.

LOUIE: It's no place to take her to isn't Dorothy's, if he doesn't want folk to know about her. Who was it?

HAROLD: I don't know who it was.

LOUIE: Oh sure.

HAROLD: Listen, that's all I'm saying about her. You just set there and give your teeth a chance, else they'll never get better. You should have had them fixed sooner like I said.

LOUIE: They weren't so bad sooner.

HAROLD: OK well you tell him about your teeth later, only right now I'm going to tell him about my early life OK? Well now: the first thing is I'm 74 years of age and she's a little bit older.

LOUIE: Only a little bit older.

HAROLD: Only a little bit right. And I wasn't born here in Bird.

LOUIE: I was.

HAROLD: I was born on a farm out near Milton Reservoir six miles east of here, and she –

LOUIE: I was born right here in Bird: number two hundred thirty eight South Third only it ain't there no more.

HAROLD: It used to be South Third but now it's South Jefferson.

LOUIE: And the house ain't there no more, there was a fire.

HAROLD: She was a local girl but I wasn't. My mom and pa, they was simple folk: I was their eldest son, but they had a girl older than me. They ran what was a grocer's store on the corner of Main and Lincoln, which was then Sixth Street. It's gone long since, it's now Joe Hagan's garage. First of all I had to get me some education, but I wasn't much of a one for schooling: when I got up to eighth grade which was when I was 14, I decided that was enough for me. So I asked my ma and pa if I could go work with my sister in the store instead, and they said yes, so that's what I did. I just worked ordinary in the store, I took care of the eggs and the potatoes and the sugar, and I packed things in and out as well. I got paid 35 cents an hour plus four dollars a week pocket money, and out of that I had to give a half back to my folks to pay for my keep. In those days at the store we used to sell 100 cases eggs a week, 100 cases cream, and maybe 75 or 80 those big bags of flour.

LOUIE: There wasn't all the fancy things you can buy in packets those days, you just did your home cooking with the ordinary things you could get.

HAROLD: And that's how we met, one day when she came by the store for some eggs.

LOUIE: Sugar. It was sugar I came by for, not eggs.

HAROLD: OK sugar, eggs, it's not important.

LOUIE: I was still at school, and my mom sent me into the store to get some sugar for to bring home after school. And I took to going into the store to meet him when I was on my way home from school other days too.

HAROLD: She didn't talk much those days either, she just used to stand there while I talked to her. I was supposed to be working, carrying things around, and she used to stand there while I talked to her. She got me into trouble for talking and not getting on with my work.

LOUIE: I never got no chance to talk because of how much he talked all the time. He used to tease me and make up tales to tell me about things he'd done and things he'd seen, see if I believed him. If I did he used to laugh and tell me I must be pretty dumb if I'd believed him. To tell you the honest truth, I didn't really care for him at all.

HAROLD: If you didn't really care for me, how come you used to stop by so often then?

LOUIE: Only 'cos I'd got nothing else to do.

HAROLD: Well, you had nothing else to do for six years. That's how long it took me talking to her, to persuade her to marry me.

LOUIE: I never knew if he really meant it or not, what's why. I never knew if he really meant anything he said to me at all. Lordy, 52 years ago that was.

HAROLD: 52 years ago that we was married, that's not bad for these days. I must have meant what I said then, when I said I wanted to be married with you.

LOUIE: You said lots of things you didn't mean though. Do you know one thing he said to me? I can remember it to this day, he said if I married him I'd never want for a new dress. And one day after we was married, I said to him I needed a new dress and I wanted a new dress, and he'd told me I'd never want for one. You know what he said? He said he couldn't afford to buy no new dress for me, so I'd better stop wanting it, then I wouldn't be wanting for a dress.

HAROLD: Well that's how it was then. You could have a new dress now if you wanted one, but in those days things was hard. When we got married, my folks said we could have the running of the store with my sister. It wasn't enough to keep all of us, but they could go back and manage for themselves on the farm if we took the store. So that's exactly what we did: we got married in the church in the morning, then after we'd had something to eat everyone together, then her and me and my sister, we went back to the store and we opened it up and it was business as usual for the rest of the day. And that's how it was, from that day onwards all we did was work.

LOUIE: We bought this little house here, and we ran the store a few years: then his sister, she didn't want to go on doing that any more so she sold out her share to us. Then it was even harder work, we had to go careful a long long time didn't we?

HAROLD: We sure did, we had some pretty hard times too.

LOUIE: We had some hard times, but there was one thing we always did, we always paid our bills. Whether it was for the store or for ourselves, we always paid our bills on the day. We're still that way, if there's one thing I don't like to see in the mailbox it's a bill. I just feel it shouldn't ever be there: it ought to have been we paid it on the nail when we bought something.

HAROLD: The other thing we did those days was no matter how little money there was, we'd always kept some of it aside for savings. She's always been pretty good at figuring so she looked after the money, and she looked after it real good. We kept our prices low in the store: we didn't go after making big profits out of folk, so we had a small business but a regular business. And even in the hardest times, she could figure how much of a quantity of something we should buy, how much we should get when we sold it and how much we'd have left afterwards to live on.

LOUIE: And how much we could put by. The hardest times were after the recession in what they called 'the dustbowl years': those were the hardest time, I reckon.

HAROLD: Those were terrible times, the thirties and through up to the beginning of the 1940s. It was like the whole of the State of Kansas was blowing right away. I can tell you, life was as tough as a boot. I've seen Main Street three o'clock of an afternoon, the air was so dark with dust you couldn't see your hand this close in front of your face. Automobiles was all stalled up with dust in the engines and wouldn't run: you had to have a kerchief over your mouth just so's you could breathe. Real tough. But in those days you took things like that in your stride, you thought nothing of them.

LOUIE: You might have thought nothing of them, but I didn't. They blew for days, you had to put wet sheets and blankets up at all the windows there to try and block up the cracks and stop it coming in. You never could though, it got into everywhere: on and on it went blowing, one day after the next.

HAROLD: You know, that dust used to get so thick on the backs of the cows, when it rained it made it solid. And seeds were in it, I've seen cattle had thistles growing on their backs.

LOUIE: That's an old farmers' tale. I've heard him tell that story a hundred times or more. It ain't true.

HAROLD: It is too, I've seen it, I've seen it myself.

LOUIE: It used to be just you knew a man who'd seen it.

HAROLD: Well still, those dust storms they were really something all right.

LOUIE: They really were. But we survived.

HAROLD: By hard work. And this isn't no farmers' tale, this is true: the only time we shut the store the whole year round was two hours at noon on Christmas Day, so we could eat our Christmas dinner. And people used to come by Christmas afternoon, they'd say 'Where were you? I thought something was wrong, I was by an hour ago for some butter and the store was closed.'

LOUIE: Hard work but we enjoyed it.

HAROLD: Every minute.

LOUIE: No not every minute: I didn't enjoy it when you went away with the truck and left me on my own to mind the store.

HAROLD: I bought me this truck, and I figured if I made the trip to Colorado for good fresh vegetable produce myself, it'd soon come out a mighty bit cheaper than paying someone else to haul it for me. Chiefly tomatoes, peaches and green string beans, and some fruits too. It was something over 600 miles the round trip, but most times you could do it in the day, if you started in the morning early enough.

LOUIE: And sometimes to Texas you used to go, for grapefruit. That used to take him all day and a night to get there, and the same to come back. I used to think he often went only because he enjoyed driving his truck.

HAROLD: Oh, it was a real classy vehicle that one was: a huge big thing, the biggest around here for miles. It was called a Diamond T. In all the years I had it, I can't once remember it ever broke down.

LOUIE: That was because you looked after it so good.

HAROLD: I did all the servicing of it myself. I like mechanical things, I always have. I learned it from watching other people right from when I was a kid: if I saw an automobile mechanic in a repair shop, I'd ask him could I watch what he was doing. That way I picked up how to do it myself. Same with everything in the house: the plumbing, the electrics, the sewering, everything that needed doing, I always did it myself. I still do. Out in the garage there I've got all the tools necessary to do everything could ever want doing. Whatever it is, I can fix it. It makes me happy that I'm like that.

LOUIE: And obstinate.

HAROLD: What's obstinate got to do with it?

LOUIE: Obstinate's got everything to do with it. Tell him about that air conditioning plant we've got in the wall there.

HAROLD: What's there to tell about it? It only needs taking down and putting together again.

LOUIE: That air conditioning there, it's getting on for 50 years old now: It was one of the first ones like that that they ever invented. When he put it in, it was just about as modern as you could get.

Now it's broken down, and there ain't a single person left living can fix it.

HAROLD: Except me.

LOUIE: OK except you: so why don't you fix it?

HAROLD: I'm going to, I keep telling you: or if I can't fix it, I'm going to put a whole new system in.

LOUIE: You're too old to put a whole new system in. Why not just call someone up and ask them to come along and put a new system in?

HAROLD: Pay some young feller 30 dollars an hour to do something I can do myself?

LOUIE: You see what I mean by obstinate? We could have a whole new house now if we wanted to, with a brand new system in it.

HAROLD: OK go ahead let's have a whole new house: only any time we talk about that, it's always you says you don't want to move, you want to stay here.

LOUIE: I don't want to move, why should I want to move, we're happy right here.

HAROLD: So then OK you'll have to wait until I get around to fixing the air conditioning.

LOUIE: And how long's it going to be?

HAROLD: I don't know how long it's going to be. Let's talk now about when the oil came into our lives huh?

LOUIE: When the oil came into our lives, that was when all the headaches came too. I sometimes think that.

TP: *What happened?*

HAROLD: Well it was a strange strange time at the beginning I can tell you, it sure was. There'd been talk for years, you know, that there was oil under some of the land around these parts. Off and on over the years one or other of the oil companies had come and done a little test drilling, but nobody ever found no oil so they went away and forgot about it again. Then when one of them came six or seven years back once more, and said they were going to start looking again, no one paid much attention to them. They drilled a bit here and they drilled a bit there, and then one day they found they had a hole that had some oil. So they said they were going to make a proper run with it, and if they found one that made ten barrels of oil a day, then it'd just about be worth their while and they'd pump it. We had some little piece of land we owned ourselves out that way, and they said they'd do a test drill there too. And that one, the one on our land, before we knew what was happening, it was making not ten barrels a day but 50 barrels a day: every day, bang, bang, bang, just like that. So they sank another one on our land and then another one. Every single one of them produced oil, some of them a lot and some of them a big lot. Came the time we had a total of 24 wells on our land, and one of them alone was producing 400 barrels of oil a day. That's going on towards nine ten thousand barrels almost a day. For each oil well they pump on your land, they give you a royalty of one eighth of what it produces, day by day according to the price of oil.

So that was it, there we were, we had a very big strike on our land. There's very few times anyone ever strikes as lucky as that. One of the oil company men, he told me they reckon on average it's once in maybe 500 times they drill that they find a well that produces anything at all. So that's how it was, we had all them wells and they was all producing, day after day after day. It got to be called Little Saudi Arabia out there. The type of oil, its gravity, its quality and that it was so near the surface and easy to pump out: all these things were what made it such a big find. They said even after five years it was still only 200 feet down from the surface. Well, it's starting to go down a little now, and it won't go on for ever, nothing ever does. Oil prices is going down too, so I don't reckon it can go on that much longer now.

LOUIE: We didn't reckon ever that it was going to go on much longer. No one else had that much oil found, but some had some: and some of those who did, they lived like it *was* going to go on for ever. But we lived just like we'd always lived, that was all. And then one day the local newspaper printed a story about it. It was nothing much, no big splash about it: and then one of the Kansas City daily newspapers got on to it, and they printed a story about it. And then one of the New York papers, and Washington, and Los Angeles, and Houston Texas, and Alberta Canada: and somebody even told us some newspapers in Europe. Which ones and where, we never did know: but what we did know was that letters started to come, cables, long distance telephone calls, it was like suddenly everybody in the world knew about it and was begging us for our help. Some of the letters, they were ten pages long: people sent us letters from their doctors telling us their whole medical histories. Or they'd get their kids to write: 'My daddy just died, and my mommy said you'd got a big lot of money and you sounded to be good kind people, please will you send her some money to help her.'

HAROLD: One guy wrote us he needed a half a million dollars that's all, to build this church he had in mind some place in South America. Or another time we had a cable, all it said was 'Desperate for money, please send all you can spare' and nothing else but that and a name and address. I mean how do folk think someone's going to respond to something like that?

LOUIE: Sad thing was you know, we reckoned some of the stories people told us about how much they needed money was true. But it was just like one of them avalanches, they kept on and on coming, and how could you tell? You'd need your whole life to sort out which was which, true or false: and we're not that kind of folk, we're just simple people and always have been. It got so bad, we just used to set us down here and look at all the letters we'd divided up into piles: those we thought were really sad and had big troubles, and which a little bit less, and those who sounded like folk who just thought they'd like money for some scheme or other they'd got. And every one of the piles, they all got bigger and bigger and we felt we were getting sick, it was making us feel like that, worrying about how to decide. So then one day someone said to us we couldn't go on like that, there was no way we could ever decide who to help and who to not to: what we should do was think of something else instead to do with our money, throw all the letters in the boiler, and not even read no more that came. So that's just what we did.

HAROLD: We set ourselves down, and we talked about this and that, and in the end we decided what we'd do. We don't have no children, so there was nothing to think of there. All we have is a few what you might call immediate members of the family, so we first of all made sure they would be all right for the rest of their days. Then we got to thinking what we could do which would be to the benefit of everyone around here, not just a few folks, but everyone. It was our feeling that the stroke of luck we'd had, we'd got it out of the ground of Auburn County and the town of Bird in particular, so what we ought to do was somehow give some of it back because this is where we'd lived our lives. To put it to you shortly, when you've got to both our ages and you've had a good life you've been happy with, there's nothing you really need or want more than what you've already got. I'll let Louie tell it you how it was we finally decided what to do.

LOUIE: I'd been to that old library of ours like I did most weeks to get me a couple of books to read, 'cos I like to read. And as I was walking home one day, down along South Adams here, I got to thinking. So when I came in that door I says to him 'Harold,' I said, 'I've thought of an idea for something to do with our money. I've just been in the town to that old library, to get me a couple of books to read. You know what? I'm getting real tired of climbing up those library steps every time I go there: it bothers my knees, my arthritis is getting real bad now. So why don't we give the town a proper decent library where folk can walk right on in and choose a book for themselves without having to climb all them steps?'

HAROLD: I thought that was a real neat idea. The more I thought about it the more I seemed to like it. So I says to her 'I think that's a real neat idea. They've got a good-looking library over in Conway City, why don't we go over there and have another look at it, and ask them whose idea it was to build it like that.' So that's what we did, we went over there and got the names of the architects, then we asked a couple of other folk if they'd do us some plans and drawings of an idea for it too. We had a talk with Mrs Oberlin and asked her what she thought about it too, and she said she liked the idea. And we all thought it'd be kind of nice in years to come, if folks went by and they wondered how it was a small place like Bird had got such a nice good library like that setting there.

LOUIE: You'll have folks tell you here and there how it was their idea for to have a library. But it wasn't their idea, not in the first place: it was mine, because of my knees.

HAROLD: So there she sets: and we like looking at it, and folks all say they like to look at it and they like going there, and that's the way we hope it stays for as long as Mr Carnegie's building's been there.

LOUIE: You going to tell him about the letter?

HAROLD: You mean the letter this week from those people out east?

LOUIE: We had a letter this week from some people in New York, what was it, the American Libraries Association or something is it called?

HAROLD: Something like that.

LOUIE: They want to make us a presentation.

HAROLD: It's no big deal.

LOUIE: They want to make us a presentation because we built the library. He won't go.

HAROLD: Sure I won't go. New York, do you know how far that is? I looked it up in my atlas, and New York, that's somewhere close on 1,500 miles away, that's just as the crow flies. How many days would that take on a train to get to New York?

LOUIE: Like I said, we don't have to go on a train, we could go on an airplane.

HAROLD: You can go on an airplane if you like, but I'm not going to. It's OK for some folk, they say they're fine and dandy. But I'm never going to get me inside of one of them things, no sir that's for sure. If they want to make a presentation to us they can come here and do it here, or they can mail it to us, I don't mind which.

LOUIE: Obstinate see, like I told you. Well I guess we'll never get to New York for no presentation, that's for sure.

HAROLD: We could go on the train.

LOUIE: How could we go on the train?

HAROLD: We could go to Kansas City Missoura and we could go on the train from there.

LOUIE: And how long would that take?

HAROLD: It wouldn't matter.

LOUIE: Look just a minute ago you were saying it was too far and it'd take too long. And anyway you don't like the trains they've got nowadays.

HAROLD: They might have some of the old sort. We could enquire. If they had one of the old sort, it'd be real good to go on a train like that all the way from Kansas City Missoura to New York.

LOUIE: They wouldn't let you drive it.

HAROLD: They might too.

LOUIE: They wouldn't let you drive it. And anyway they don't have that sort. Do you know what he's talking about? He's talking about them old steam trains they used to have, the ones with a big chimney on the front shaped like that, and a cow-catching gate, and an old steam whistle that you pulled the chain and it went 'Woo woo'.

HAROLD: 'Woo woo woo', that's how they went: they went 'Woo woo woo'. You know, when I was a boy they used to go across the plains, I could see them in the distance from the farm that we had, you'd see them going across the skyline. That was the Union Pacific Line, the Union, Topeka and the Santa Fe.

LOUIE: It wasn't nothing of the kind, you're getting it all mixed up with the words of that song. And anyhow, you couldn't see that railroad from there, it was a hundred miles away.

HAROLD: I could too. Anyhow, I could see *a* railroad and I could hear those whistles. And you know, those men who drove those trains, they could play a tune almost on those whistles of theirs. They'd go along all day long like that, and they were, they were playing a song. And the smoke from their chimney going up in the sky, it was a beautiful sight, they sure don't have trains as beautiful as that these days, all they've got are those real ugly diesel things with their horns and big engines all full of black smoke. Sometimes I reckon you know if I'd been a young man when we had all this money come to us, maybe only half the age I am now, 35 or 40 or somewhere around there, you know what I reckon I might have done? That was the one thing I always wanted: and I might have gone off and bought me one of them trains, and driven it all day to my heart's content. I'd have said to Louie here, I'd have said 'Louie I'm going off for a while, I'm going to get me a train and drive it across the prairie some.'

LOUIE: I shouldn't believe all that if I were you. He just makes things up as they come into his head.

HAROLD: I didn't make that up about that train and its whistle, I've always wanted one of those.

LOUIE: I know you have. But all that about going off and driving it around the prairie, that's just talk. On your own: you'd have wanted me to go along with you and sit in the carriage behind the engine and cook your dinner for you, that's what you'd have wanted. One day of going off and driving the engine and pulling the whistle, that'd have been enough for you: as soon as you got hungry or had a hole in your sock, you'd have come hollering for me.

HAROLD: Well. Well maybe I would and maybe I wouldn't. You never can tell. Say all this talking we've been doing: I'll go see if we've some beer or something.

When he'd gone to the kitchen, I asked her any way she could see having money had changed him. She thought for quite a while before she replied.

LOUIE: Not one bit do I see it's changed him, not how in any way at all. He's just exactly what he always was, ever since I've first knowed him: a sweet, nice, gentle, man.

11 *Out at Garland*

Opal Richards

– I'm an old old lady, I'm a vat-dyed Kansasite, I don't mind the wind or the winters or the mosquitoes, I like walking barefoot, and I love the prairie because out in the middle of those big big spaces you look up at the big big sky and feel tiny but you know you're close to God. And one of its real great glories, that prairie land, is its wild flowers: the buttercups, primroses, wild daisies, pansies, wild onions, all the hundred different pretty little colours that there are. And each one of them lasts a few days, two or three days that's all: then they go till next year, and if you missed them this time you've got to wait till next.

Well, my little home here at the end of the street in Garland, it might be not so smart and it's tumbling down a bit, but it's been my home for 44 years. I came here as a bride. I was the country schoolteacher, and my husband he worked in the filling station out the north side of the highway. Them days Garland was twice the size it is now. No, what am I saying to you: it was ten times the size, a real little town with a drug store, a bakery, a grocery store, a Post Office, a church: everything you could need for this world or the next. But then in the end we lost our school: by a state law you had to have 80 pupils to continue, and we had nothing like that. So they closed the school and bussed the kids into Bird, and that was Garland's finish: over the years after that it went down and down till it's what it is now, a place with a handful of old timers like me, and the rest all the ragtag and bobtail of the world. Don't get me wrong though, I like living here, wouldn't want to live nowhere else. When my dear husband passed away two years ago, my dear son and his wife, they came asking me to go live with them in Great Falls, Montana. I told them No thank you, my home's in Kansas, I was born here 77 years ago, I've lived here my whole life, and I sure don't want to go to Montana to end my days.

He's a good boy though. See, here's a picture of him and his sweet young wife and their two fine children, in that silver frame right there on the mantelshelf. My husband and me, we wasn't able to have no children of our own: so we adopted him just one week before his first birthday. Now he's 42, and him and his wife and children, they come to see me three four time every year, all that way from Montana. Look I'll show you something, it's a verse I keep in my Bible here: I don't exactly remember now where I got it from: I cut it out from some magazine ten years back or so, it just caught my eye. Read it out for you? Sure I will. It's called 'My adopted child' and it says it's by 'Anonymous'.

> 'Not flesh of my flesh, nor bone of my bone,
> But still miraculously my own,
> Never forget for a single minute
> That you didn't grow under my heart,
> But you are in it.'

That's a beautiful poem uh? We've always brought him up to know he was adopted. He asked us one day around when he was seven or eight what the word meant, so we figured when he asked he was ready to know and we told him. How his mother had loved him very much, but was a person having a hard time: so she gave him to someone else to find a home for him, because that's most of all what she wanted him to have. Now and again sometimes when he was little, he'd ask us a question about her: we told him what we knew, which wasn't very much. He never said he wanted to meet her: and so far as I know he's never ever done so since he was married. I don't know if she's alive, or who she is, or where: that's up to him if he wants to try and find her, he's a grown man. But my husband and me, all through our life he's brought us great happiness: he's given us his love and we've given him ours, and I sure hope we helped him to be not too unhappy.

Another thing he doesn't do, is he doesn't not come with his wife and children to see us in Garland here. Oh you'd be surprised: there's more than one person not two spits from here, their parents won't come to see them not while they're living here. Don't you hear about Garland from the folks in Bird, how everyone here takes drugs and's an alcoholic and divorced, and on top of that living with somebody else's husband or wife? Well I'm not any of those things myself, so maybe I've missed out on a lot of fun because of it.

But what I do know, let me tell you, is I've got friendly people all around me here, some young people with young families, they're good people. They know I'm an old woman living on my own, and they're for ever caring if I'm OK and I've got enough to eat and am I comfortable. Every day there's not one person but six persons at least come in through that door there, all of them asking me 'Hi Opal, everything all right, you OK?'

It don't matter to me if they live with somebody else's husband and they smoke a few drug cigarettes now and again, what's that got to do with me? It don't mean you can't be a kind person with a kind heart. There's several deserted women here and young divorcees: this is where you come if you're down on your luck and looking for a cheap place to live. No one's going to look down their noses at you if you're on welfare either and having those food stamps. Me, I've never understood this idea that's around that poor folk must have brought it on theirselves, they ought to have made provision or something. Life's not simple like that.

There's a mixture of folk here like I said. But like it should be, the younger ones'll look after the older ones if they know they're on their own. Not just me, I'm not the only old person here or widow. This is why I didn't want to go to Montana to my son's: I'm perfectly happy here, safe and happy. I got friends, lots of them, they stop by any time they're passing. You going to meet some other Garland folk and talk to them? Anyone'll talk to you. You just go and knock on any door you like, say to them Opal sent you: I know what they'll say to you. You see if they don't: when you tell them I sent you, their first words to you'll be 'Well then come right on in.'

Ellie Lou Harburg

– Yes sure I'll tell you what poor is, poor is very poor, poor is very very poor. I'm 27 years old, I've been living here five months in this tumbled-down house that's dirty and lets the rain in and lets the cold in, and I'm paying cheap rent for it because it's not fit to live in. The guy who owns it can't be bothered to knock it down, so I'm very grateful to have it to live in. That's what poor is.

I came here January from Tulsa, Oklahoma, with a guy who said he'd heard there was jobs going in Hammond in the rig maintenance business. Opal got this place for us, we didn't know no one here but someone told us go see her. She's a great lady: we said we needed help and she helped us. She called up the guy this place belonged to and asked him for us could we have it a while.

This guy I came with, you could say his name was John. For all I know, that could be his name, it could be John. So he goes off to Hammond to see about a job, then he comes back and tells me he's found work starting Monday. Only he says it's long hours and night work and all that, so he'll have to stay in Hammond Monday through Friday. So he stayed in Hammond the week, and the weekend Friday through Monday, then the next week and the weekend, and that was the last I saw of him.

I wasn't all that shook up by it, to tell you the truth I hardly knew the guy anyway. It's always seemed to me if a guy's going to move in with you it's because he wants a certain thing, like someone to wash his socks for him or something like that. And if he moves out, it's because he's found that certain something some place else, like someone washes his socks more the way he likes them washed. But there'll always be some other guy comes around before long looking to move in with you. If he's got some money and pays his way, so what, I don't mind. I don't have guys bumming off me though, I don't allow that. They keep me, not me them.

If you mean did I have a service in church and a gold band on my finger, yes I've been married. In Cleveland, Ohio, when I was 16. I was born there and he was a kid from down the street: he was 16 too, we'd been at High School together and I was going to have his baby. My mother said we should do the proper thing: I didn't mind if we did, I shouldn't have minded if we didn't. I suppose he was a nice kid, or a dumb one, depending which way you look at it. It lasted just one year including the fighting and all the arguing we had. We were living with my ma, and one day he didn't come home. The sad thing was though the baby only lived a few hours after it was born: there was no reason we should have got married. When the baby died he turned against me: I think he thought somehow me and my ma, we'd kind of tricked him into marriage. It's an awful long time ago now, I don't have feelings about it, it's like it happened to another person. One thing it meant was I couldn't have no more kids afterwards. Maybe that was good, I don't know.

After that I left my ma. Correction, she left me, she went off I think it was Pittsburgh some place with a guy. Since then I've managed somehow. I've learned to look after myself from an early age and I do OK. I don't know where she is, I'm not bitter about her the way some people are about their ma. I guess my pa must have given her a hard time and it was that that made her like she was.

Right now I take the welfare. A lot of people don't talk about that, they think it's something they should be ashamed of. That's the way the SRS make you feel, that you should be ashamed of it, welfare saps a person's motivation to find themselves a job. Up till just recently they gave you a card: you had to have it signed at five different places a month, to say you'd been asking them for work. Then next month another different five places, and on like that. Now they've stopped that but toughened up other ways. You have to prove it to them you've no money and that you're in a deserving situation. They look at it there's them that deserve and those that don't. Last month the guy at the SRS office there, he said to me why didn't I go to Hammond to look for this guy'd been here with me. Then if I told them where he was, they'd go after him to send money to me. Otherwise he'd think he could leave all his problems to the State of Kansas and they'd pick them up for him.

Then he started saying to me how often did the guy come back to see me, say like night when there was no one around? I said never, he'd never been back to see me. I said what did they think, he came back from Hammond in the middle of the night and got into bed with me, then he creeps out again before it's dark and in the morning I find he's left some money for me on the floor by the bed? The guy just laughed:

he said 'Well it's only six miles from Hammond, lady.' Then another one comes from SRS Baxter, and he starts along the same lines: he said to me was it someone else dropped by now and then and gave me some money? I said to him 'What are you saying, I'm prostituting or something?' He gave me a look and he said 'Well, you're still quite a pretty lady.'

You know, I think it was that word 'Still' made me mad, it made it sound like he was propositioning me himself. But prostitution, that's what they'll ask you about if you're a woman and you're taking welfare. They say 'Well you're not working, so what *are* you doing for money, where you getting it?' It's much more the woman they come down on. A guy goes off to Hammond or wherever, they know they're not going to find him: or if they do, they'll likely find there's some other woman he's giving his money to, and maybe another and another. Or he could have kids some place and be sending money for them: so it's easier to keep knocking this woman, making her feel she's being watched all the time, not the man.

I guess I'll be moving on from here pretty soon, more or less any day now. I don't like it around here: I don't mean the local folk, they're OK: I mean the people in the SRS office. If some guy makes me an offer to look after him a while, I'll move on. You don't have no choice about it really.

Wayne Standish

– Uh huh yes I'm a Kansas man, I was born at Lewis, Cameron County, Kansas 111 miles southwest of here. I'm 31 years of age and I came here seven years ago. It came about this way: I'd been a patient in the County Hospital Whipsburg, I'd been six years there having treatment for nervous illness. I left there because I wanted to get myself on a federal programme for people who've been hospitalised a long time like I had: then you move on from there to what they call a protected environment, you go to work and you live normal, only they have people who are like social workers and nurses, and they help you look after yourself.

At that time my mother, she was living in Baxter. Things didn't work out the way I hoped though: my mother and me, we didn't get on, and I didn't get on the programme like I hoped, so there was no reason for me to stay there. I had a sister living in Lewis: she and her husband they worked a farm there, and they said I could go stay with them. They had four children and they didn't have a lot of what you might call living space, so that didn't work out too good either. So then I was wondering what to do next, and then my mom died. She'd had some money that she left to me and my sister and my other brother, and I used my part of it to buy me this house here, so I could live in it. I look after myself, and once in a while I go see my sister in Lewis. I didn't use up all the money was left me by my mom, I was careful about that: I just bought me a place that was enough for what I needed, and the rest of the money I've invested and things. It gives me some to live on, and I get by OK.

I'd sooner live here than in the middle of Bird, I think the folks here are more easygoinger than they are in town. I'm not saying they're unkind to you, nothing like that: but if you've been hospitalised a long time, like I have, you get a label hung round your neck that says long-term psychiatric patient. That makes people, well kind of leery about you. You have that word in England? It means kind of cautious right? I used to think it had something to do with King Lear: he was kind of mad and suspicious that way wasn't he?

You have to forgive me, my memory's not all that good, I've forgotten where we were at, it's all these pills and stuff. Oh yeah about the folks in Bird. Well this here's like the edge, the shore you might say: Garland's where folks wash up. Bird is a place where people don't like to have too many loose characters around. Garland's not like that: there's all sorts around. But it's handy for getting in to town. I go in and out a couple of times a week to Gover's food store. And I guess the last time I ever go to Bird, it'll be to see Mr Demarr. Least I like to think it'll be Mr Demarr, he's the undertaker, and if he buries you that shows you're respectable. I have an arrangement with him, I've given him some money to give me a proper funeral in the town cemetery there so everything's OK and as it should be.

Folks here's mostly good folks I'd say, they look out for you. That Mrs Opal Richards she's a nice lady, she makes cookies for me. Everybody's friendly and knows who you are. I can set on the porch out front there, and folks go by and we all greet one another. 'Hi how are you Mr Standish? Oh I'm just fine Mr Mailman how are you?' I like that, and sometimes a person will stop and visit for a while. 'My goodness Mr Standish, isn't it a real hot day? Certainly is Mr President, too hot for governing the country eh?' That kind of thing. If I go into Bird they're friendly too though: lots of folks know my name, if I go into Dorothy's Cafe when I'm in town they'll tell me Hello and that. Only they seem to like it more at a distance somehow, they don't say to you drop by at their house some time. Are folks like that in England?

– Last time you came to visit with me you said for me to think about ten years from now: how I thought it might be with me, where I'd be at and stuff like that. You know, after you'd gone I set and I thought, and I thought, Isn't that strange, I've never thought about that before? You can go all through your life can't you, and not get around to asking yourself that: where am I going, what am I doing, what's it all mean? I had the idea you see, that's what you was really asking me, what did I think did it all mean, was that right? Well you know I guess I can't answer that. If there's God up there I guess he could, but I can't. My life's been a very funny kind of a life so far, I know that. When I was in that hospital such a long time, when I was there I met a very pretty lady: she was a patient like I was, her name was Benjamine. We used to sit and visit, they had a room where the male patients could meet the female patients each day for an hour or maybe some days two hours.

I used to think one day, perhaps her and me we could meet when we wasn't in hospital. We both had been in that place a long long time, and I didn't often have no one come to see me: and she sure never talked about no one coming to see her. What we talked about mostly was being in hospital, and we used to make up stories, sort of fairy tales to tell one another to make each other laugh. And you know that's a question I never asked her, what do you think it all means, your life, where do you think you'll be ten years from now? Then one day I didn't see her, she didn't come into the like a big sitting room it was, where we used to meet. She didn't come in the next day, or the day after that. I didn't like to ask what had happened to her: they don't tell you those things in hospital any way, they say if you want to know about people you must ask them yourselves. Only I couldn't do that could I, because she wasn't there.

And then it was a few days after that and I'd almost decided to forget about her: and she came in and she came over to me, and she put her arms around me and gave me a great big kiss. You know what she said? She said 'Wayne, I had to come and see you and tell you goodbye. My husband's come back for me and he's taking me home.'

I felt kind of sad about that. I mean I was happy for her, but I was sad for me. She sure was a pretty lady. Wasn't that crazy? All that time and I'd never asked her was she married and things, where would she be in ten years, stuff like that. Me, I'd have to say something like I'll still be here, I've got no place to go except that last trip I take see Mr Demarr.

I've enjoyed visiting. Any time, drop by.

Herbie Kohl

– Well I'll tell you, it's 76 years ago come Friday I was born in a little place in south east Kansas called Parsons, that's in Lubbock County. I went to country school there for a while, and I had seven brothers and sisters and I was the youngest. Then my daddy moved on to Kansas City Kansas, and we all lived there for a while, then we moved on to Hiawatha. Then moved again, right back over the west side of Kansas, a place called Colby, and I went to High School. Some of my brothers and sisters, they moved on along the line, got themselves married and things like that. Five years in Colby, then back to south east Kansas in Garden City. Next thing I recall after that is being in north east Kansas at a place close to the Nebraska State line.

The time I'm telling you about then, I was working and I'd got me a wife too. We went to Manhattan, then Topeka, then Wichita where they make the airplanes. Let's see, after that Dodge City, Syracuse, Lebanon, Hoisington, Emporia a while, St Joseph . . . you want any more? I been nearly every place in Kansas there is, pretty near, and I'll tell you the reason for it. The reason for it was I was like my daddy, an auto mechanic: and I was a welder, an electrician, a carpenter and a yard worker in timber too. What they call a jack of all trades, and if I didn't like what I was doing or the folks I was working for, I just upped and moved on. I knew wherever it was, the next place I come to there'd be someone waiting for someone like me and would be glad to give me a job.

Moving always moving: but I'd say I'd had a real good life. Lucky for me I married the woman I married though, because no one else'd been able to live that kind of life and enjoy it. Never liked to be staying too long in the same place: many the time she was the one, it was she said to me 'Come on Herbie, we been here near three months now, I'm tired of this place, let's go some place else.' I used to tell her she must have gypsy blood in her. We never had no kids, so we could live like that all our lives and please ourselves.

She passed away three years ago, God bless her soul: the finest wife any man could ever have. It wasn't long after we'd come here to Garland. She just said to me one night when we was going to bed, 'I don't know Herbie,' she said, 'I feel so tired tonight.' Never had a day's illness in her life: and when I woke up in the morning she was lying beside me cold. She'd gone, kind of slipped away just like that.

It was like kind of someone'd drawn all the shades down over the windows, you know how I mean? I just set in this chair here days and days: people came, people went, there was a funeral but I don't remember much of it. I didn't feel sad or anything: it was just like she'd gone out the house a while and was coming back, and I was setting waiting for her. I can remember thinking she'd gone for a walk or something, through a forest with a lot of trees, along a path. And I used to think she'd turn around looking for me, and when she saw I wasn't there she'd come back for to get me and take me with her. I still get that kind of a feeling: each night I go to bed in there I think maybe I'll be going on after her. I say in my mind, 'Yes I'm coming Violet, I'm coming, won't be long.'

We weren't the sort of folk ever had much money: we'd lived mostly in rented places, mobile home parks, places like that. This here's the first place like this that we ever paid out money for and bought us as a place of our own. Now I'm going to stay here, because this is the place Violet knows I'll be. Only don't get no idea I'm a lonely person. I'm not. I got a lot of memories, each day I got a different lot of memories to think about. I don't get myself all sad and crying about them, nothing like that. I just set here and I say to myself 'Emporia' or 'Lawrence' or some place: and as soon as I said it, that's my memories for the day. I don't know if I'm much a Christian man, I don't go to church or read my Bible or anything. That big feller up there, he's the one would have to decide if I was a Christian or not. But I do have this belief this life isn't the end of things somehow, there's got to be more to it than just like you was turning out a light. That's why I'm pretty sure Violet's there waiting somewhere. That's a good feeling to have.

– That other day after you was here, you know what I got to thinking? I got to thinking how you was telling me about Bird and you staying there and talking to folk: and I thought how long was it since I'd had a walk around the town myself? So you know what I did, I did just that, walked around the town a while and looked at the folk there. Must be a year or more, you know that.

Well what I got to thinking about it, I'll tell you: might sound kind of crazy to you though. I got to thinking it wouldn't suit me to be living right there in the town, I'd sooner be here in Garland. It's all kind of tidy there, tidy people living tidy lives, everyone like they'd pick up a beer can or a piece of wrapping or something, soon as they saw it in the street. And another thing was I liked the kids: they smile, they say 'Hi' to you like they meant it. When you get to be an old man, you're always thinking you know that kids ain't what they used to be like: they're noisy, they ain't polite to old people no more. Well they weren't like that Tuesday, that's all I can say. There were some real nice kids there in town, the way they look at you and speak to you when you go past. And what I thought was kids weren't what they was like in my day, that's right, no they're not: they're a whole lot nicer than that now.

And you know what I'd have done? I'd have come back here if Violet had been here, and I'd have said to her 'Violet, let's ask some kids in sometime, ask them to come around with their friends for a soda or something.' Isn't that a crazy thing?

Anne Wheater

– I paint and I paint and I paint. My sister says I make a production out of art: I don't know I'm sure what she means, but that's the way she describes it. What I do know though is that it's only now when I'm 65, I've been able to do what I really want to in my life which is spend all my time painting. I only really got into it maybe ten years ago: but in that time I've worked and worked, and I've done something around 200 canvases, most of them real big canvases, of Kansas landscapes.

Nowhere else but of Kansas, mostly entirely. I was born in Nebraska: my dad was in the agricultural machinery business, but we moved to live in Deerfield 12 miles south of here, when I was little. And you know, what I'm getting around to saying is although I've lived most all my life in Kansas, the more I've been painting these last ten years the more I've seen there was to paint in the Kansas landscape all around me. Not just the obvious things, the surface things like colour and form and light: it's the graduation of things, the way things when you come to look at them aren't what you first thought they were. The prairie at a certain time of the year, say in the late summer when the temperature's been up more than 100° for weeks like it often can be: you look at it, you think it's all arid and dry and brown like some kind of colourless desert. Then you go on looking and you think to yourself: 'Heh wait a minute, there's this kind of brown and there's that kind of brown and there's *that* kind of brown.' And you look some more, and there's four more kinds of brown: and you look some more still – and for heaven's sake what do you see, you see another *six more* kinds of brown. And you think 'Heh what's going on here, am I going crazy or what, where are all these browns coming from like this?' Where they're coming from is inside your head, inside your eye: and you think 'There's 50 different colours of brown here, how on earth am I going to mix them all, never mind get them on my canvas?' I do, I get really excited about it just talking about it as you see. And I never do get even a half of them reproduced how I want them: not a half or a quarter. But it sure is one great feeling to try.

I exhibit and sell all around western Kansas now. I have pictures in the permanent collections of most the museums and art galleries in the area, and some places individual people will buy a picture of mine. It's always a big thrill to me if someone would want to have one of my paintings hanging on the wall of their home, it really is. Fran Webber who I think you know, at her little place in Main Street she's going to try and see if she can sell some there. Maybe she will, maybe she won't, I dunno. I don't make a living out of selling paintings, I don't sell enough for that. But it's a supplement to my income, and quite a good one. You see that little white and pink painted thing like a small barn out there, under those trees? Well this house was an old farm building when we bought it when we were first married, that was one of its outbuildings. My husband's restored it and painted it up, and now I have one end of it for my studio where I work, and the other end a little gallery for hanging my work. But all the materials and everything that was needed to fit it out, that was all paid for out of proceeds from my sales.

What I am originally is a teacher. After I'd graduated from High School I went on to university in Baxter, and I took a degree in English and art. While I was there I met the boy who I married and he went on to be a schoolteacher too. He's now retired, and it's good having him around the house all day, I like that. We have two children both grown up and married: when they were younger I combined being a mother and homemaker with part-time work teaching. Usually it was pretty easy for me to get jobs: there weren't then, there still aren't now, all that many art teachers around in this part of Kansas. And with the job I got access to materials I wouldn't have been able to experiment with: acrylic, crayon, poster paint, all kinds of stuff. I taught the kids how to use them the same time as I was learning to use them myself.

The other thing I learned teaching kids was how not to rush. They always wanted to, they were always impatient to see the finished product. Me too, I was the same: but I had to teach them to work slowly and carefully, to look and look and look again, then make notes, sketches, take photographs, plan the spatial relationships. Get the foundations right before you try to build the house or paint the picture, whichever it is. That way I slowed myself down too, made myself methodical.

I may not be the greatest painter in the world, I know I'm not that and never will be. But what's important to me is the pleasure I get from working as though I was, that's what's important. I might not be able to get onto canvas anything near good enough to what I can see: but the fact I can see it's there, see it with the painter's eye if you like, that gives me great great pleasure.

Here where we live, on our own piece of land just out of Bird, on the edge of Garland, this is where we came 40 years ago and we've never wanted to live any place else. We like living not quite in Garland and not quite in Bird, and we've got good friends in both places. Earlier on in the first days there were stores and a school in Garland but they've gone now. There was much more of a sense of an independent place to it then. Now there's lots of transient people moved in because the property's that much cheaper, and the older folk like us and Opal are getting fewer. But it's still a good place, even if it's getting a reputation for itself as somewhere where everyone's into drugs and living on welfare. There's people in Bird talk about it like it was Sin City of Kansas or something, but that's ridiculous of course.

Our family come to see us now and again with the grandchildren, they come and stay in the summer a while, at Thanksgiving and so on, and we like that. I'm a very happy person. A happy painter, that's when I'm happiest.

Annie Vee

– It was until last year I was at this bar, a small place, a kind of drinking club, the entrance to it was near the corner of Lincoln and Main. Then it closed down because the guy and his wife who owned it, they bought a restaurant over at Conway City. He offered me a job to go there and work for him but I turned it down: the working conditions, the hours they expected you to put in, the wages they were offering, none of it was good. He gave me the usual stuff: we pay you low wages you declare, the rest you make up on customers' tips, that way the Revenue don't know about it and you don't pay the taxes. It still meant me driving 19 miles to Conway City every afternoon and 19 miles back at night, not coming home here till four or five in the morning. I didn't fancy that, not with two kids. So I decided I'd give me a break, take a vacation for a while.

I have this place to live here, I share the rental with a friend. She works as a clerk at a store in Deerfield, she's got two kids too: I baby-sit for her and she lets me share her place with her in return. Mostly I live on welfare, only that's not easy. I have a little money comes in too once in a while: it's a sort of maintenance payment for the kids from my husband, except it's irregular, it comes when he can send it or when he remembers to. The sort of thing you don't tell the SRS about, else they take it into account like you got it all year round.

I'll tell you about the bar I worked in in Bird, but obviously I'm not going to tell you names or things like that. For one reason, the guy I worked there for, he might come around and ask me to work for him again. He wouldn't be too pleased about it if he heard I'd been talking about it. So don't describe me or anything, just leave it I live in this house here in Garland OK? I ain't going to be here long anyway, I've got plans of my own to move on, but I don't want to tell about where.

I'm not from Kansas, I'm from Utah: Salt Lake City, around there. When you say Utah, Salt Lake City, folks think right away Mormons. Shall I tell you something? I spent nine, ten years there from when I was born and I never met a Mormon in my life. Maybe it'd have been a good thing if I did: I'm not too crazy about the ideas of Mormon people but I guess if you've got a faith like they've got, it kind of stays with you all through your life.

Then I lived in California a while. My mom and dad separated and she lived with a whole lot of different guys. Me and my sister, we never knew which new guy she was going to have living with her when we got home, sometimes it seemed like three different ones the same week. You know really I think she was kind of sick: she drank a lot of alcohol, she took a lot of pills, and one day when I was 15 they found her some place dead. Sometimes I think she'd OD'd. My sister was two years older than me, and she had a guy and I went with them to Santa Monica. That's a place where there's a lot of guys and a lot of girls and so long as you're friendly there'll always be someone'll look after you. We did OK and it was a good life, all them big houses and swimming pools and stuff: children of the sun, know what I mean?

Once I even had a screen test. There was this guy he said he could get me a screen test: I said yeah yeah, that was OK I knew all about that, he didn't have to bother giving me that stuff, I didn't even want to be in movies. He must've thought I was some kind of screwball or something, everyone wanted to be in movies, that's why they went there. I did the screen test though to keep him happy. I didn't get in the movies though.

Let's see, where'd I go after that? I think it was Arizona maybe: Nevada some place, somewhere like that. I had my little girl then, Kristy. I was working in the clubs, what they call a hostess, which is the polite name for something else. These clubs, they're not in Vegas but they like to pretend they are. The clubs are an industry, an industry that produces money. Folk produce money out their pockets and other folks work to take it away from them by telling them they're having a good time. It's kind of funny: people want to give you their money, don't ask me why. You wouldn't believe the number of guys I've met who just wanted to give me their money: that's what they wanted more than anything. All they wanted to do was talk: if I just listened to them, that's what they were most happy with and they gave me money for it. They talked about themselves, their lovely wives back home, their lovely kids: then come out with the pictures of their kids. I even had one guy, he had a tape recorder with his kids singing songs on it: right there in the motel room, he played me his kids singing songs, to show me what a nice guy he was. So what's a nice guy like you doing here in a motel room with a girl like me? You know?

I came here two years last February. I was ill, I'd got something with my chest, I just wanted peace and quiet. My friend that I came with, she'd had a lot of troubles too: we seemed to get on OK, so we made what you call a conscious decision to try and get both of our lives straight. She had this guy and he was the one who brought us here to Kansas, to Baxter. Only of course it wasn't long, then he faded away. We were going to move on to Kansas City Missouri, then she got this job in Deerfield so we decided to stay on awhile. A few weeks after that I was in Bird and I got talking with this guy and he said someone had walked out on him, he needed someone to tend bar evenings at this place he had. So I said I'd give it a try.

I couldn't believe it at first, it was a real kind of a weird place, I mean really weird. It was so dark you couldn't hardly see who you were serving to. Maybe that was the idea of it, that no one could see anyone. A guy'd come in, and whoever it was he'd got with him, he always made sure she should sit right away from the bar over in the corner. He'd take the drinks over and they'd sit there and they'd talk in whispers. They didn't like it if you went over and said would they like another drink or something: the guy who owned it, Bill, he told me to stay behind the bar and not take empty glasses off the table or anything, not until the person had gone. Some of the guys they knew one another all right, they'd be at the bar at the same time and they'd say Hi to one another: but they didn't introduce the other guy to who it was they'd got with them, nothing like that. It was, it was real weird.

I gave up last year and I've stayed here since because I like it. A time or two I've been in town and seen some guy I recognise from when he came in the bar: course I never say anything and he doesn't either. I'd think he doesn't know who I am anyway, he never looked who was behind the bar. Dark lights, no names, having a drink with someone and she's not your wife: that'd make him a real fast liver in Bird, and he'd sure not want no one to know about it.

12 *Them that deserve and those that don't*

Alan Ford

– Like I said, I'd really have preferred it if you'd submitted me a list of questions you wanted answers to.

And I want to repeat right here at the beginning of this interview so that we understand it, you and me both: you don't give any personal information about me, or personal description of me, or have anything I could be identified from. Now we got a clear definite understanding on that OK?

Right, well we can start with saying we're talking in my office here, at the SRS offices in Baxter: and yes, that I'm the SRS officer who deals with Bird and that I'm over there twice a week, yes. SRS is the abbreviation commonly used for Social Rehabilitation Services, and it handles the social stroke financial part of our federal welfare system.

I don't know anything about your English system of Social Security, what you say's called unemployment benefit payment, or National Health Insurance. Maybe if you could outline it to me a little, I could tell you more about the differences and the similarities.

OK yes I got it, I think. Then the first big difference is as we might expect, one in terminology. Here in the US what we call 'Social Security' doesn't sound much like what you call 'Social Security'. Ours is more like a federal pension sort of a thing: from the day you're born you have your own individual Social Security number and it's like your ID, your identification number which you carry with you all through your life. When you grow up and get a job, you give it to your employer: when you're employed, contributions are paid from your earnings into a central fund, and when it comes time that you want to retire, or you have to retire say on grounds of health, then that contribution is paid back to you in monthly sums for you to live on. So if you've had a good and regular working life, you're going to be looked after from your Social Security payments when you come to need it. The amount you get, well that depends on what you've paid in: it's a matter between you, Federal Government and maybe God comes into it too. No like I said there's no fixed rate: what you get depends on what you've paid in. But I have to repeat to you what I've said is a very simplified description of a very complicated system.

What you've described to me as Social Security payments in England, that would sound to me like financial payments here made under the heading of what's we call 'Welfare'. You've already used several words for example that don't come up too often in the US, such as 'benefit', 'rights' and so on: we do have 'entitlements' though. I'm sorry no, I can't give you information about those, because it's something we're not allowed to do. They vary from individual to individual and situation to situation. To work out your entitlement you and I would have to fill in a very long and detailed form, in which you would have to give me in full detail all the information I wanted. We try for uniformity of interpretation of the rules: and they're set down here in specific and exact detail as decided by our legislators, in this massive tome which has its place here on my desk, never more than six inches away from my hand. No, I'm not allowed to let you have a look at it, that's one of my conditions of employment. Even certain members of my staff below a particular grade, they're not allowed to see it either. When I've made my assessment, my interpretation of the rules is final: you can appeal against it over my head, but I'm not allowed to give you material or information of any kind which you might be able to use for your appeal.

Yes, you could if you wished say it was part of the American ethos that every person who is capable of working should be pushed quite hard towards fending for themself. But if you do quote that, I should like your assurance that you'll make it clear the words were yours and not mine. I might agree with the philosophy on a personal level, but it absolutely in no way represents either state or federal policy to incorporate agreement with the words – or for that matter to disagree with them. That's right: I don't accept them and I don't contradict them either.

The main purpose of Welfare is to ensure that dependent children are fed and clothed to a minimum standard. A woman with a child or children, she's no need to feel that she's going to have to prove her children are dependent if her husband or the man she's living with has left her. We don't expect her to work while she's young children to care for, and a cash payment would be made to her for the children without too much difficulty. She wouldn't get an additional payment for herself though necessarily: it's assumed unless proved otherwise that she'll provide for herself as well, out of the payment for the child or children.

Additionally she might get food stamps, to a varying amount in each individual case: these are vouchers which can only be used in food stores for basic food purchases. I wouldn't know if that system's abused or not: some people will tell you yes it is, they've seen food stamps used to purchase toiletries or cigarettes. Other'll tell you they've seen women with their shopping carts piled high with 50 dollars' worth or more of food and magazines and luxuries, paying with cash and foodstamps. I think it'd be wiser if we didn't get into that area.

Most of my work I'd describe as pleasant, it's rare to meet an unpleasant or difficult individual. I try to be fair is what I would say basically: and when I say that, I mean I'm all the time conscious in my mind that I must be fair to two people, not one. On the one hand the person in front of me: if that person is in genuinely difficult circumstances and has made a full and honest disclosure of all money they have and get from whatever source, and especially if they've got a dependent child or children – that's one person I have to be fair to. And the other one, very importantly, is the taxpayer: at the bottom line, it's his money that I'm paying out. He's very likely a hard-working guy: out of his own money he's looking after his own family and his own dependents, and making sure they don't become a charge on the state or the government. So it's natural for him to feel with these other folk, well why aren't *their* family looking after them, how come it's got to come out of my pocket? It's to be fair to him, that my job also has to be to make 200 per cent certain you aren't giving handouts to people who are deceiving you, or people who are just too goddam lazy to work, and they make their living bumming off others.

I see myself as an impersonal assessor: an assessor of income and means, and of eligibility. No I wouldn't accept that it's policy to discourage people from turning to SRS for help: that was your question and not my statement. But it's no part of my occupation that I have an obligation to give people information about entitlement: my obligation is to make sure they have neither more nor less than entitlement. Repeat, to be fair. I guess there's not much more I can tell you: I hope it's been of assistance.

Patti Oliveri

A small woman in her fifties, with short dark curly hair, and a lively hand-gesticulating manner. We talked in her office in the courthouse.

– I'm a children's Social Worker for a section of the SRS. I work out of this office here in Bird and the area I'm responsible for is the whole of Auburn County. This is my base, but I live 40 miles north west in Baxter, and I drive here every day then back there every night. I've been here two years now and I like the work very very much indeed.

I have five children, all grown up now. I got married right after High School and stayed home and brought up five kids. Ten years ago my husband passed away: I talked about what I should do, and what I wanted to do, which was go to college at Baxter University as a mature student and take a degree. We lived just down the road from there so it was handy, and the older children looked after the younger ones, and it took five and one half years. But I did it, I got my degree in social work. I worked first as an office clerk, then with a company which wholesaled goods: it wasn't interesting, but it made an income. At college they let you arrange your necessary study hours the way it best suits you: so what I did was worked in the warehouse three till midnight, then went to bed until six in the morning, then went to school from eight o'clock until two o'clock. After my degree, this is my first post: but if something comes up where I can work out of Baxter, then of course I'll go for it.

The caseload I have, which I share with another worker who does the adult side, is something around 20 to 30 children in custody, and on top of that another 20 families where we're trying to avoid taking their kids away from them. The problems we mainly face are neglect, cruelty and abuse: we have statutory powers, but wherever possible we try to get parents to co-operate with us voluntarily. We do individual counselling with parents and with children, and we run groups too. Most parents co-operate, but if they persist in not doing, then we have to apply in front of Judge Hertzog upstairs here for a custody order.

In that case, if we get the order, the State of Kansas has residential homes for children, but we also have the foster home system. Wherever possible we prefer that, because it means the child is brought up as part of a family instead of an institution. The foster parents have full power, under supervision, to bring the child up as one of their own in all matters of discipline and upbringing, except that under no circumstances do we permit physical chastisement.

Some of the Kansas State homes, they're pretty big: and they do have in them a high proportion of young offenders who've been through the courts. It gets kind of tough sometimes: a lot of people feel if a child or young person has turned to crime it can't be their fault, there must have been a wrong upbringing. That may be true: but in some cases the damage that's been done is severe and irreversible, and so what you've got is the juvenile equivalent of a hardened criminal. They're only a few in number, there usually aren't parents in the picture that you can aim at trying to restore them to, and so we have the responsibility for them till they're 18. But sometimes children who have no criminal propensities, they do temporarily have to be kept there with them. That's sure something we're always fighting to avoid.

Who like that'd be put there? I'm thinking of the sort of case, say, where you've a persistent absconder from foster homes. I guess in your country you don't have quite the same kind of problem as we do here because of distances. Just last month we had a girl in our care who was 13: she ran away from the foster home where we'd put her, and finally she turned herself in at a place on the state line in north Minnesota. That was coming close on 2,000 miles away from here, as far maybe as I'd guess London is from Cairo. She said up there she wanted to come back to us, and we said we'd be happy to have her. So that was one thing: but the other one was we had to arrange a total of 17 different escorts for her, from one state district to another. It wouldn't have been realistic for me to go get her myself, that'd have taken me away almost a whole week from all my other cases. Well we got it sorted at the end.

But this kind of case, well it's serious and it's very distressing: a girl of that age going a distance like that, on her own and on the road and riding in long-distance trucks and all the rest of it with men. She'd had a bad childhood, hadn't seen her father in years: and it was him she said she was trying to find. It's sure hard to talk to a kid like that and try and get her to see what the realistic situation is, that most likely she'll never find him ever. If she'll wait five years, then she can take off wherever she likes: but right now we can't let her do what she did, and she's very near being put some place where she just won't be able to run from. But I know to be truthful about it, it can't be long before another day comes and she'll hightail it off over the horizon again. We know, you get to thinking sometimes how you wish somehow she would find him: even if he turned around and sent her on her way, least then the kid would know what the true situation was.

A lot of my work is out of the office, and I'd sooner it was. I don't go for a lot of report writing and telephoning and that side of it. That's not to say I don't do it: I do, I have to. But I don't like asking clients to come here and see me in my office, I like it better to go and meet them in their own home. Quite a lot of them are women on their own with kids, their husband or whatever has deserted them. So I have to go see them: they don't have cars, the kind of public transport there is from outer areas into town and back is non-existent, so I don't have the choice anyway.

The job's strenuous, right, it sure is. But it's what I like doing: and I make no secret of it, I owe it to my kids that I can. They were the ones who made it possible during the time I was at college, by looking after themselves so's Ma could go do her studying. Not one of them, not ever once, did any of them complain. We laugh about it sometimes, at what they didn't say to me though they could have: 'Heh Mom, how come you're neglecting us so's you can go to college to learn how to look after neglected kids?' They were great, all of them, and they still are.

Alma Wise

The group of small, low, red-brick apartments was arranged in a semi-circle. It stood on a patch of flat ground at the edge of town, a hundred yards back from the highway at the end of a driveway. A tall young man with long black hair down to his shoulders was guiding a lawn mower over the neatly kept grassed area in front of the entrance: he waved a greeting and pointed to the office at the end of the buildings.

– This is called Hill View Apartments and it's a low-income housing project for elderly people. It has federal, that's government, funding but it's administered by the Bird Housing Board. My name's Mrs Alma Wise, I'm pleased to make your acquaintance, and I'll tell you as much as you want to know: or maybe I should say as much as I can tell you, because I might not have some of the answers. I wasn't here when the project first started up as an idea, which I believe was sometime ten perhaps 12 years ago: I joined it just when it actually got opened to take in residents, which is now eight years ago.

How I got the job was right at the last minute, in a kind of a panic you might say. Someone had been appointed, better qualified than me which wouldn't be too difficult: and they were right at the point of opening up when her husband took ill and she had to drop out. I was working as clerk receptionist for one of the doctors in the town: it was known he was soon going to retire, so in desperation Leonard Demarr, who knows me and who's on the project's Board of Management as one of its trustees, he called me up on the 'phone and said would I come to this job and help them out, least to begin with. So I said OK: I'd been thinking I might even retire myself, but I'd come temporarily till they found someone more suitable.

And that was it. I've been here temporarily eight years. So far they haven't pushed me out, and I guess I'll stay here till they do. I'm supposed to work five half days, from eight in the morning until noon. But I enjoy it so much I often forget that and find myself still here at four in the afternoon, or even on from that. And the days when I don't come in, I really miss coming. My husband's retired himself and he's happy at home and he looks after himself in the day: he says so long as

I'm happy and I'm home evenings, I ought to be doing something and this suits me so why not keep doing it?

We have 27 single bedroom apartments and 3 two-bedroom apartments. It's a non-profit-making organisation, and to come here you must be at least 62 years old, or elderly handicapped or disabled, or a registered war veteran. It's subsidised with a federal loan over a period of 50 years to the town of Bird: when that's paid off it becomes Bird's own property. And one of the very first things happened was oil was found under this piece of land, and drills were put down right outside my window here, and another one by that tree over there. The royalties aren't what they were because the oil price has gone down: but from them we've got money which keeps us up way ahead of our loan repayments, so that's a happy situation.

If you want to be a resident, you make an application or have a relative make it for you, then you come along here and we talk over what your needs are. Like whether the place is suitable for you on your own, or whether maybe if it's you and your wife, or two brothers or two sisters, one of the double apartments would be suitable. Then we sit down like you and me are doing now, across this desk here, and we work out your income and your savings, taking into account Social Security, any investments you might have and anything else. Then we have allowable deductions for the cost of extra medical treatment you're receiving, bills you're paying off, and a whole list of other things. Then out of the balance of what's left, we calculate what rent you'd be asked to pay here: and it's the same for everybody, 30 per cent of the balance between income and outgoings. It means a whole big range of payments: you can see here by this month's list, we have two people here paying only 30 dollars a month rent each, someone here paying 90 dollars, this person paying 344 dollars.

We make it clear always to our residents that we never disclose how much rent a person pays to other residents. And what do they do? They all the time tell each other and have discussions about it. 'You're paying two hundred a month? Well what do you know, I'm only paying one forty.' But I can say this without any contradiction: they all know how the rents are calculated, and I've never had one person complain to me ever that they're paying more than someone else. There's a real good spirit in the place.

Rent includes electricity, air conditioning, heating in winter, and there's a coin washing machine area. Cleaners come in four days a week for two hours, and they'll do your washing for you if you want. An apartment has kitchen diner, sitting room, bathroom, separate toilet, and bedroom: also there are built in closets and cupboards and everyone has a telephone and television. There are two alarm call pulls, one in the bedroom and the other in the bathroom, and the police drive around the whole area once an hour through the night. The young guy you saw out there with the mower, Pete LeRoy, he's employed to be around the place and keep it tidy, or do repairs or whatever people want. All the old ladies make a big fuss of him: and he does of them too, he's a really kind and helpful guy and a very popular person.

You can have a certain amount of your own furniture, and there are no restrictions on friends or relatives coming to see you any time you want. We have one or two elderly people, they have sons or daughters come to see them and stay here with them a few days, and that's OK: we've one lady, her son's so far been here a week. We have voluntary car helpers who drive folk into town for their shopping, and we like folk to feel their apartment's their home. We have a communal dining room and sitting room: you can use them or not, the choice is yours.

Next step after this is the old person's home at North Creek, and the step after that is hopsital. But as long as it's physically possible for someone to stay here, we do everything we can to help them make out. Sometimes folks come here because they can't carry on any longer on their own: and you think, and their relatives think, it's only going to be for a short time. But it's truly amazing what a transformation it makes in some people, they seem to take on a whole new lease of life. That's a really great thing to see, we've several folk who've been here since we first opened up in fact. That's what makes me feel this is a real worthwhile job.

Dana Rogerson

– I'm 38, I'm separated from my husband, and I live here in Bird with my two children: both girls, one 16 and one 14, and they're at the High School. It's where I was born and grew up, and we've lived back here ten years now. My parents are both alive, they live here also, and I guess for me now it's here I am and here I'll stay. I don't have any idea of remarriage in view or anything like that.

My former husband's a doctor and before our divorce I worked in the paediatric clinic he had in a hospital in Baxter. I'm a fully trained registered nurse, so that was a convenient working arrangement for both of us. Then when the marriage broke down and I moved back here, it made life kind of difficult for me: I didn't want to go on working at that hospital, so I started to look around for something nearer home. Because my children were young and he was paying me towards their upkeep I wasn't under great financial pressure. All the same I was glad when I did get a part-time job: apart from helping with the finances it gave me a feeling of being independent to a degree. I had a part-time post at North Creek Retirement Home, and I worked there until just last year. I did 20 hours a week and there was one other trained person also there on the same basis, and we were able to work out days and times between us as we wished. Because of my qualification I could give medication, and I was in a supervisory capacity over the general staff of nursing aides: they were people who'd taken short basic courses and were only allowed to work with someone like myself in charge of them.

The first thing you have to remember about a place of that kind is that it's a business: it's run on a basis that it's there to show a profit. There are hundreds, I don't know many thousands maybe, all over the United States. They have to be properly run and administered, they're from time to time inspected, and they can be closed down if there are complaints about them or they're found not be giving proper care to the required standard.

North Creek I'd say was one of the best. What made it that way was the man who owned it, he was a businessman but he was there himself in residence as the administrator of it. He left the medical side to his medical staff, and concerned himself with the welfare of the patients. He took a real interest in them and had a real concern for them.

The numbers of patients or residents as we preferred to call them, varied but it was usually somewhere around fifty. Depending on the fees they were paying they had either their own private room, or were in shared rooms with two or maybe three others. There wasn't a lot of opportunity for them to have any of their own things around them: the bedrooms were comfortable, but plain and functional. The same with the dining room and sitting room: the main emphasis was on spotless cleanliness, which is very necessary when you have old and not always fully capable people there to be looked after.

We only accepted people who were beyond looking after themselves to some degree, but who only required simple medical treatments. Some few were entirely bedridden, quite a number were incontinent: and a few, again, were mentally disturbed. They came within the range of what's defined as 'intermediate care': that is, people who couldn't manage on their own, but weren't bad enough to be hospitalised permanently. If they required heavy skilled nursing, or suffered from too disturbed a mental condition, they had to go on from us to hospitals.

A lot of folk in Bird give time to be voluntary helpers there: the range of who came along and what they were prepared to do, I always used to think it was quite astonishing. You'd get some of the pupils from the High School, usually girls, who were maybe thinking of going into nursing as a career later on themselves: they'd come along once or twice a week and help with feeding a person who was too infirm to handle it themselves. Car drivers of course, we had many of those who'd take residents out for rides; a couple of ladies who came along and played the piano, all the old favourite songs for them; a lady who came in twice a week to lead a simple activity group; organised social activities, people who came just to visit for an hour with a person who was lonely. Also some of the ministers from the different local churches, they had a rota system they came in on. There was always a whole lot of things going on all the time.

It's a place that could be described, I guess, as one which gives care and pleasant surroundings to those who're elderly and to a degree infirm. I think it's inevitable all the same that it could seem to an outside visitor rather an impersonal place, with the emphasis on material standards. And it's sure not inexpensive, either for the patient if they're paying for it themselves, or the patient's family to have to find the money for. You'd be looking at upwards of 500 dollars a week basic, plus medication and nearly all personal extras, in most cases.

Because it's registered as a properly conducted and administered home, the SRS does accept to a degree that some folk there are in need of welfare supplement payments: maybe half those there do get some form of help to some extent. Others are very wealthy in their own right, or their families who are paying for them are. And you also get certain organisations in the town, or from outside of it, who will sometimes take a particular person under their wing and make themselves responsible for them.

The worst problem there I'd say is what you might call social isolation. If they had families who could care for them, or would care for them, obviously most folk would prefer that to being there. I don't criticise the standard of the medical and nursing care, but it does have to some degree to be impersonal because at least the way I see it, on grounds of expense not sufficient trained staff are employed. As a result the personal side of things gets left to good-intentioned people from outside: and OK so what they do's much to their credit. But if you're an old person and all your contact with the outside world in a week is a half-hour visit from a school kid, and a half-hour singalong in the residents' sitting room with a whole lot of others like yourself, that's not what you'd call a very stimulating environment.

Do you have things better organised in your country?

13 *Thursday morning*

Debbie, Sharon, Kim
Charlie, Karl, Mark

DEBBIE: We're six High School seniors, three boys and three girls, and you asked us if we'd take part in a discussion group with you over two sessions, one this morning and another one a few weeks on from now.

You gave us a list of the topics you'd like us to talk about with you, and you said we could take them any order we liked. After we'd read the list and talked about it between ourselves, we decided to follow it straight down the line, take them in the same order you put them in. The list of topics you gave us was this:

Number 1. Our school here, what we think's good about it and what we think's not so good and could be improved.
Number 2. Living in Bird, what it's like, and what we think are our community's strengths and weaknesses.
Number 3. What our own individual ambitions are as young people, what we want to do after we graduate from High School and what we want to achieve in our lives generally.
Number 4. How we look at religion, its importance or unimportance in our lives.
Number 5. Sex. How we regard it, what we think standards of sexual behaviour should be.
Number 6. America, what we feel about being American, and how we think other people see us.

We've put another one in at the end if that's OK with you. We'd like to ask you some questions about your country: none of us have ever been to England and there's lots about it we'd like to know, OK?

SHARON: OK well I'll be the one who starts. The first question was what do we think about our school: I'd say that I think it's a pretty good school.

DEBBIE: One thing is, we didn't find this out until we started talking to each other about it, but none of us has been to any other school. So this one we don't know how it measures up with other places. But I'd go along with what Sharon said, to me it seems good.

KIM: I'd say the kind of basic general education you get here is about right. I talked a bit with my ma about it, she went to High School in Colorado: it looked like they were pretty much the same to both of us.

CHARLIE: The thing I think is that you don't really get into education properly until after you've gone on from school.

MARK: What are you saying, you're not properly educated unless you've been to college?

CHARLIE: No I didn't say anything about going to college, I said after you'd gone on from school: whether you go to college or you don't, that's when you really start learning things.

DEBBIE: Like about life you mean?

CHARLIE: Right.

DEBBIE: I don't know that I agree with that necessarily, I think some kids learn a lot about life quite a while before they end their schooling.

SHARON: Maybe. Only let's stay on the subject of what we think's good about school. The first thing is the teachers: I'd say they're the ones make a school what it is.

MARK: Most of the ones here, they're OK. They're friendly, they don't shout or stuff like that.

KIM: It's like they seem to enjoy what they're doing, which is good.

SHARON: And most of them treat you like grown-ups, that's another thing: it gives a good atmosphere all round. They keep some discipline but not too much, and they do that most often by leaving it to you to discipline yourself.

CHARLIE: Nobody gets hit or things like that: we don't have corporal punishment in the school and I think kids respond to that by not feeling they have to behave, but by feeling they want to behave.

DEBBIE: You want to come in on this Karl?

KARL: I guess we must sound like we're a lot of goody goodies.

MARK: Maybe we are: but if we are, we are because we don't want to be any other way at school.

SHARON: What are the things we think are not so good?

KIM: There's no privacy. It's a small school and things get around pretty quick. You start dating someone, everyone else gets to hear it.

KARL: Yeah or you get into trouble for low grades or something, everyone knows about it, all your friends, everyone.

CHARLIE: It's good though that it makes you feel you can talk to anyone about it. Least I think that's a good aspect of it, I don't think you could feel lonely here.

DEBBIE: I think after graduation I'm going to miss the feeling of having so many friends. Kind of sad about it, even if it's part of growing up. We had a class discussion about this the other day with Mrs Eagleton, she asked us did we think school was a protective environment.

KARL: Did she say protective environment? I thought she said protected environment?

KIM: They're not all that different. The thing was though that everyone agreed when you get outside of it, when you go to college or whatever, you're more on your own and life's not as easy as it was.

CHARLIE: It's like what I was saying about growing up, being more adult and more educated after you leave school.

SHARON: Bad points about the school, any other bad points? Do we like it that everything you do, even when you're out of school, it seems somehow you can't get away from it?

DEBBIE: You mean like everything that happens, it happens because it's to do with the school – outside, sports, parties, dances?

SHARON: Right. There's only the one school, everyone goes to that school so school kind of dominates everything.

CHARLIE: I don't see how you'll ever get it different, not in a small town. I don't think that's a bad point to the school. It might be to the community though.

DEBBIE: Well that's the next subject on our list, the community: so maybe we can take it on from here, like living in the school to living in the community and how we feel about that.

SHARON: I was the one started first about school. Let's have someone else begin on this one.

KIM: Well, what we were talking about how everyone knows everyone and things can't happen without everyone knowing about it, it's more or less the same way in Bird generally. It has advantages and disadvantages the same way, and you get a lot of community spirit. I'm thinking like when Mary Hanover's father was killed in that road accident last year, how everyone got together to raise money for the family because they knew they were having a hard time. That would be one example of the good side to living in a place where everyone knew things about other people, how they were fixed.

KARL: Yeah that side of it's good. But there's the other side where you get certain groups or clicks of people. Mostly it's based on families, and if you and your family are not in with the right people you can get to feeling a bit left out of things sometimes.

DEBBIE: I don't think there's too much of that goes on, not more than you'd get most other places. I don't think Bird's all that different. If you've been here a long time and your family's been here a long time, that gets you respect. But I think that's right, specially with the older people.

CHARLIE: I think the family gets the respect because of what they've done.

MARK: You mean in their job, or whether they've made a lot of money, or what?

CHARLIE: No I was meaning from what they've done for the town. I don't think people respect Mr Albert because he's got a lot of money, they respect him because of what he did for the town, giving it the library.

SHARON: Yeah, you compare him with Mr ****. He's got a lot of money too but folks don't respect him too much.

KARL: No, because he's got a drink problem. People aren't too sympathetic about that.

KIM: Sure, why should they be?

KARL: I'm not saying why they should be, what I'm saying is Mary Hanover, her father he gets killed in a road accident: but the guy we're talking about who drinks, his kids don't get a lot of sympathy for it.

CHARLIE: What're you saying, we should have a town effort to raise money for him so he can go get more drink or something?

DEBBIE: OK we can all have a laugh about that. But I don't see it's what we're really talking about here, or supposed to be trying to. Do we like living in Bird, what's it like?

KIM: It's OK if you like sports and outdoor things, going to the lake and stuff like that. It gets kind of draggy in winter though: there's no cinema, no entertainment, no place where you can go and have an ice-cream or soda and meet your friends. Only Dorothy's, which is more for grown-ups.

KARL: You have to go 40 miles to Baxter for anything at all like that. That's bad.

SHARON: My dad told me they used to have a lot more here than there is now: a bowling alley, a pinball arcade, a cinema and everything.

MARK: I think this is the fault that there's such a lot of old people here, they want to keep the town quiet and respectable. They're not going to bring things in that they think might give trouble.

SHARON: I think we all think it's no place for kids here because there's nothing to do, right?

MARK: I mean if you do go out to Milton Reservoir or some place, take a few cans of beer to have a good time, like we were saying word gets around and you get into trouble for it.

DEBBIE: Another thing we should say is it's a pretty friendly place. If new folks come to live here people try to make them feel welcome. It's a problem though that there aren't many reasons for people to want to come here to live. There's not a lot of jobs and places to employ people. I guess most of us are not thinking of staying here the rest of our lives: if we go away to college or whatever, we won't find much to bring us back here workwise.

SHARON: We were saying it's quiet. It is, so it's a good place to live. But I wouldn't want to go on living here for ever, not like a lot of folk say they do.

CHARLIE: It's mostly older people say that, that they want to live here for ever. I think it's a kind of a place you like coming back to when you're not here: but if you think you're going to be here for good, it's more a place you want to get away from.

MARK: That sounds real profound.

CHARLIE: I only just thought of it too.

DEBBIE: So next is our ambitions, what we want to do after we graduate.

MARK: I want to make a whole lot of money.

KARL: Me too.

KIM: I want to get married.

CHARLIE: I want not to get married.

SHARON: Yeah I want not to get married too. Least not till after I've done lots of other things. I don't want to be one of those women who by the time she's 20, she's got a husband and two kids and what she's looking at out the window is the end of her life.

DEBBIE: That's what people expect of you though if you're a woman, that's the way of life you're supposed to want to conform to. My mom said to me 'The great thing is to be satisfied with what you've got in life. If you've a good husband and good kids, you be thankful: you've got the most important things in life.'

KIM: I think that's OK, I really do. You have a nice home and everything, what's wrong with that if that's what you want? Everybody can't all be the same.

SHARON: But that's making everyone like they are the same and all want the same things.

KIM: I think everyone does. Happiness, anyway: and if that's your idea of happiness.

DEBBIE: Well so far this is just us. What did you say you wanted Mark, to make money?

MARK: A whole lot of money.

DEBBIE: What for?

MARK: To have everything I want.

DEBBIE: Which is what?

MARK: Money.

DEBBIE: No, come on.

MARK: Well what we're talking about is security right? A secure home life, a wife and children, and never be poor. I'd be happy with that. I wouldn't care a lot about my job, I'd just look at it like it was something which gave me the chance to have an ordinary good life.

KARL: I think I'd like a job that was a bit more than that: it would have to be something had a certain amount of interest to it. But I'd go along on the security angle, I think that's pretty important.

DEBBIE: Why'd do you say you wanted not to get married?

CHARLIE: It was me said that. Getting married's not high on my list of priorities, I think people who get married young are ones most likely to end up getting divorced. I'd want to be 30 or somewhere around there before I got married.

SHARON: Play the field first you mean?

CHARLIE: You could say that. I sure don't think you should marry the first person you're attracted to or fall in love with or whatever. And I don't think that should just be for guys either, I think a girl should do the same.

KARL: We were talking where we were saying about a woman having a home and two kids and looking out the window, and that's her life. I think it can be like that too for men sometimes: you know, you get yourself married, you get a job, you have a nice home, a good car, your wife has a dishwasher and all the rest. And that can kind of be the end of it for you too, except mostly you're the one who has to do the figuring and the worrying, and make sure you bring up your family as good as the guy next door's doing. That's a kind of a trap for the man too, to have to do what's expected of you.

KIM: Yeah but like I said, just because it's expected of you, if that's your ambition, that's what you both want, then OK.

DEBBIE: What if the woman wants to have a career?

KIM: Then she should have a career, that's up to her. But if she's happy staying home she should stay home.

SHARON: I think it happens a lot these days the wife has to go to work to help out with the family finances, so it's got to be a good thing if she's got some qualifications to do it with.

DEBBIE: There goes the bell. That's a good point for us to finish at, we talked about three of the things on the list, which is halfway. Let us know when you got the second session fixed for us, OK? You're welcome.

14 *Keeping up a profile*

To be a preacher: Revd. Norman Ortenshaw

His offices were modernly furnished and equipped, on the ground floor of a newly built administration building at the side of the church. He was small, soberly dressed and quietly spoken.

– The way I see it, much of the work of the church here is keeping up a profile: not just my own Methodist church, but all the others too.

I guess you've noticed, as you drive into town from any direction, there's a board on the side of the highway with names and addresses of all denominations' churches and their ministers. We have what we call ministerial alliance: we have a monthly meeting, usually at breakfast-time in one of the town's cafes, where we all get together and talk about mutual problems and experiences during the previous month. We also have a small joint financial fund, available for use by any of us if we're approached by needy travellers passing through. I think if you asked any of the other ministers they'd all say the same thing: we all work together, and our working together this way is good both for us and for the community.

Tell you something about myself personally? Yes willingly, if you think it'll be of interest. To be a preacher, that has always been my ambition, I'd say from around 16 years old on, when I was in High School. I don't know why, it wasn't tied in with any particular experience: but from that age I had no doubt at all that was the direction God was pushing me. I heard the call very clearly: and I've often said since I've never questioned God's call, but I have at times questioned God's judgement in picking me. Because although I always wanted to preach, that side of it is something I've not ever found easy.

I was born in the south east of Kansas, and after graduation I went to a Methodist university in Texas and took my master's degree in education. I didn't go straight into the ministry: instead I taught in rural schools and junior high schools. From time to time I did some preaching: but that aspect like I said was hard. I liked, I still like, the pastoral side. But in character I've always been somewhat of an introverted person: I don't find being socially outgoing easy. So that's the difficulty, almost a contradiction. I find doing actual physical things comes more easily to me. Even now all these years after, when I'm working on a sermon in my head, I like to be working at something with my hands while I'm doing it, woodworking, something of that sort.

My first church of my own I ever had was in a small place called Garwood, over in Joplin County, west of here. So I've always had what you might call an affinity with this part of Kansas. Then over the years I went on working and preaching mostly in southern Kansas: and finally it was two years ago I was offered this church. I prayed, and I felt led: this was where God wanted me to come, here to this community. From the moment I came I really loved it. At present I'm 58 years of age: I shall retire when I'm 62, and if God wills it that I should stay here till then, I'll tell you nothing will make me happier.

We've a large modern church here, with excellent additional facilities such as our large hall, several smaller meeting rooms, and a very well-equipped kitchen which serves meals for functions and parties. Weddings, yes: but we make a feature of it being available for use not just by our church, but any organisation in the community whatsoever. There's a whole lot of activities go on here which have nothing specifically to do with the Methodist church at all: children's play groups, women's club meetings and dinners, pretty well anything and everything the town people want the use of it for. It's partly because it's so much in use I have one full-time staff member, and a number of part-time workers also, we're all always busy.

I think we're what might be called a traditional and conservative church: we uphold traditional values. I know that Methodism in other countries such as England often involves itself in a number of issues to do with social questions, working in poor areas or with prison work for instance. It does to some degree too in the United States in the big cities, but there's not much opportunity for that kind of thing around here. From my own personal feeling I'd say there's a danger that those who want the church to politicise itself more are lessening concentration on spiritual matters, which ought to be the first concern. From that you'll gather I regard myself as someone who shares many of his parishoners' convictions: I'd say that's what they want in their minister, they wouldn't be all that happy with someone who was more radically inclined.

In this part of the country we're not quite in the area that's known as 'the Bible belt', but we're on the edge of it. Religion here is still considerably more fundamentalist than in a lot of other areas. Any church has discussions and divisions within it, it wouldn't really be a lively or a living church if it didn't. But when I read of some of the things going on in some of the so-called sophisticated areas like the East Coast, I wonder what people here would make of it. If it's not a contradiction in terms, there's quite a bellicose element out east in our church: it wants the church to move towards pacifism, particularly over the issue of the use of nuclear weapons. There are even so I'm told people who want to entirely remove from our services the singing of such hymns as 'Onward Christian Soldiers' for example, or 'The Battle Hymn of The Republic', because they think they're inappropriately militaristic. I sure don't feel ideas of that sort would be very well received here. But I can't feel either that it's something which is going to be what you might call an imminent issue of contention in Bird any time now.

I don't want to give the impression that we as a church, or any of our individual parishioners, don't want to bother with such matters. But the reality of daily life here is that there are many more immediate concerns, such as the price of wheat and cattle, and the economy generally. Ordinary people take pride in working and achieving financial security, and not having to depend on or ask for charity. They're still very charitable towards others who need help, and I think the community as a whole is a very good example of Christianity in practice on an everyday level. They're not bothered with East Coast politics.

Little by little: Revd. Susan Raynes

She was tall, with long blonde hair: wearing jeans and a T-shirt she sat cross-legged on the floor of her small gloomy office at the back of the Congregational church.

– I'm 27, I was born in Illinois, and I went to Divinity School at Yale, where I graduated last year. It's hard to say what brought me into the church: I guess to be completely honest I'd have to say in some ways it was almost a decision by default, there was just nothing else I wanted to do. I'd studied literature and religion, and about the only thing I knew was I'd sooner be in the ministry than be an academic. I can't say any one person was specifically influential on me: except generally perhaps my father, who taught me ideas are not much good unless you try and do something with them.

A lot of churches wouldn't consider having a woman, and such a young woman at that, to be their minister: so I was fortunate to be invited here. They had one woman minister here before though, but that was 50 years ago almost: so I wasn't a completely new departure for them. I came for interview with my husband Dave and we both liked the look of the place: there was some concern about how I'd handle things if we started a family, but people seemed ready to judge me on what I could do rather than what I was, so I was really delighted when they decided to take me on. I needed to get started into my first job: and I feel if I stay here maybe three years or longer, that'll help me as a candidate in future jobs.

Divinity school was a big college, and Bird is a small town: their populations in fact are around the same size, so that was a plus for me not to be coming to a place which was large and outside my experience. So far I've enjoyed my work very much, though I'm not entirely happy in being an administrator as well as a pastor. The ministerial alliance here, they've been very helpful and supportive to me, which I wasn't sure they would be: men in the church are often very conservative and I didn't know how they'd take to a woman. But I didn't need to have worried about it, they've all been absolutely great so that was another plus for me.

It's interesting and a little bit amusing that people all round are rather more restrained towards me because I'm a woman. They're very polite, very gracious and very kind, but they do treat me with kid gloves a little. Like they're still uncertain what they can say in my presence: I don't mean they don't swear in front of me, which of course they don't, but something wider than that. Certain subjects, they don't know if they ought to mention them even: abortion would be an example. But I think gradually they're coming to realise I haven't lived my whole life in a very sheltered and protected environment, and I think this'll change. In many ways this is a far more sheltered community here than I've ever lived in anywhere, and quite often it's me who isn't sure whether I ought to bring up certain subjects with them.

Well an example of that would be for instance that at college I was something of a political activist, and into the peace movement very much. I feel the work of a minister should be to encourage in a church's members a concern about war, about poverty and hunger and inequality and so on: they shouldn't be content just to put another dollar in the collection plate and leave it to other people to think about the problems of society and the world in general. To me it's being true to the gospel to be aware, to be radical, to want change: and Bird is hardly a hotbed for that sort of thing. Equally I know there's the argument that says nobody's going to make a big impression on the world or change it a lot from a small town in the middle of the United States. But I'd like to try and open up, just here and there in a few people, some sense of a vision of their own possibilities, and encourage them towards a desire to bring about even a small degree of change. So far I have to say I've not met anyone at all whose ideas coincide with mine about the peace movement for example: there may not be anyone, come to that. But I shall go on hoping and trying to spread a few ideas: keep working at it, and there's no way of telling – attitudes might be changed, little by little.

On the other side, I'm conscious that being here and in my first job, I'm in a learning situation too. I can't just criticise people whose ideas don't match with mine, I have to go someway towards meeting and learning to understand them. I hope to be of some good for people, and but equally I have to remember they can do me good too.

Where I'll go next from here isn't a subject I've devoted much thought to yet. It's a very pleasant place to live, the people are as nice as you could find anywhere. I could well see that for someone older, it could have a great sort of seductiveness to it: it wouldn't be too hard to persuade yourself that you'd found your niche, come into harbour or whatever phrase you like to use, and that this was where you were going to settle down and stay. There are times when the idea's very tempting: and if I had a family of growing children and had to take account of schooling for them and things of that sort, I'm sure I'd give some serious thought to it as a place for our future. Some days I'm not too sure either I mightn't get around to that way of thinking completely.

But as of today I'd have to say I don't think it's a very likely immediate future road for me. To be here's a great experience and one I can learn a lot from. But after this I'd like my next post if it was at all possible to be in a city or a large town, and perhaps in a deprived and underprivileged section of it. I'd like to have a church that played an active part in the life around it, that was excited by challenge and change. Or even, but this is no more at this stage than just a possibility Dave and I've talked about a few times, I might if the opportunity arose go outside the United States, to a country in somewhere like central or south America, some part of the developing world, and try to be involved and help things along there. This all ties in with how I see the church's role, as an agent for change: that's why it's the place for me to be. Dave works freelance and I think he always will do, so we have an ideal partnership in that way which would allow me to go almost anywhere where I felt there was need and opportunity.

An import from Ireland: Father Damien

– Well welcome to my humble abode: or humble palace more like you may be thinking, when you see the extent of this huge mansion I have. The church and the house were built together only just a few years ago, and what exactly they had in mind for one lone bachelor priest to live here I don't know. I've six downstairs rooms, all of them big: my bedroom, the kitchen, and the office. Then there's a housekeeper's bedroom if I had a housekeeper which I don't: upstairs four more big bedrooms plus three separate bathrooms. And then down underneath us the basement, which is the full width of the house and's used when necessary for meetings. I have a part-time secretary, a lady comes in to do the cleaning, and another one four times a week to cook my noon and evening meals. To tell you the truth of the matter it is, it's sometimes a wee bit embarrassing to be having all this: particularly times like these, when there's people struggling to bring up families on very modest incomes from their farms, or even some of them losing their homes all together.

Still, this is where my Bishop assigned me six years ago: and maybe next time it'll be somewhere much much smaller and more modest. It'll be somewhere else in Kansas, that's about all I know: that's where I've always been, ever since I came to America, 21, newly ordained and fresh as a pie, 30 years ago. A whole day and a night's train journey in a cold windy October to Kansas City: nothing to be seen out of the window but mile after mile of grass and bare trees. I didn't know they made train journeys that long, the furthest I'd ever gone before was from Dublin to Cork. No houses to see, no people, nothing but space and then more space, and then still more space after that. I'm not ashamed to tell you, I sent up a prayer I did: I said 'Oh Lord please turn this train around and let me go back home to Ireland.'

I hadn't asked the seminary to send me to Kansas, I'd just said I'd like to go anywhere at all in America. I was one out of 11 brothers and sisters, and I knew some of them were in the United States, so I thought it'd be a fine idea. I thought of America like Ireland: Chicago, San Francisco, Miami, to me they were the same as Galway or Limerick, just a little bit this way or a little bit that. When they told me the first diocese I'd be in was Wichita in Kansas, and Kansas was about in the middle, that sounded just right.

So there I was, come to America, an import from Ireland, one of the two principal ones that Ireland exports to the States: priests is one and fat cattle is the other. Over the years, I've managed to see some of my brothers and sisters, just once in a while we've visited one another. I'm the only one of the family in the priesthood: they're here propagating the Irish race and I'm here propagating the faith. I go back now and again to Ireland too: I used to go many times to see my mother, but she died 20 years ago and I've not been there so often since.

And now I'm a naturalised American, so that makes me a stranger when I go to Ireland. I never thought I'd become one though at the beginning. I thought America would be an English-speaking country you see: but when I came at first they could no more understand me than I could understand them. I decided straight away that part of my mission must be to teach the natives to speak English. But I think I've failed miserably to be honest with you: I've hardly ever met a Kansan who speaks it with my accent at all.

I like it now though, of course I do, I love it. I'm completely American, and I wouldn't want to be anything else. I'd like it even better if they could just put themselves to learning the simple art of making a decent cup of tea, but that apart there's not a lot of improvement I'd wish for. Yourself, have you since you've been here tasted such beverages as powdered cinnamon tea? And iced tea? And what they call 'Sun Tea', have you experienced that? All of them, you have? Well all I can say is you still look remarkably healthy, and we'll perhaps talk no more of that subject shall we?

Now what else can I tell you about this great land of ours that you'd be wanting to know? Do I feel American? Well yes I think of course certainly I do, after so many years. I don't feel at home in Ireland when I go back there. I am an American, with all of the privileges and obligations that that brings: and as a priest, when we have our little get-togethers once every week or two of the whole of the priests in the area, I'm very conscious of being at one with them all, and most of them are American born. It's such a great country America isn't it now, with so many different races and peoples all in the same melting pot? Which makes it that you can feel American, and be American, all of you all together, wherever you or your father or your grandfather originates from it in the first place. There's a kind of what shall I call it, a kind of informality and we're all the sameness about America and Americans, which I think is very appealing and one of our great strengths as a nation.

And Bird, yes, I'd say that I thought in many ways Bird was the sort of epitome of what America represents: a kind, decent, honest, upright community, with a clear sense of values, a strong idea of right and wrong but also a readiness to tolerate another person's point of view, so that everyone gets along together. I think there are strong moral values too: there's very little gossip or talk of scandal, and that's not just because people think those things are wrong to talk about, it's because they're wrong to do and most people don't do them. There's an old saying about hating the sin but not the sinner: I think that showed itself when there was the incident, or rather the incidents, with the High School girls who had the babies.

Another point's important to say is that people have charitable hearts, and they show it. If there's a family with a child in hospital, or where a parent's been lost, there's fund-raising for them from the whole town. Catholics or anyone else, it makes no difference, everyone joins together to help: I think that's something to be very proud of.

Will I stay here or not is something I don't know and all I can tell you of that is I'll go where my Bishop sends me, and be happy to. Now can I be making for you for once a real genuine proper cup of tea?

OK I hope with Him: Gary Long

On a Saturday morning he was sitting at his kitchen table: in front of him were a Bible, a tape recorder and a pad of paper covered with notes. He was round-faced and lively: he wore grey slacks and a colourful shirt with a large check pattern.

– When I was called for the draft, the two years' Army service which was compulsory in those days, I went to the Reporting Centre and there was a sergeant there with a great long form. 'What's your religion?' he said to me. I said 'Christian.' 'Sure,' he said, 'But what sort of Christian?' I said to him, 'No sort of Christian, put down just that: "Christian."' That's how it is with us: we say no creed but Christ, no book but the Bible, and no name but Christian. Our only guide is the words that are in the Bible, both Old Testament and New. Whether that'd be what some folk call fundamentalist I don't know: or Baptist, or what, you could give it any name you chose to. But to us it's simply and only Christian. We control our own Church ourselves: we don't have superiors we report to, no one else owns it but us, we hire and fire our own preachers, and everything else that there is.

And in it we have just two titles only: Elders and Deacons. Elders are folk like I am, responsible for guidance, and Deacons are ones who carry out the administrative work. Together with our members we ordain our own preachers. The last one we had, he wasn't a graduate from a Bible college, nothing like that: he was a self-taught man, and that was what we liked about him and why we chose him. He understood the working life and the spiritual life, and how sometimes for instance the former has to take precedence over the latter. If your job's your life, as it is in farming say, the Lord knows that. He's not going to blame you if you're too busy for church and have to get on with work at certain times of the year. Ours is a religion for everyday living, and we don't involve ourselves too much with abstract theological matters.

Right now we don't have a preacher at all for our church here. We're looking, and we've had one or two come, to see if they liked us and we liked them. But so far we haven't made a decision. The one we had moved on, and we don't know yet who the Lord will send us to take his place. He will send though, and when He does, we shall know.

Because right now we don't have anyone, and because I'm an Elder, therefore it's up to me to fill in, and preach until we have a proper person to do it. The nearest I could be called would be a lay preacher: only I'm not really no preacher at all, I'm just an Elder that's all. But I guess if you're an Elder, if it's necessary you should be able to stand up and give a message to the people. So that's what I'm doing here right now, in preparation for in church tomorrow morning. But it's hard to do, I don't find it easy, no sir. I have my Book here, which is the good one, the one and only one: and I make my notes and read it into the tape recorder to see how it sounds, then I listen to it played back and try to improve it. There's a message here in the Book, I know that: and it's no more and no less than the Word of the Lord. The message is simple and clear and direct, because His word always is: and that's all I'm trying to do, just to convey that. And I hope the Lord understands that, that that's what I'm trying my best to do: and if I don't stray too far from what the Book says, then that'll be OK I hope with Him.

I'll sure be a whole lot happier when a better preacher comes along though, and maybe one who'll at the same time be our church minister. What he'll do then, when the Lord sends him, is he'll minister, just that: to all of us in our congregation, to the sick, and do the pastoral side of things also. This is what we're missing out on right now because we don't have a full-time appointment. But you know, it could well be for instance the Lord was setting a little testing time for us here. He tells us that in life He will test us, it says so in the Book: and that if you survive the test, your faith will be stronger. I'm not talking here about a crisis of faith, not anything of that sort: like everyone else I've had a few problems in my life now and again, but I couldn't say any of them had gone that far, to make me doubt the faith I was brought up in. I should think whatever came, or I should certainly hope that whatever came, my faith would endure. I've never had cause to worry along those lines ever in my life. Religion after all, it's the rock on which your life is founded.

The number one thing I'd say about our faith, without any doubt, is the happiness of it. I sure feel sorry for those who don't know the Lord, who don't know how many things you can do for Him and how many things He'll do for you in return. If you let Him into your everyday life, that's where He belongs: and if only all folks everywhere would understand what a difference it would make to them if they did that, then we'd have a whole lot less of the world's problems.

It's hard for me to understand that not everyone can see that, because I know it from my own experience, this happiness of having God in your life that I'm talking about. I'm sorry they haven't yet had the same experience, because I think everyone should live their life to the full: your religion's the basic part of it, not just the most important part but the only part there is. When you look around our church on a Sunday and you see all those people there, with their eyes shining with deep deep happiness, then you can actually see it in a way no words can describe. You can see how full of love for God they are, and He's in return filled their lives with His love for them. It's sure a truly wonderful thing, it surely is.

15 *Veterans of foreign wars*

Eldon Simmonds

He owned and ran a one-man agricultural machinery repair shop on the outskirts of town. A tall heavily built man with cropped dark hair and glasses, he talked sitting on an oil drum in his unlit office, a lean-to structure of corrugated metal against the building's side.

– Nam sir, yes Nam I did two tours there. I'd go back again tomorrow if they asked me to, yes sir I would for sure. There's unfinished business there and we ought to go back and finish it. I have a wife and two kids and I'd go back there for them, that's the way I'd look at it: I'd be fighting to keep the world safe from the Commies. Best time of my life when I was there. You don't join the Army for a soft life, you join it to be a fighting man and to go where your country needs you and do what your country asks of you, right or wrong.

Always wanted to be a soldier: that's why I joined the Army, because it was what I wanted to do all the way up through school. I wasn't much interested in my books or in sport: since right back from when I can remember, what I liked most was watching war films on TV. So as soon as I could I went to Baxter to the Recruiting Centre and said I wanted to sign. My ma didn't want me to. My pa, he'd died when I was five: but I always thought him and me'd have gotten along pretty good, he'd have approved of my way of thinking.

The Vietnam war was on and that was the reason my ma didn't want me to join, because she was scared they'd send me out there. Which was the same reason exactly why I wanted to join: because the war was on and I wanted to go out there and fight. It wouldn't have had half the appeal for me joining the Army wouldn't, not if there'd been no war for me to fight. I told them what I wanted to do most, which was fly. So first they sent me to Missoura for training, and then to Alabama for more training: I learned helicopter maintenance and then I was sent off to Vietnam as helicopter crew. I was with what they call a Medivac unit, that's medical evacuation work. You went in where the fighting was, and you either set down and landed or if it was too dangerous to do that you let down a winch, depending on the circumstances.

We carried machine-guns for self-protection: if you didn't, you were just a sitting duck. The Cong didn't pay no attention to whether you had red crosses painted on your sides or whether you didn't: made no goddam difference to them, soon as they saw you they'd just take you out. So we always went in firing and taking fire. The first year we got shot down twice, but we weren't ever captured: once a gunship came in and saved us, the other time it was a back-up Medivac copter that took us away.

After that, they sent me back home a while and that's when I met Louella who's my wife. We got married, and after that it was back to Vietnam again for my second tour. I was with a gunship unit, but still crew on a Medivac copter. By then though the war was phasing down: in ten months we saw action only three times.

Now let's see, what happened to me after that? Oh yeah, after I came home again I went to a training school for officers, but had an injury to my leg and had to drop out of that one. I volunteered to be a Recruiting Officer then, and I was after a particular job in Baxter. But they gave it to the other applicant for it: he was a black man from Nicodemus, so being in a minority group he had an advantage over me. That finished me for the military and I came out: that'd be 12 years ago now.

I was a custom harvester a while but that didn't suit me too good, so then I bought me a truck and built up my own haulage business. I was happy doing that, but it had the drawback to it I'd be home say only once a month. I was all over the United States, sometimes driving 4,000 miles or more in one week. I liked driving though, nothing better: and the best time of all was driving at night, I could just drive and drive, I sure got a great feeling out of it. I still have the haulage business, only I stay home more. Getting to be more the family man, with growing up kids you like to be around. So I have this repair business here now, and I'm happy doing that.

Thinking back on Nam, I'll tell you what I feel now, and it's pretty damn strong. If you want it in one word, I think we was betrayed, that's what. We weren't allowed to fight the war the way we should have fought it, we all the time had one hand tied to our backs. We went there for the right reason in the first place which was to fight communist aggression, and we should have gone on until we won and did what we'd set out to do. But it got into a situation back home where it had become a political and financial war, with people making money out of arms selling, and trying to improve their own positions. That's why Johnson was into it, no other reason.

And what happened then was a blot on American history. Nixon came along, and he was a really good guy: a very wise man, a very fine man, someone who was honest and entitled to respect. He wanted to get the war over: and get it over good, and get it over quick. And if he'd been let go on with the bombing like he wanted to, we'd have won it and South Vietnam would today be a free country. But he was forced to pull out. The peace movement, or what it should be called more rightly the anti-American flag movement, they forced him to stop. He was made into a public scapegoat by the newspapers and the television, which everybody knows are owned and run entirely by lefties. People don't all realise that. What they done to Nixon was a shame and a disgrace.

And what they done to us who were the soldiers out there, that was the same. We were in combat, getting ourselves killed or risking it: and what did we read in the newspapers that was being sent out to us? That there were big demonstrations organised by the Commies in Washington, protesting the war. So why didn't they come out to Vietnam, and organise and protest it to the Commies? No one's ever answered that. Right at the end we had to leave in a hurry: and you know what? Within two days of arrival at our base in Texas, we were issued leave passes to go off camp: and me and two of my buddies, there's a crowd of these people outside the gate shouting at us 'Baby killers, baby killers' as we went by. American people, they was supposed to be. Well let's have this straight OK? Sure we killed babies: some, that's war. And some women, and some old people. But what we killed most was gooks – a whole lot of them: and if we'd been able to kill a whole lot more, every single one of them there, then Vietnam would have freedom.

You got that word on your tape recorder now have you, loud and clear? That one word which I want you to have, how I feel: betrayed?

Thompson Ketch

In his mid fifties, he had light blue eyes and a mass of curly white hair. He sat in the cool of a summer's evening, outside on the veranda of his small house on South Garfield Street.

– I'm not one of those guys you could say believes all that stuff you sometimes hear, you know my country right or wrong. You'll still meet folk of that sort so they say, but I don't think you get so much of it these days. I saw a book in the library a few months back, reproductions of posters of one sort and another, one of them was that one 'Uncle Sam wants YOU', you know the one I mean? My way of looking at it now is if Uncle Sam wants me, he's got to tell me first exactly why, and then I'll make up my mind whether I'll go along with it.

I wasn't this way when I was younger. Oh no. At the time of the Korean war I was a young feller of 20, just starting to make my way in life: I was working with an insurance company in their office in Conway City, and my future was looking fairly bright. There was a girl lived here in Bird, we'd been at High School together, and there was talk the company were thinking of opening a branch office here. I thought if I could get a job in Bird with them then, prospects would be even brighter.

Then came the war and the draft: and young men my age, they were among those who were the first to go. You weren't sure what was going to happen to you, no one was: so me and my girl, we decided the best thing was to get married, I'd go off and do my military service, and then we'd start our proper life together after that. I remember it was put to us at the time that the Korean action, it wasn't like a war in the old sense, it was more of something might be called a police action: we were going in on behalf of the United Nations kind of a thing.

That seemed a good reason. My wife and me weren't happy about the idea of separation: it was an inconvenience but then a lot of other folk were being inconvenienced too, so we had to take our share. Getting killed and dying, that would have been too big an inconvenience all together, so I made up my mind I'd try to be pretty careful and not let it go as far as that.

Let me tell you though, I got a little upset after I'd been only just a few weeks in Korea. A new edict was brought in that as far as our American military was concerned, if you were married you'd not be sent to Korea. We were sitting around a table in a tent, about seven of us: and there was one guy reading out pieces from the newspaper from home to us. He was a guy had a reputation as a joker. We all knew it, and he'd now and again make up something and read it out, keeping his face straight to see if he could get us believe it. And he read this piece out, about this new law and married guys not having to go to Korea. Well we all laughed out so loud we nearly blew the tent down didn't we? We were all seven of us married, every one. So this guy he lets everyone go on laughing, and then he didn't say anything, he just folded up the newspaper where the news item was and passed it to the guy next to him to read. I'll remember that scene for ever. The guy he'd handed it to, he read it, and he stopped laughing just like that. He passed it to the next guy, and the same: and so on, and it ended with the seven of us sitting around that table all completely silent. All of us thinking the same thing: we was the last married guys to be sent to Korea. That really got to us.

I think it's correct to say the other thing that got to us later was this was a United Nations action, right? But the country that took the most casualties was the US: and some of our so-called allies, they were still trading with North Korea. I know a lot of the guys there at the time, they felt pretty sore about that. Soldiers in a war, there's always long periods when there's nothing to do but yap: and there was, there was a lot of talk about that.

Well, I'd gone out there like I said not wanting to be killed or win myself any medals for being heroic, and luckily that's how it worked out. I was chiefly concerned with supplies and stuff, and not in a position where I was shot at. The nearest it ever came to me was over the other side of the hill. You didn't have much choice mind: you were told what to do and you did it. I was only John Doe, the ordinary service guy marching around, taking orders and saluting people, and I never got commissioned up to officer nor ever put myself forward to be. Once for a time I was in charge of 150 men: but that was my only experience of command, and they were enemy prisoners so I guess that doesn't count.

Your memory fades you know. It's a while since I've even thought about it, not to mention talked. What'll it be now, 35 years back? I was in Korea 19 months and the biggest danger I was in ever was I might have died with the boredom of it. Like every other place, in town here we have our own VFW club: that's Veterans of Foreign Wars. But I guarantee you could go in there, sit around, have a beer, visit with someone: and all the talk you heard, if you don't know where it was you were, you wouldn't be able to guess. The guys in there, most of them have gone for the company and maybe to get away for a while from their wives. But not for sentimental reasons, not to reminisce together about their fighting days, nothing like that. Some of the younger ones, those who were in Vietnam, once in a while they get into how their country doesn't appreciate them and start sounding off like they was Rambo about the MIAs: you know the prisoners who was listed as missing in action and never came back? Some of them'll tell you they reckon there's around two, two and a half thousand of them still there: and we ought to do something about it they'll say, we ought to get a platoon, go get them back. But it is, it's just Rambo talk is that. Myself I reckon if there's men still there, they've got a reason for being. I wouldn't necessarily like to say exactly why, but everyone knows there was a lot of drugs out there, a lot of men getting into things the military would no way have approved of. If they went missing presumed killed, well it could be that was a way out for them, and quite a convenient one. Deserters, men taking to the jungle and living with girls they'd got for themselves: there's a number of reasons why a missing soldier wouldn't necessarily be all that too happy to see a bunch of his old comrades parachuting down from the sky come looking for him.

These summer evenings like this, after a hot day we've had like today, they can be real pleasant eh? Talking of war, halfway round the other side of the world, so long ago: it seems like a dream now you know, it really does.

Calvin Hughes

A small, stocky man in a suit, with a white shirt and a black velvet bow tie, he lived with his daughter and son-in-law in their large house on North Adams Street.

– All these years and you know what I've hoped for most of all? That one day I'd take a trip back to your country and see some more of it. It was 1944 I was there, for just three days: and two of those I spent on a barge on the water of some harbour I can't even recall the name of. Could be we weren't even told it: all I know's it was near some place would it be called Way Mouth Bay? We were taken across the Atlantic by plane, a night in a camp in Dorsetshire, on to this barge and the next time our feet touched land it was in Normandy, France. So I don't have too much idea of your scenery and I never met none of your people. This would be around what they called D-day plus five, not the actual invasion thank God but soon after it: I was with a support company behind the primary assault forces, on the beach that had the name given to it of Omaha.

And you know, the funny thing is, in past years my dear wife and I, we've been back six, maybe seven times to France: to Normandy itself, to the beach where I was. Very very different from how I remembered it, it sure was, I can tell you that. The French people, they've done a great deal of redevelopment there to make it into a holiday coast. I remember the first time, she and I were walking along and I came to a spot and I stopped, and I made a cross in the sand with my foot. It was about there, just about right there I told her, that I took my first step on the Normandy soil. Well I can tell you now, it doesn't matter: I was making it up, I didn't want to disappoint her after we'd come all that way. But it could have been there: it could have been anywhere, I couldn't orientate myself.

We went back several times after, and I always told her one day we'd go to England too, see if I could find where I'd been there as well. Only sadly she passed away three years ago, so there don't seem quite the point to it now.

The place in France I remember most of from World War II is the Ardennes. We got into some real hard fighting there in what afterwards became known I think I read it referred to as the Battle of the Bulge. They only get these names afterwards: you don't have no General coming round in a jeep saying 'OK men, now tomorrow you're going to be fighting the Battle of the Bulge.' The end of December it would be if my memory serves me right: north France, east and south of the Meuse River. Very beautiful countryside it is now, when we revisited it. But when I'd been there in wartime, the time before as a young man in a tank support group, it didn't look too pretty then, I can tell you that.

I was not long out of school, straight into the Army, did my training and then right away over to Europe and into combat. I read a book the other day, I think it's called *The Good War*, interviews with people by Studs Terkel, have you come across that? Person after person there, they were saying how when they were in it, they all felt the same, that they were part of some great event. Maybe not all of them, but many of them said that. I didn't feel about it that way myself, for me it wasn't a good war but a horrible brutal one. Following the tanks, you saw too much of death in their wake: cattle lying at the roadside in heaps, piled on top of one another. And then you'd come to a village maybe, or what had maybe been a village just a day or so before: and you'd see a figure hanging out the window of a first floor room, like a doll someone'd thrown away, limp, hanging forward like that. You'd look at it as you went by, and the thing was it always took time: leastways for me it did, it always took time for it to impress itself on my mind. 'That's a dead person, that's a dead body: a while back it was a living person like I am. Now it's not.' It didn't make me want to throw up, be sick, nothing like that: but it was like you were wandering around on a location they were getting ready for a film. 'We'll have a dead body hanging out that window there, another one there, another one over there.' All completely unreal to you, you know?

I've always thought of it as a slaughterous war, and to tell you honestly about it, one I've never felt too proud that I belonged to. We had more men than they had, more machines, more equipment: and we just went on throwing them at them until finally they backed off. Didn't matter who they were, soldiers, civilians, men, women, children. We were doing it to them this side the same time the Russians were doing it to them that. A good thing we won in the end, I've always felt that. But to me there was nothing heroic about it, it was just a matter of which one of us had the most we could afford to lose.

I met a guy once in Denver Colorado, my wife and I we'd gone to a photographic convention there because photography was our hobby. In the lounge of our hotel we were sitting one night having a drink, we got talking with this young feller who'd been too young to have been in the war himself. I was saying to him something like along the lines I've been saying here to you. About northern France and those places, telling him where I'd been. He said to me, 'Heh,' he said, 'just last night right here in this lounge, I was talking to another guy and he was telling me the names of these same places, about all the fighting he'd been in around there, what a time he'd had and how like life had never been the same since.' He said he'd go see if he could find him, bring him back to visit with us so we could like exchange with each other our experiences. I said to him no, I didn't want to meet the guy: if he felt like he said he did, then no thanks, I'd sooner not visit with him. The war hadn't been no fun for me, the more I got the further and further away from it, the happier I was.

After the war I was a teacher, and I always used to tell my class if it came up the same thing: I didn't think war was all that good a way to settle quarrels, if you could find some other then you should. Necessary sometimes, you can't avoid it: but not unless you really really have to, no.

We came here three years ago to retire and because our daughter and husband and their three children are here. Bird we liked, though we're not Kansas people, we come from Maryland. The thing I regret most is my wife wasn't able to be here long enough to get the flavour of the place, and sometimes I get lonesome. My son-in-law, he said to me a while back 'Pa,' he said, 'why don't you go to the Veterans' club, meet some of the guys there who were like you, in the war?' Which is just what I don't want, and I told him. I think he understood.

16 *Couples*

Larry and Patsy Lawrence

LARRY: We've lived on this farm here out the edge of town since we married 19 years ago. This is my family's farm from three generations back. She came from eastern Kansas, around Wichita, and what brought her here I sure don't know.

PATSY: You sure do: what brought me here was you. I was at college at K State University training to be a teacher, and I was rooming with a girl from Bird: he came to see her and that was how we met.

LARRY: She sure was a nice girl and I had in mind marrying her. But then this one clapped eyes on me and decided I was too good to let pass by, so that was it, I never had no chance at all.

PATSY: He did real good for himself if you want the truth. You want to contradict me?

LARRY: OK maybe not, I'll only suffer for it later and the kids don't like it if we fight. We've five of them, three boys and two girls: youngest two, oldest 15.

PATSY: We should've had six: our first born was a girl but she died at birth.

LARRY: And that's something you don't forget, I think folks don't realise. The doctor at the hospital, he said to us 'Well you're young, don't upset yourselves, you've plenty of time to have more.' That was a kind of a hard thing to have said to you when your first child's died only ten minutes before though.

PATSY: I've liked having a big family, it's how we've always wanted it. I do a bit of substitute teaching if someone on the staff's sick, and I go back to college once in every three years to keep my credentials up to date. So I could always work any time again I wanted to.

LARRY: She does work: she takes care of the kids and she keeps all the books for the farm and our business. All that's work: you're on the library board and everything, so don't say you don't work. We both work real hard. We have two and one half thousand acres here, we grow wheat and milo, or maize as some folk call it, and we have 400 head of cattle. Our other business is house moving, we decided a while back with the farm economy being how it was we ought to diversify, so that's what we did and it's coming on nicely. House moving is just what it says, moving people's houses for them: the whole house, contents and all. You lift it up and you put it on a transporter, and you take it wherever folks want it and set it down for them just where they want it on their patch of land they've bought. Let me show you some photographs we've took of houses on the road while we was moving them.

PATSY: You have to do a lot of thinking and a lot of figuring and a lot of measuring before you start. You plan it all out and when you're sure you've done it all and it's all right, off you go. We figure we can move a house 125 miles or so in a day. A lot cheaper than waiting to sell your house some place and building a new one some place else.

LARRY: I'm getting so I think sometimes I like the house moving better'n farming. More excitement, more variety, more fun.

PATSY: But hard work that's for sure. Some days he'll leave home around five in the morning and I won't see him no more till nine or ten o'clock at night. I say to him sometimes why doesn't he take a break, and he always tells me the same thing: moving houses is a break from farming, farming's a break from moving houses.

LARRY: Be careful now, any minute he's going to be asking us how we had the time to have five children.

PATSY: We've had plenty of time to have five children, and they've given us a rich life. When they're all grown up we hope they'll look back to their upbringing here and feel they had a good childhood. We might not have been one of the very rich people, but we do OK, we make out, none of us goes short. I get kind of impatient when I hear folk talking about the economy and how times is hard. Too many of them spend too much time sitting around in diners or beer joints or in implement dealers, and all they're doing is talk talk talk. OK so some times in a year, a few weeks, we have to work ten twelve hours a day seven days a week. If it's necessary, harvest time and times like that, or we've got three different folks all want their houses moved for them all in the same week – well, we'll do it. We don't neither of us sit around telling other folk how hard times is though, that's one thing we don't. And we do other things too, community things. He's on the school board, I'm on the library: we find time, we make time and we enjoy doing it.

LARRY: The most important thing we have is our partnership, and if we didn't have that feeling together, nothing would work. But with the partnership feeling we've got, we feel we can do anything. I'm no businessman: but Patsy is and she keeps everything in line. She negotiates the bank loans, deals with the government on subsidies and taxes, and goes through all the information and figures with our accountant. He's a man myself I've never even met.

PATSY: We're not even one of those families where we've had oil found on our land and that way got extra revenue to carry us along. We had one drilling once, that's all and it was a dry hole.

LARRY: It's difficult to say what our problems have been. We've always been plumb downright happy with each other since the day we was married, and I can say that right here in front of her and she knows it as a fact.

PATSY: I think the only real problem I've ever had was just in the first few years, with your mother. But that was years back and only at first, and once we had that sorted out she and I have gotten along good and now we're real good friends.

LARRY: And you know, me being a man and all, it was all going along right over my head and I didn't know it. Not until the day once after I'd been working and I dropped by to see her: and she was cooking something for my pa and I told her it smelled good, so she put it in front of me and I set and eat a big big meal. Then when I got home here, Patsy had cooked a big meal for me too, so I had to set and try and eat that one as well. I couldn't get it down, there was no way it'd go: and she stood in front of me, watching me and getting madder and madder.

PATSY: I did too. But I wouldn't now. I guess she was trying to get her boy back, least that's what I thought. I wouldn't think that now though, I'd think OK he can eat at his ma's every night if he wants to, less work for me.

LARRY: You would not, you're just saying that.

PATSY: You want to bet? Give it a try sometime, see what happens.

LARRY: I'd sooner eat your cooking.

PATSY: Well there now, what d'you know?

Wilbur and Olive Sawyer

In their house at the south end of Harding Street, they sat on high-backed wooden chairs at a formica-topped table in the middle of their sitting room. He was thin and his hair was sparse: she was dark and her voice was slow and small.

WILBUR: I'll have to do most of the talking because Olive, she don't hear too good. I'd best say to begin with I'm not from Kansas, I was raised in an orphan's home in Denver and I never went out of the state of Colorado until after I met her 30 years ago when I was 32 and she was just past 50. So that makes it now I'm 62 and she's 73.

OLIVE: I ain't 73 I'm 72. Maybe I don't hear too good Wilbur like you said, but I can still count all right.

WILBUR: OK 72 it's no big deal. My dad had left me in an orphanage when I was a kid: from there I was put to work on a farm from when I was 12 and all my life as a kid I had a pretty hard time of it, not like her. Ain't that right, as a kid I had a hard time but not you?

OLIVE: Yes that's right, it is. I was born and reared on a farm but I had a wonderful life when I was a child. There was 11 of us, and as I recall it there wasn't a day when the sun didn't shine. I got married when I was just a girl, and I was married 27 years but then my husband passed away. Then one day I went to Boulder to see my grandaughter who was studying there at the university, and there was Wilbur painting some buildings they had, up in the sky in one of those cradle things. I got talking with him and he told me he'd been single all his life: but I thought I'll soon change that my man, and I did. I got my son-in-law who was lecturing there at the university for to ask him to come over and I cooked a meal, and that way I got him. We were married just 21 days after we met, on the 4th of July. I don't know about him but I've been so happy since then, and this year we'll be celebrating our twenty-fifth year.

WILBUR: Oh I dunno about marrying, I was just looking for a housekeeper and a cook that's all and she seemed to fit the bill. I was painting the university and I was living in an old boxcar down by the railroad there, and I needed a person to look after me because I had this here bad luck. Just my joke. I hadn't reckoned on moving and coming all this way here to Bird though.

OLIVE: We came because I had children and grandchildren here, and stepchildren too. When I first married at 19 I had three stepchildren, and they've always been wonderful to me they truly have. Their dad died in 1960, they're all grown up and married with children, and since then we've all been closer and closer still.

WILBUR: This house here, this is our first and only home. Before that it was trailer homes, boxcars, shanties, anywhere I could find that went with a job. Neither of us has very good health now: so this house we have here, it's small but it's home, and here we'll be we hope the rest of our lives.

OLIVE: I feel like Bird is home and I think he does too. All the folk around here are friendly. When he had a heart attack and was hospitalised five weeks, all the neighbours came round and brought things for us to make sure we had everything what we needed. And our Uncle Joe as we call him, which has the Bank, he took our house as collateral for a loan for two years even though he didn't know us too good. It took us two years to pay him back but he never once hurried us for money did he?

WILBUR: That's right. We've always done good and got by, and if you can say that, that's the most important thing.

OLIVE: We've been hungry and there's been days we didn't know where our next meal was coming from. But it's like Wilbur says, we've always got by.

WILBUR: Let me tell you something. This girl here, she's the connivingest person you could ever wish to meet when it comes to fixing a meal out of nothing. I'll tell you without a word of a lie, she can make a feast for anyone out of a cupful of beans and just some flour in a pan. Isn't that right Olive? Your bean pancake, I'm telling him that that's one real treat.

OLIVE: Oh don't exaggerate, it's just something to eat. But most of our times, they haven't been too bad. We reckon if we have a hundred dollars left at the end of the month that's pretty good. He has a little service pension from when he was in the Army, and he has his Social Security and I have mine, so we do all right. We're not big people for entertaining or going places, we don't have no car: but we have children and friends stop by, and he does his paintings to keep himself occupied, so we're happy enough. Tell him about your paintings Wilbur.

WILBUR: There's nothing to tell. They're just paintings I do, watercolours, that's my hobby for my spare time. That one there over the mantelshelf, that's one of mine. Cowboys attacked by Indians, I copied it from a magazine. And you know that one they call the *National Geographic*? Well over there look, the one on that wall, that's one I copied out of there. An old print of the great fire of Chicago, it was done by two guys whose name I've forgot. What was their name Olive, the guys who did that print originally of the great Chicago fire?

OLIVE: Currier and Ives was it, some name like that?

WILBUR: Yeah Currier and Ives. I tell you this girl you know, she's like a dictionary, anything you want to know, you just have to ask her that's all.

OLIVE: You tell him how you like it living here Wilbur, tell him that.

WILBUR: She wants me to tell you because when we came here first, I said to her I'd never want to live in a place like this. I'm from Denver, the big city right? I thought how would I make out in a place like this one, where nothing happened from one day to the next.

OLIVE: And do you want to go back to Denver now?

WILBUR: I sure don't girl, I sure do not. All the noise and the traffic and the dirt in the streets, everyone shouting and hollering. You step off the sidewalk there, and some guy in a big automobile he shouts at you 'Watch where you're going you, you stupid son of a bitch!' Everyone's got red faces with their bad tempers all the time. No thank you, no sir, back to Denver or any big city now, I do not ever want to go.

OLIVE: You don't even like to go to Baxter when one of the children takes us there for shopping or just a ride around. Here in Bird you've settled in pretty good I'd say.

WILBUR: We'd neither of us want anywhere or anything different now would we, from what we have?

OLIVE: I'd like to be able to cook more than I do, that's all. But I have the rheumatism and the arthritis and all those things you have when you're getting old, and I don't move around the house too good. So Wilbur does most the cooking now and cleans the house. But that ain't right really, that's the woman's job.

WILBUR: We look after each other, next year when it's my turn I can't move, you'll look after me. That's how it should be: a husband and wife, that's just how it should be. OK, is that OK for you now?

OLIVE: Could I just say one thing please? He said a word there a few minutes back which he shouldn't have. I'm not going to say it myself, you'll know the one I mean. He don't talk that way himself, not ever he don't. I know he said automobile drivers in Denver say it, but when he repeats it, it makes him sound like he's not a gentleman. And he is, Wilbur himself is a gentleman, so please don't make it sound like he talks that way himself. Would you make sure of that please?

Fanny and Greg Petersen

Both were in their thirties. She was plump, fair-haired and brown-eyed: he was tall, thin, angular, with glasses and going bald. The house they lived in was round the corner from the High School, and was sparsely furnished with the impersonal air of rented accommodation.

FANNY: Greg's here on a two-year contract with an oil company in Baxter. Our home's in Ohio and we left all our things there, we didn't feel it would be worth it to bring everything here for such a short time. Right now my sister's living there and looking after it for us. I have a small part time job three days a week at the school: something to do, more than anything else. Next month we go back again to Ohio, so we've been here 22 months only, which isn't long to have gotten much of an impression of the place to tell you about. But I think we've enjoyed being here, I'd say. When you talk with him ask Greg how he feels about it, but I guess he'd probably say the same.

The biggest difference for me's been the small size of the town. Cincinnati where we were, that's a huge big city: you could live there all your life and you still wouldn't ever meet one half of one per cent of the population. Here it's only been two years and I feel like we know everybody, or everybody pretty near. That you walk a block to where you work, two blocks to the bank, two blocks to the library, things like that make you realise. Last fall in the evenings some times we'd go out and walk around in the cool air for a while: after an hour at most we'd been everywhere there was in the town to go, so we'd come back home again. That took some getting used to: at first it was like living in that place what's it called, Lilliput land, Brobdingnag or is that the one where everyone's tall?

I don't know if Greg would go along with this too, but you kind of feel, at least I do coming from a big city, that because the place is small the outlook of the people who live here, it makes that small too. This is their world and they're not too concerned with what goes on outside of it. I guess the answer to that's why should they be, it doesn't make a difference to them how people in other places look at things, so why should they bother? But you do get the feeling once in a while they're very what's the word, 'circumscribed' in outlook is it? It's a feeling it's hard to describe or give you an example of. Let me see, let me see if I can think of something. Yeah well I suppose the nearest example I could give you was a couple of weeks back, one of the teachers at school when I said something to her about India I think it was, she said it was a place she'd always wanted to go. When I said to her well why didn't she, just for a moment she looked quite kind of scared at the thought, and she said oh no, she never could, it was too far. Only the thing was, just last Christmas she'd been to see family she had in Vancouver.

Well to me, Vancouver from here would be pretty far. Not like India I guess, but one's only a few hours further on by air that's all. I'm not explaining this to you so good, but what I'm saying is that to her Vancouver didn't seem far because they were all white people there who all spoke English: but India isn't, it's all brown people who don't speak English. So the way she meant far was it was a long way away from her ordinary everyday lifestyle.

But then against that you do have to set the great kindness of people, the way they make offers of help to you immediately if they know you're in trouble. December last year Greg had a slight accident in his car in Baxter: he wasn't badly hurt or anything, but he had to stay a night in hospital, just one night. The husband and wife from across the street there, I didn't even know we knew them: and I don't know how they found out, but they came over and said they'd take me to Baxter to the hospital. I said no really it was OK, Greg had called me up and he sounded fine. You know truly, they looked so disappointed I was turning their offer down I finally said well Yes I'd go, I couldn't help worry about him. So they took me all the way to Baxter, waited an hour at the hospital then brought me all the way back. Let me tell you what I got from Greg: from him I got 'Heh are you crazy, what in hell are you doing here, I told you not to come!' I said, 'Greg honey, I just had to.'

So I guess those are the two sides of Bird to me.

GREG: I'll try and not say the same things Fanny said the other night when you spoke with her. She told me what she remembered it was mostly, and I'd go along with her views I'm sure. She has a better idea of living here in the town though than I do of course: she spends her days here, while I'm mostly only actually in Bird evenings and weekends. Like she does, I've found it a big contrast from living in Cincinnati: I guess changing from big city life to life in a small prairie town in the mid west is about as different as you can get.

She told me she told you about the time I had to stay in hospital a night, and I still think something like that's pretty remarkable.

And there's the other side to life in a small place that's good too, like not having to lock up your automobile if you leave it standing outside at night. And not having to worry about Fanny if I'm late coming home from work, knowing she's perfectly safe everywhere she goes, walking on her own. There's many parts of many big cities, and even not so big cities, where you couldn't say that.

I've been thinking about it knowing we were going to talk, what I could say to you else about the town that I'd noticed which I didn't think was so good. I thought if there was one thing I'd say, it would be something about the cohesive social identity of the place, for want of a better phrase. Everybody knows everybody, and this brings advantages but disadvantages too. For example every disagreement or conflict has a personal face: so when it does happen over something, as it's bound to, I think you get people taking sides not on a basis of who's right or wrong, but on which person they like best.

There was the time you'll have heard of I'm sure, you couldn't be in Bird and go long not hearing about it, when three girls at the school became pregnant and had babies. On the one side when you hear about it, it all sounds like a very open-minded and tolerant approach: and you think it was a pretty good example of right behaviour, and perhaps a bit surprising and unexpected some place like this. Don't get me wrong over this, I'm not criticising the behaviour, I'm glad the town took it that way, and so they should. But I just have a kind of question mark in the back of my mind about it. All of those girls, I don't know their families personally, but all three of them were from families very well known and highly regarded in the town. I just wonder if the same kind of tolerance would have been given, even say to a woman living on her own, who didn't have that much social standing in the community as they did. I don't know if that's true, or if it's a fair thing to say: all I do say is sometimes I have wondered about it.

We don't live here though, and I wouldn't say really we've got too deeply into the life of the town. We were talking the other night about it, I think it kind of followed on from what Fanny'd been telling me about her talk with you. We got around to asking ourselves would we like to live here permanently: and we decided no we wouldn't. Not because of anything to do with Bird though: it was to do with us, with the sort of people we are, coming from the city and so on. And Fanny said yes, but feeling like that, how come when we came we didn't rent ourselves a house in Baxter instead, if we wanted a bigger and more sophisticated place to be living in? We laughed, we couldn't answer that: we remembered how when we came we just liked the feel of Bird. And that's the point of it, we still do.

Jenny Ash and Jarrett Viner

JENNY: We've been ten years here now. We were both married and divorced, when we met I'd been on my own a couple of years and his divorce was about coming through. This was my house, it still is my house: and when we met and decided to get married, he just sort of moved in ahead of time you might say. Everybody looked at it we were going to be married in a little while, a few months at most: so I think they thought what the hell, sort of decided they wouldn't notice it.

JARRETT: I guess we were that way ourselves about it. We had every intention of marrying, it was just somehow we never get round to it.

JENNY: Sure, that's right, yeah: we never had the idea of making a public declaration about it, like announcing we were going to live together in defiance of convention, nothing like that.

JARRETT: Right. It's still the way, we take it for granted now that we're not married. Somehow after a length of time like ten years it doesn't matter too much one way or the other.

JENNY: If either of us had children, either from when we were married before, or children of our own, then we might feel different about it. But we don't, so that's not something that's made us have to think again about it.

JARRETT: We're both local people, that might have something to do with it too. I'd been away when I was married, I was out west in California eight years and me and my wife lived there. But Jenny lived here all the time with her husband, then he went off with someone else to where, Flagstaff Arizona?

JENNY: Around Flagstaff, yeah. So everyone here knew he'd left me and I was a woman on my own. And most folks thought, well I did myself, I'd move back home with my parents who'd moved to Kansas City Kansas. But then Jarrett arrived and I stayed here instead. When you said we were local people, did you mean so everyone must have known what our situation was or what?

JARRETT: Yeah partly that: and partly too that you were well known and liked in Bird, folk knew your husband had taken off and left you, so they were a bit more what you might call sympathetic to you and your situation. They were more ready to give you time to sort yourself out and make a new life for yourself, things like that.

JENNY: Could be: but are you saying they're still taking it that way, still now, ten years later?

JARRETT: No I guess not now. I think by now they just kind of take it for granted. Or maybe they think probably sometime we did get married, like a few years back and we didn't mention it.

JENNY: No no they don't think that, they know we're still not married. I mean we don't go around pushing it at folk but there's certain people know, they have to.

JARRETT: Like who d'you mean?

JENNY: Well like the bank for one, the girls in there they all know we have our two separate checking accounts in our two different names: and in the stores and place, if you write out a check or I write out a check, we use our own names but we have the same address. I never get any funny looks about it though, do you ever?

JARRETT: I can't recall one ever anytime, no. And no one's ever asked me are we married or not, and if not why not: nothing like that, have they ever you?

JENNY: No absolutely. Do you think if I went in Dorothy's tomorrow and I asked the first person there I knew, would she like to know if you and me were married, and if not why not: I wonder what she'd say?

JARRETT: Ten dollars to a dime she'd say no she didn't want to know, it was no business of hers. I think they just accept it and don't think about it and don't want to think about it. They accept it and they accept us.

JENNY: No they don't.

JARRETT: I thought you just said they did?

JENNY: It they accept: but not us. We're not church people and we don't go to church: but no one's ever asked us to, least not me they haven't. And the sororities, the women's clubs, no one's ever asked me would I like to join those either, not one.

JARRETT: You want to join a sorority?

JENNY: No I don't, that's not what I'm saying: I'm saying I never get asked.

JARRETT: Go along sometime, ask if you can be a member.

JENNY: No, because that would put them in the awkward position of having to decide whether to have me or not. I guess none of them would come right out and say it to my face, but they'd take a decision not to have me. And then they'd choose one to come and tell me that, and she'd say it wasn't her had decided, but she was sorry the answer was no I couldn't join.

JARRETT: Heh you've got this all worked out haven't you?

JENNY: I'm pretty sure that's how it'd be. We stay like we are and they'll look the other way: they won't mention it so long as we don't, I think it's like that. Thinking on a bit from that, what do they call you?

JARRETT: Jarrett, Jarrett Viner, what else?

JENNY: 'Mr Viner'?

JARRETT: Well, someone, sometime I guess. I don't think I see what you're getting at.

JENNY: Just this: I hadn't noticed it before, not till we're talking now about it. Nobody ever calls me Mrs Viner, not in the stores, not anywhere. It's always 'Jenny'. Kind of odd. And another thing too: when folk ask me about you, how are you or something, they always say 'How's Jarrett?' Never 'How's your husband?' Always 'How's Jarrett?'

JARRETT: Well it's the same with me, that's right. 'How's Jenny?', right, not 'How's your wife?' This is real kind of weird you know, talking about it now like this. These little things you take for granted, things you haven't noticed.

JENNY: Like I said: 'You don't push it at us, we won't push it at you.'

JARRETT: You know what'd be good? One day we have an

announcement made we're going to get married, then we'll have a big party and everybody's invited to come. Imagine it.

JENNY: We'd never do it. It'd be too embarrassing. For them. They haven't embarrassed us all these years, so the least we'd do is not embarrass them. If we were to get married we'd go to Kansas City or some place, get married there. Then we'd just kind of let it get around after we came back that's what we'd done.

JARRETT: Interesting you see: it's what you could call a tacit understanding isn't it, on both sides, us and the community. Not something they talk about or we do. Don't push it, yeah.

JENNY: Which is why we asked you no address where we live, no descriptions of us please. So as not to cause embarrassment all round.

Pete and Helen LeRoy

Their small house was near the end of South Jefferson Street. A well-used children's slide, a seesaw and a swing took up most of the small patch of worn grass in front of it. He was tall, well built, with an olive skin and long black hair: she was fair-haired and blue-eyed. They were in their middle thirties.

HELEN: We've lived here 13 years now, my mother lives in Bird but I was born and went to school in Fort Marsh, that's 60 miles east. I went to college at Independence and that's where we met first.

PETE: I was supposed to be the bright one in our family. My idea was eventually I wanted to do some sort of social work, so I studied psychology and sociology. But my grades weren't good and I needed to get work because I'd eight brothers and sisters at home. I came over to the area looking for work in oil, to do with rigs or something, and we met again then. She was a lot different from any other girl I'd ever known, I just hoped she'd agree to marry me. And so she did.

HELEN: We came here to live, which was hard on him because there wasn't much work. Our first five years were pretty tough.

PETE: I took a job at an alfalfa plant at Deerfield 12 miles from here, then I worked with a trucking company at Hammond, then with another company erecting and dismantling rigs. With that one the money was better, but there was a lot of travelling: sometimes I'd be maybe a hundred miles or more away and have to find my own food and accommodation, and paying for that cut my wage a big lot. Finally I decided I'd sooner be back here with Helen and the children, even if it meant not much security and only odd temporary jobs wherever I could get them. I shovelled snow, did yard work, anything: if someone wanted something doing and'd pay me, I did it. Then the middle of last year I ran into Mrs Wise one day in town, and she told me she was looking for someone to be a handyman around the place out at Hill View, the old people's apartments: so I went there and I've been there ever since. I like it, it's real good: I do maintenance, carpenting, repairs of electrics, everything. The money's not all that big, but I like the work and by now I've got real fond of the old people who live there.

HELEN: Them of you too. You're good to them, anyone wants something fixing, Pete stays till it's done, eight or nine o'clock at night sometimes. It's because everyone's so friendly up there, everyone looks out for one another, there's no prejudice against him.

PETE: Me being an Indian, lots of other places in Bird we do have it a little, I'd say. I'm not exactly an outcast, but it's a very conformist society here and to a lot of folk a mixed marriage, well she's done something that's not quite as it should be.

HELEN: Caucasians, whites, they take themselves as normal: if you marry into a different race like I did, they're not sure how to treat you. They somehow can't talk easily with you. I notice this more because I was born and grew up here: everyone used to be at ease and friendly with me. Now I'm a white woman married to a Red Indian and with two children: and to them now, that's something else. Through Pete and what he's told me and we've talked about, I've got books to read about: so now I know much better about the Indians and their way of life and how we exploited them. But if you talk about it, it's real funny how uppity some white people get. Only just a few weeks back, I'd been in Gover's and when I came out there was a woman I knew on Main and we visited a while. We got around to talking about east Kansas, the land round there, and I said something like how originally it'd been Indian territory and we'd stolen it from them. I didn't mean nothing by it, I was just making a comment. But she looked real mad, she said 'Well you can't blame me and my generation for that, none of us was even born when that happened!' I hadn't been meaning I did blame her, I'd just made a comment that's all.

PETE: What I am is a White Mountain Apache Indian: my people originally came from the Rocky Mountain area in Colorado. There's an Apache reservation in Arizona, but that's desert land and it's not where we really belong. It's the white man designated it as belonging to us, like the whites do in South Africa: they take a land that's not rich and call it a tribal homeland and send people there. It was the same here with us. They took the land where we were originally away from us, signed treaties with us to say we'd sold it to them, and then afterwards told us we couldn't go there any more. But buying land, owning it, that was a white man's concept, not an Indian's: to Indian people no one could anymore own the earth than they could the sky. They gave us one of three choices: to migrate and go away, to stay there and adapt to white ways, or to perish. Only you know this isn't a subject you find a lot of folk want to talk about, not in a small town like this: or anywhere else much either.

HELEN: One thing I find is a lot of people, they tell you about their ancestors coming here, that they came from Germany or Scandinavia or Bohemia or wherever, and they research everything they can find about them, old photographs and everything. But what they're not interested in at all is the original people who were here before that, which were the Indian tribes who roamed the plains. The buffaloes who were here, yes those they're interested in: but not the tribes who hunted the buffaloes and who depended on them for their living.

PETE: Well that's not quite true, not quite entirely. There's a guy up at the apartments, he asked me to lend him some books about my people. And I did, and that old guy he's really read them, he asks me to stop by once a week nearly, and anything I can tell him at all, he gets really interested in.

HELEN: That's more than anyone's asked me about ever. I get the feeling a lot of folk'd sooner not mention the subject to me of Indians.

PETE: You're sensitive about it more than I am. You know, like you were saying, you've taken the step across the divide: but with me, it's not like that for them. I haven't made a choice to be an Indian, I am an Indian: but you've made a choice to marry one. Maybe it's something like that.

HELEN: People are just people.

PETE: Sure, I know that and you know that. But they don't: there's their kind of people and there's other kinds of people: they're happy with one kind and one kind only, which is their own.

HELEN: Well, discrimination: don't let's be too strong about it, don't let's say it's too bad. It isn't. If it was we wouldn't live here, we'd go some place else. It's something we live with and we're conscious of it that it's there, but it's not much more than that. We're an oddity. When folk stop to think about it we're an oddity, but I guess most times they probably don't really think about it. Maybe even not as much as we do huh?

PETE: Sure.

17 *Two Lives (3)*

A no good vagrant bum: Gus Boot

It took a long time to get any kind of properly recorded interview with Gus Boot.

It wasn't that I didn't meet him often: I did almost daily, and sometimes twice a day. He'd frequently be immediately and unexpectedly round a street corner, just as I turned it: after a while I began to imagine he knew I was coming and was lying in wait for me. But after I'd seen him several times when he hadn't seen me, standing alone at street corners and then spontaneously greeting and talking to the first person, anyone, who appeared in front of him, I realised it was just his way of life.

The other place I met him regularly was in Gover's Supermarket. Coffee there was free to customers: they had a large automatic dispenser you helped yourself from as and when you wanted to. Gus Boot spent almost as much time in Gover's as he did on the streets, pushing an empty cart slowly up and down along the aisles, looking round thoughtfully, sipping from a polystyrene beaker until it was empty, and then going back regularly to refill it and resume his walking inspection. I never saw him actually buy anything, or even so much as take something off a shelf and look at it as though he might be considering buying it. But obviously Gerry Meister and his staff interpreted the meaning of the word customer liberally, extending it to include anyone who could possibly be one sometime in the future. And just as obviously that was what Gus Boot took it to mean too.

Whenever we met, Gus greeted me every time with a wide open-mouthed grin which comprehensively displayed his large collection of blackened stumps of teeth. He always enthusiastically shook my hand even if we'd previously parted only an hour or two before. He then launched instantly into a rapid monologue, the exact subject of which I invariably found very difficult to identify. The reason was it always seemed to have started some time earlier, several minutes or possibly hours before. It was like hearing words coming from a tape recorder, of which he'd pressed the 'Playback' button anywhere at random. I used to think at first that if I listened carefully I'd eventually get some idea where it had begun, and perhaps divine the direction it was going in, and even be able to put in a few words to help it along towards its conclusion. But it didn't work: after a while I discovered the only way to bring any meeting with him to an end was physically to put one foot in front of the other and start to walk away. This never seemed to offend him, and the result was always instantly the same. He'd halt his monologue at once, lay a lightly restraining hand on my arm, and say 'Before you go Tony, here's another little joke for you, I know all Englishmen like jokes right?' What then followed was always and without exception an anecdote of short duration, with a beginning, a middle, and an end. It was also always without exception in the early days of our acquaintance dirty, in the middle weeks of our time filthy, and towards the approaching end of my stay close to scatological. It was inevitably concluded with a roar of mirth on his part, and quite often with the facial expression of a prudish prune on mine. But he never seemed to notice or mind that either: he would give me an affectionate farewell pat on the shoulder, and allow me to go on my way. Where on earth he'd obtained the information, obviously a basic tenet in his lexicon of handling international relationships, that all Englishmen enjoy dirty jokes, I've no idea: it can only be one of those common folklore generalisations which the English themselves never indulge in about other nations.

So the difficulty of getting a properly tape-recorded interview with him wasn't, as I've said, that I didn't see and meet him often. Nor was it that he wouldn't agree to be interviewed: that was no part of the problem. In fact, if he had refused, I wouldn't have been in such difficulty. The problem was the reverse: he always immediately agreed to the suggestion of an interview, but it then didn't happen. Our conversations about it became stupefyingly repetitious.

– Sure, yeah, sure you can interview me Tony, I'd be glad for you to, just say the word.

– All right, but like when?
– How about tomorrow?
– Tomorrow? Sure, fine. What time?
– Seven in the evening, how about that?
– Good, great, yes. Where?
– My place. OK?
– Right. Ideal. Where is your place?
– How about I meet you and take you there?
– Fine. Where shall we meet?
– South side of Main, corner of Monroe?
– Tomorrow evening, seven o'clock. OK?
– Sure OK.
– You'll definitely be there?
– Sure I'll definitely be there. Look forward to it Tony. Heh just before you go here's a good one for you, there was this lady and she had these huge tits see, so she went to her doctor and she said 'Doctor' she said, 'as you can see, I've got these huge tits' and he said 'They don't look all that huge to me, you better let me. . . .'

And the next evening at seven o'clock I was at the corner of Monroe on the south side of Main: and he, like Macavity, wasn't there. At first I used to wait half an hour, before long I reduced it to fifteen minutes, and finally more out of interest than anything else I'd go along and look, not see him, and go straight back to our apartment.

Yet the day afterwards or the day after that, whenever we next met, he always came out with his warmly friendly greeting and then went straight on with his usual monologue. Sometimes I'd get in a question about his not having kept our appointment: his invariable unabashed reply was 'Yeah that's right, I couldn't make it' and he'd then swiftly resume his talking. On one or two occasions I did manage to ask him did he mind the idea of being interviewed, or would he really sooner we forgot about the whole idea? He always responded affably that far from minding, he positively wanted to be interviewed on tape. It was only a matter of finding a time when he was available. I asked him to suggest days, soon to come or far ahead: and times, an hour away or 24, midday, late in the evening, very early in the morning, or whenever he liked. Nothing ever materialised, though his offers of tentative possibilities or firm appointments alike were both numerous and frequent.

I was very obtuse. It was not until only a few days before I was due finally to leave Bird that when he said 'I'd be glad for you to, just say the word' I responded with 'How about now?'

There was a slight pause: and almost uniquely a short silence. Then he smiled and said 'Why not?'

We were standing on Gover's parking lot, and I asked him if he wanted to come and sit in the car while we talked. No he said, he didn't care for anywhere public like that: come on, we'd walk around to his place.

An inconspicuous terrace of small wooden houses, long unpainted and now not far from dereliction, huddled almost out of sight behind a row of neglected willow bushes at the far south end of Monroe Street. Most of them had planks nailed over their front doors, their ground-level windows boarded over and their upper ones glassless and open to the weather. Round the back, broken wooden porches at back doors were just visible among tangled bushes and straggling briars: everywhere was overgrown with grass. We could sit on the veranda steps of one of them said Gus: but we'd better not go in because other folk might be there.

– I got to go soon and work while I'm able. I got this that they call osmotic oedema in my hands see, which means sometimes I can work and other times not. There's not a lot here for a skilled craftsman, nowadays it seems folk are more interested in knocking things down, not so much in preserving. But me I'm an individualist you see, and some folks well they just don't like that.

Right now I'm working for a guy out west of town on his farm, looking after his horses. And I'm looking at an old barn he wants for me to restore for him. What he wants mostly from me is advice you know, he doesn't have the financing for doing it this year. He says next fall if I'm around this way he might have, it depends on the harvest. Only I told him I can't wait around: if he's got the money and he pays me, fine I'll do it for him.

I've often thought I'd like to write a book myself you know. I've had a whole lot of things happen to me. I reckon I'd be 55 years of age or

56, somewhere there, but I don't have a lot of birth certificates and things. This time last year I was in Columbus, Ohio, then I went to Richmond, Indiana. I guess that tells you something right? Right, that I'm a wanderer, right. Minneapolis Minnesota, I was there. North Dakota, South Dakota, Lincoln Nebraska, Omaha, Topeka. That's a lot of places. Now I'm heading for California.

You want to know where I originate? OK sure I'll tell you, I was born in New Mexico, a placed called Artesia. My mother's folk were Irish, and that's kind of peculiar you know, you don't get many Irish as far south as that. They're more city people and places of that sort. You ever heard of Mayor Daley? Well now my mother, she always used to claim kinship with him through someone related to her father. She was poor though all her life. It shouldn't have been that way because of the silver, but that's how it was.

You want to hear about the silver? OK well I'll tell you. This is how it was told to me but I don't know I have all the details right. It goes back to one of her ancestors, the one I was telling you about came from the Cheviot Mountains. I'm talking about more than 120 years back, when he emigrated here he didn't come out west, he stayed in New York City. He started himself a business concern there, it had to do with the importing of silver. All through his life he gave out that he was a poor man: but when he died they found a valise under his bed and it was full of silver ingots.

So then one of his drinking acquaintances, a man by the name of MacPherson, before anyone else could claim them he went off with the silver ingots, he said they were a gambling debt and they'd been promised to him, and he went I think it was to Detroit. Now from here on in, the story becomes a little complicated. A lady comes into it: and if it's anything to do with a lady it's always complicated right? Sure is Tony. Her name was Malley or Mulley, something of that sort: and she took advantage of MacPherson and took everything he had, his money and all the silver ingots, and she went to Texas some place. In her turn she had a daughter whose name was Maureen, and when she died she bequeathed everything she had to her. And now this is the important part: this daughter whose name was Maureen, she was taken advantage of as they say by a man from New Mexico.

So that's how my mother came to be there in Artesia, New Mexico, where I was born. She spent most all her life trying to find these people to give her back what was rightly hers. It was there somewhere, I'm convinced of that: and I have all the names and dates still here in my head, so it's my hope one day I'll find the silver. I reckon it'll most likely be in a safe deposit box some place or a bank under an assumed name: none of these folk was living in luxury so I'd say the capital sum so far's not been touched.

Honesty and independence is the other important thing with me. You'll never meet anyone anywhere, and I've been a whole lot of places in my life, but folks will always tell you the same. I'm proud of my honesty and I value my independence. I'm not one of those people goes around stealing and taking drugs, nothing like that. I like to have a beer once in a while like everyone else, but I can handle alcohol, that's no problem to me. And I've never taken anything from someone that wasn't mine ever in my life. Stealing, that's something I'm against all the way down the line. And bumming off folk, you know, asking them for a handout, Brother can you spare a dime and stuff like that Tony, everyone's got their pride. If someone was to give me a dollar or two that's different, but I'd never ask. That way you lose your independence. What I live on is what I've worked for, I don't have no Social Security or pension, but you can get by without if you know what to do. The health side of things is important, you have to look after that. In another week or two I'll be moving on, I'm heading for Grand Junction, Colorado: I'm due for a hospital checkup there in the fall. After that I usually like to winter in San Diego or some other place in California.

Oh sure yeah I've been in hospitals for different things: a slight nervous breakdown one time, you get that kind of thing a lot in independent people who travel around because of the hassle they get all the time from the officials of one sort or another you know? Move on, don't stay here go some place else, that kind of thing. They're not such nice folk a lot of them, you keep away from them.

Bird? Well one place is much like another you know, I wouldn't say here was any different from the one before or the one coming up next. A small town and the usual story to be told about it of how there's good things and bad. They don't trouble me, I don't trouble them: but I walk around, I keep my eyes open, I reckon I'm a pretty good judge of character and you can learn a lot you know just from watching folk. I wouldn't do anything illegal, hiding behind trees or peeking in windows or nothing of that sort. But you know the old saying, you see a guy walking along the sidewalk with a spring in his step and he ain't heading in the direction of home: well then in that case he's on his way to meet a lady or he's looking for some place to piss.

It's been a pleasure talking with you Tony, and that's real nice of you: I didn't do it for money though you know. See you around: oh and say, here's a real good one I've been saving for you.

There's this guy joins the Foreign Legion see, and he's posted to this fort way out the middle of the desert. There's no one there but other soldiers, and sand in every direction as far as the eye can see. And after a week or so, he starts to feel real horny see, so he says to the sergeant, 'Heh, what do you do for women around here?' So the sergeant says to him, 'Don't worry,' he says, 'the camels'll be here Sunday.' And then Sunday this guy's in the compound, and an Arab comes in leading a string of camels: and he just leaves them there and he goes off again. So this guy thinks to himself 'Oh well,' so he makes one of these camels go down on its knees, and then he goes round the back of it and fucks it. And just as he's finishing the sergeant comes out in the compound and he shouts at him, 'Heh, what in hell d'you think you're doing?' And the soldier says, 'Well it was you told me about the camels.' And the sergeant says, 'Sure I did. They're to take anyone down into town who wants to go pick up a girl.'

It must have been hard for Gus to choose one of the less vulgar stories from his repertoire to be recorded: but this was a good example of one of his more delicate ones.

In the cooler: Kendon Prender

His cell was up on the sixth floor of the courthouse. In its end wall there was a square of wire-meshed glass out of reach ten feet up, and from the entrance there was nothing to be seen through the bars of the heavy metal sliding door except the white-painted brickwork of the corridor outside it. A burly young man with long gingery hair and pale blue eyes, wearing orange dungarees – he sat on his bunk with his legs stretched out in front of him. His voice was a quiet flat drawl.

– Well nossir I do not come from around these parts at all, that's right no I do not. My home town in Elgin, that's 30 miles south of Baxter, right on the Tipton County line. That's my home town where I was born and where my ma and pa are, but I guess now it's two years or more since I been down that way. I don't have much to do with my folks and they don't have much to do with me, and that way we get along pretty good. My pa he's a drinking man and I'm kind of a drinking man too you could say: we have some awful fights if we get together when we've both been drinking, so most often we try and keep ourselves apart. That way no one gets hurt and my ma she don't get to cry.

Well sir I have two brothers and one sister: I'm 24 and I'm the oldest one of us. As far as I could tell you I'm the only one's been in any kind of trouble, least not the last time I heard. And my pa no, he's not been in no trouble, he's a regular hard-working man is my pa. I sure don't know what's different about me, and I can tell you I wish sometimes I did. Then I'd maybe know what to do about it, only the way I'm heading right now it's getting to be just one thing after the other, and that's sure worrying me some.

This last time that Judge gave it to me straight, she said I was lucky it was only going to be 12 months here in the County Jail, and maybe I wouldn't have to do all of it if I behaved myself. She said next time she was going to send me on in front of the District Judge and he'd give me a heavier sentence for sure. Drunk driving she said was something she regarded as real serious, specially this being my third time in court here for it: but 12 months, I think that was real heavy of her. I had in mind more like she'd give me maybe 6 months, or 6 and 6 months suspended, something of that order. To tell you the truth I was kind of surprised about it because I'd not been in front of her before. When I saw her I thought she was a real pretty Judge with nice-looking legs: but there you are, that didn't make no difference when it came the time to sentence me. Kind of makes you think about these things, something like that does: makes you think the next time you go drunk driving, don't do it around Auburn County, else you've got big trouble for yourself.

I don't know that I can make a good job of piecing my life story together for you, but I'd sure be happy to give it a try. Only I'll have to think some first, just give me a minute to think some first and kind of get it in order OK? Well I'm 24 years of age for a start, did I tell you that? Yeah well that's what I am, 24. And I have two brothers and a sister, did I tell you that too? I did, yeah. It gets kind of when you sit here on your own all day, you don't do all that much thinking you just kind of set. I'll think a little more OK? You know maybe if you could ask me some questions or something that might help some.

Went to school, yeah I sure did. I went to Junior School and to High School both, that was in Overland. My dad, he worked for a trucking company and Overland was where we lived. It was later on that we went to Elgin after my dad and my ma split up and got divorced: the guy there I call my pa, he's the man married my ma after her and my dad were divorced. Sure, I liked going to school but I never got good grades and stuff and so I didn't go to school that much, I'd sooner stay home or run around with the other guys. We didn't have gangs so much, just groups of guys running around. What did we do, well we didn't do very much of anything, I'd say chiefly we smoked: smoked marijuana chiefly I'd say, yeah. I'd say I started using like most kids do, around 11 or 12 somewhere there: the usual age but not younger than that: I guess I was different from most kids a bit, because after I started I didn't stop. Nossir I never have stopped, I still use now when I'm out. I kind of like it you know, it gives you a nice feeling: I've never had heroin or cocaine, I think those things are harmful to you, but I sure do like to smoke marijuana. I had a girl friend once, now she was all the time shooting and wanting me to as well, but I just didn't go along with that. That stuff can give you bad health and all sorts: I do, I keep right away from it. What I chiefly like when I smoke is it relaxes you and makes you amiable towards folk: it gives you a kick but it's a kick into relaxation, which is sort of good. You talk to anyone who smokes, they'll tell you the same.

Let's see now, my family: well I'd say they were an average family, that's about all there is to say. I think my ma was kind of unhappy most times and my pa was unhappy some of the time, I'd put it like that. He drank a lot: I wouldn't say he was an alcoholic but he was going that way if you know how I mean. A very silent man most of the time, he didn't talk much to anyone, not to me nor to my brothers and my sister. Me and one brother, we have the same father: then the other brother and my sister, they were his children that he had with my ma. I think I've got that right, I'm pretty sure it was that way. Only you kind of forget: when you're young and you all live together you don't take too much notice of that kind of thing.

Well yessir that is right: from somewhere around 12 on, I didn't spend too much of my time home, no I did not. I spent my time with my friends, and mostly we lived in different places on our own that we found, like kids do. Places with no one in them, empty buildings, garages, places of that sort. We never did nothing very bad, like I said we were just running around. Well yes, I dabbled in a little stealing, yes I did. But nothing great, I was mostly into breaking into workshops and garages and stealing tools of that sort. I never stole nothing there wasn't somebody wanting it, no stealing for the sake of stealing, I didn't do that. You could get a good set of tools for an auto mechanic, and you could sell that for a good price that'd give you enough to keep yourself living for a while: then you went out and stole something else if you didn't have money. But stealing just because something was lying around, whether you really needed it or not, well that was something else. You could get caught for stealing something, and you'd get into trouble for that, and you hadn't had a need for it anyway: I could never see the sense in that.

Yes I did, I got caught a time or two. Then it was mostly you got fined, so you had to go steal something else to get the money you needed for the fine. You had to pay the fine off before you could settle down again. Or they'd send you to the juvenile probation officer and he'd tell you you were to go to school and go back to your folks to live, which you'd maybe have to do for a while. That way I'd sometimes have it where it could be a whole week in school, and living with my folks: but then everyone kind of stopped bothering you anymore.

I guess I was first sent away it must have been when I was 14 or 15, something like that. They sent me to a big school in Topeka that was for bad boys. If you add it all up, I'd say I was there it must have been close on one year all told. That was because of the system they had. They had I think it was nine levels, or maybe eight: you started at number one, where you were locked up and you couldn't do sport or swimming or nothing. Then after some weeks, if you'd done OK there you went up to level two, which was where you could watch the TV at night until eight o'clock. Level three you could go outside the building and walk around the place: and level four, level five, you went on up like that. Only if you did something wrong, they put you back down level one and you had to start over. I guess the highest I got was level five or six, somewhere around there.

They had school lessons, yes a bit of schooling yeah: but mostly the emphasis was on exercise, physical fitness, gymnasium: climbing ladders, hanging on a rope with one hand you mustn't fall off else they threw a bucket of water over you, stuff like that. The thing was to show them you were a pretty tough sort of a person, whatever they could throw at you, you could take it and not let them think they could break you down. You didn't learn much except things from the other guys who were there, about ways of breaking doors, taking automobiles and ways to steal most anything there was. Like a sort of college education for you in crime. That was what I mostly learned there.

Then after I'd got out from there I got caught again, and this time they sent me to another place, I think that one was in Kansas City Kansas. That was more of a prison sort of a place, they kept me there six months I think it was. That time it was for drugs, they said I was a dealer. But I never, I wasn't no dealer, that was wrong. I might sometime let a friend have something, but I was never in it in the way of business. It wasn't too bad that place as a matter of fact: they mostly just left you alone.

Then what happened . . . oh yeah I had this steady girl and times were good for a while, yeah. Around then I was 17 and she was 18: she didn't use drugs at all, her thing was drink and I moved off drugs onto drink myself. We used to go out in the country driving around, with maybe a few cans of beer and a bottle of bourbon or so, and we had ourselves a real good time. Her and me we used to work together real good: we'd go in a filling station for some gas, and one or other of us would catch the attendant's attention and the other one take a few things. Our method was if it was moveable and common and saleable, we'd take it and dispose of it some place down the line. We worked like that in stores too. The important thing was not to keep it very long: they always say for every person ready to steal something, there's three more that won't take the risk themselves but are waiting to buy it from you, and I'd say myself that was about right.

I can't recall for you that girl's name, Dawn, Doreen I think it was some name like that. She was a sweet girl though and together we were real good, I do remember that.

What I was getting into then was drinking alcohol, and I started getting arrested then for DWI. That's driving while intoxicated, it's called. The first few times I did OK, I said I had a drink problem and I needed help. So then they put you on a detox programme. Usually that's say 30 days in a unit: alcohol counsellors give you talks and you talk about your problems in a group, and you get some sessions where you talk with the doctor on your own. Sometimes in some of them folk from outside come along, people from Alcoholics Anonymous who've had problems with drinking themselves: they tell you what are the signs to look out for when you're outside, if you want it you can have what they call antabuse tablets to take when you go out. Everything you want to help you, they provide it for you: I reckon they do a pretty good job at it those people, they surely do.

Oh no, sure it worked: it worked with me every time, four or five times, things was just fine. One programme I got, it was 45 days in the unit plus I think it was another two months afterwards as an outpatient three times a week. It took me off alcohol, that was what, three, three and one half months? It worked real good. But it was always the same problem for me, when I finished the programme I'd take a drink because I thought I'd learned how to handle it, and in maybe two days or sometimes three I'd be drunk again. And then I'd go driving and they'd arrest me again for DWI. If they don't have anything else against you, usually they put you back on another programme again. I used to get good reports from my programmes, about how I'd been co-operative with them and it looked like I'd succeeded, and they thought it was worth for me to try again.

Then sometime around there was the only time I was in serious trouble. It was for a robbery I done, only this one was serious. There was this guy I knew and I needed money real bad: I asked him if he'd loan me some but he wouldn't. He was a neighbour of my ma and pa's, and he knew my pa would pay him the money back if he wanted it. I think it wasn't much I was asking him for, only 200 dollars or so. But he said he wasn't going to give it to me. And I needed it real bad. He had a dry clean business, the type where you put coins in machines and operate it yourself, and at night he used to go get the money out of them and bring it home in a box. So one night I waited for him at the street corner near where he lived, and I had a stocking over my head. I didn't have a weapon, nothing like that: I just ran at him and pushed him over and took the box with the money and ran off. I guess the stocking was too thin or something, because he recognised me. I'd gotten the money hidden in a garage some place, so when the Sheriff's Department people came around I told them I knew nothing about it. I said it couldn't have been me that done it, I was way way away over the other side of the country that night at my girl's place. She backed me on that. But I was pretty dumb myself: they kept on asking me questions and things, and they promised me if I told them the truth, and where the money was so they could go get it back, they'd give me a break and nothing serious would happen to me. They went on that way all the way through a whole day. And so in the end because they kept making me these promises and telling me to trust them, all they wanted to do was help me, so that was it, finally I said yes and told them everything they wanted to know. I really buried myself and I got what I deserved, I surely did. They gave me nine months in gaol with one half of it suspended. Next time around I'll not be as dumb as that, I'll not believe what people tell me about how they're going to help me, nossir I will not.

You could say it was quite a light sentence for something like that, yes I suppose you could. Only if the guy'd lent me the money you could say too I wouldn't have done it. And he didn't have very much in the box, only 100 dollars, something like that. This guy when he came to court and they asked him, he said he knew my pa and we were neighbours, he didn't think I was bad but more foolish: that's what his words were, something like that. He said I'd learned my lesson. I think that was right myself: the lesson I learned from it was something like that's not really for me, and I'm not really for it. I'm not successful at those kind of things.

Well, I guess what I'd like most is for to get out of here: it's sure awful boring being locked up here all the time in the cooler. Where are we, level four or five is it? I'm the only prisoner they got here, and I'd like someone to talk to once in a while: it gets like you feel some night they might all go home and forget they've left you in here. I have three meals a day: the food is things like hamburger, potatoes, chicken, beans or corn. I don't know where it comes from. Someone brings it along that corridor to me, I guess they send out for it from the Sheriff's office. They don't let me out for exercise: there's nowhere for me to go to have exercise, I just walk up and down the floor here about ten minutes once an hour, something like that.

No, I don't have no visits, it's too far for my ma or pa to come here from right the other side of the state. I have a girl writes to me once in a while, but she's not been to see me yet. Some place here there's a library I think, they send books in for me to read. Mostly westerns is what I like best, one of the clerks from the office here, she asked me what I liked and that's what I told her so that's what I get.

They might let me out soon, I mean before the end of my time: they do that if you've behaved yourself good. I couldn't exactly say when that would be, because I don't know exactly when it is now. Sometimes the Sheriff comes along to ask me how I'm doing, and he loans me his newspaper to look at: I don't know just when the last one was so that's why I'm not sure of the date and things. The way I see it, it don't matter a lot right now to me though.

Well what I do mostly in the day is I set here and wait for the time to pass. Sometimes I do yes, I try to think to myself why I'm like I am and what the cause of it is, but I never have the answers. So far I've not had a lot of success in my life, but I don't think it's because I'm stupid or nothing like that. I think the chief thing is I'm a loner. What I mean by that is I never seem to get very close with anyone, and no one gets close with me, not girls or anyone. The people I've liked best were the people I've done my drinking with: we've always gotten along OK. To answer your question straight, I guess that's because they seem to take me as I am. Nossir, I've never met no one I could say who'd given me good advice: lots of folks have given me advice, I mean I've had advice from most everyone I've known including myself, but somehow it just doesn't seem to count. Last time, right there in the courtroom here, a guy came up to me and asked why didn't I try and see if God could turn my life around for me, ask God if he could run my life better for me than I could myself. I don't know what he meant properly, maybe praying and things like that. I thought maybe I might give that a try sometime.

Yessir it's sure been nice for me talking to you too, and yes I'd appreciate that, I really would, if you would send me something in. They don't let me have drink and I don't smoke, but maybe some hair shampoo or a packet of cookies would be good, something like that. No it don't matter what sort of cookies, I'd like it if you were to surprise me with what sort: any kind except chocolate chip, I don't like them, that would be great, I'd appreciate that.

18 *Looking back*

Lucille Richmond

Lively and quick-talking, she wore an old striped T-shirt and paint-spattered jeans. She was on top of an eight-foot ladder, vigorously scraping old paper off her sitting-room ceiling.

– Oh my, that's what happens you know, I guess I must be getting old I'm so forgetful these days. Is today Tuesday? I thought you said you were coming Wednesday. OK OK it don't matter. Clear a space for yourself to set down somewhere while I go clean myself up. OK OK thank you, you don't need to bother about me, I've been climbing up and down a ladder all my life: it always shakes that way but it's like me, good enough yet for a few more years.

– The thing I remember most is the dust storms, you heard about those? All the top soil of the land blew away in the wind, it came in everywhere, you couldn't keep it out. There was only poverty and dust: and near starvation for anyone trying to make a living from farming like my Pa and Ma. Our place was out north, towards Hammond: I had four brothers and sisters, and I was the oldest. I'd set my sights on being a doctor, so I worked hard at country school and High School, and then one day in my senior year Pa told me there wasn't enough money for me to go to college. I didn't blame him, I knew we weren't people with money: but that day I did, I thought the world had come to an end.

Still, I guess when you're young there's times you're realistic: you're often more realistic about life than you are when you're grown. So the way I thought was well if my parents couldn't help put me through college, then it was up to me: I'd get myself work and save my pennies, and that way or some other way I'd get to be a doctor in the end. Another thought I had was if I took a job at something like a live-in domestic servant, then my parents wouldn't have the expense of keeping me and it'd save them money too. So I went to the house of a wealthy man in Hammond and his family, and I was their housemaid. I cleaned and I polished, and I washed and ironed and swept floors, and on top of all that I looked after their little boy for them too.

Because they were giving me my keep, the way they looked at it was they didn't need to pay me much of a wage as well: so the situation was I was working hard but saving nothing, or near to it. Then one day there was great excitement here in town: a woman was coming to open a beauty shop. You have to remember this was 50 years ago, and folks really thought that was something in those days. So I left housemaiding and went to work for her.

The wages were better and that time I saved some: but the years were going by and it takes a long long training to be a doctor, so finally instead I went to college for four years to be a hospital laboratory technician. While I studied I worked as well to keep myself, and it was finally when I was at the age of 30 that I got my qualification. By then my brothers and sisters had all gotten married: and what happened almost at once was that my Pa died, and I had to come home to look after my Ma. Right here in this house which she'd bought. She was frail and her health was poor: so for 12 years after that I did nothing but care for her. I nursed her and cooked and cleaned and papered the house, and when she died she was 101 years old, and as clear in her mind to the end as she had been all through her life.

So there it was, and by then I thought life had kind of passed me by. I'd had a couple of boy friends while I'd been away at college, but nothing came of it with either of them. I'd have married either of them, though, if they'd asked me to. One of them was a very sweet man in every way, and for 12 years I'd loved him every second of the day: but he had nervous trouble and was in hospital for treatment for a long time. He'd been married once very unhappily, and he said he'd never marry again: but I was always hoping and hoping he might change his mind. I loved the other man too, I don't think if you're not married you just have to love only one person. If he'd shown any interest in me, well things might have been different there: but he never did, so nothing came from that either.

Oh my, now why I'm talking to you about all this I don't know. They're just my memories and reminiscences the same as everyone has: times long ago, and I suppose when you're my age you find yourself doing that more and more, looking back. Sometimes I think maybe I didn't love either of those men enough, you know: maybe that was it. With either of them if they'd asked me to marry them, I'd have gone with them any place in the world. But it could have been I never made my feelings to them sufficiently clear, and they couldn't find the courage to ask me in case I turned them down. Sometimes I think that.

From that comes my one regret in life and it's my only one: that I didn't have no children of my own. I would have liked that I know. I've a dozen or more very precious nieces and nephews, and I love every one: but to have had children of my own as well, I think that'd have brought me even more richness than ever.

Only like they say, you can't have everything so be thankful for what you've had and what you've got. My mother was a very fine and remarkable woman: and I not only loved her, I always felt I'd been privileged to have her in my life so long. A lot of folk haven't been happy with their parents always, but I wasn't one of those. When she died it badly affected me, and it was a year or more before I could find any interest, because she'd been so very much my centre of things. But now I'm past that stage, and I still enjoy painting and decorating and keeping a nice home. I'm happy, or maybe I ought to say instead content: and if you can say that at 73, you sure must count yourself as being a very fortunate person.

James Youngman

A tall distinguished-looking man with iron-grey hair, he sat in an old leather high-backed chair in his small book-crammed study in his large house in North Washington Street.

– I'm an attorney, or I should say since I'm now retired that I was an attorney: like my father before me, and his father before that, and our family's practice has always been here in Bird. I would have preferred to go on working, but in answer to my wife's pleas I finally gave up, and now I spend my days chiefly in reading: and most of my reading is still to do with law, because the subject to me's still as fascinating now as it has been all through my life. It's something which is constantly changing, new aspects of things are seen, or old ones suddenly reappear in a new light, and there's always mental challenge in reading and studying it.

Until a few years back I was the County Attorney. We now have a young woman, or in comparison with me she's very young: and a very able and capable person she is too. Sometimes for the pleasure of the atmosphere I go into the courtroom and sit and listen for a while, and it gives me pleasure to see the way she handles her work. I guess prosecuting can't avoid giving you a somewhat jaundiced view of the world around you, because you're facing almost all the time people who've done wrong in some way.

In my time when I was younger we had prohibition and much of my work was in prosecuting bootleggers. I wasn't myself teetotal and never have been, and I was often not entirely happy in pressing for convictions under a law I didn't at all agree with. But that was my duty, and I carried it out. All down the years as you may know, Kansas has had the reputation of being a pretty blue-nosed state when it comes to drink laws, and it still has some today that other folk regard as peculiar to say the least. At the end of the last century and in the early part of this, the Temperance Movement in the state was very strong. There was a lady whose name you may have heard, Mrs Carry Nation: she used to go around with a hatchet physically smashing up drinking saloons and bars, and spent many times in prison for her activities. I've often reflected on what my father's told me about those days. One of the things the temperance people said, I recall, was that alcohol damaged the brain cells: so we should remember that. Imagine, if your Winston Churchill hadn't drunk so much alcohol, who knows he might have become in some ways quite a brilliant person.

But Kansas has its other kinds of luminary too. One of the most interesting to me was at the time I was in college, and we sometimes went to the Karl Menninger Foundation in Topeka to listen to lectures on mental health by Dr Menninger himself. I thought he was a great man. I remember him telling us once to remember always that whatever the outward appearance, our country was not sick or crazy, our civilisation was not disintegrating, and our society was not now more violent or criminal than it used to be. What had happened was that we were nowadays far more aware of things that were not as they should be or might be: and this in fact was a sign of a society that was a healthy one. An important thing that he did also was to try to get people to understand that much more could be achieved by treatment than punishment. He wrote a book about this, that was very influential in its time called *The Crime of Punishment.*

In recent years my wife and I have had more time and opportunity to travel. We've been several times to Europe. Our foreign languages are not too good so most often the place we've visited and enjoyed the most is London. Whenever I go there I make a particular point of paying a long call at the bookstore there in Charing Cross Road called Foyles. It's a really amazing place, an Aladdin's cave of treasures: if you looked long enough I'm sure you could find there every book there's ever been. Another favourite place of mine I go is the second-hand bookstalls around the legal area Chancery Lane. I have a collection of cartoons of legal luminaries in the English judicial system in the past, and after our talk I'll show them to you. Each time I go to London I purchase a few more for my collection, and I could happily spend my whole time there in its bookshops and print shops. My wife though, she likes to look at your many fine historical buildings and landmarks, so we devote some of our time as well to that.

Our life in Bird has been a happy one and I've never given thought to the idea of living some place else, not ever. It's the town where my family belong, we're old established here. I see it's in many ways somewhat inward-looking, but it's always been that way and I can't see much change coming. How I would feel if I were a younger person living here, and at the beginning of the time in life when they're growing up and wondering about what to do, I'm not sure. It has to be said that the future of the town's not very brightly shimmering ahead, and it would be hard for a young person to see into it with any confidence, I'm sure. We have a population of residents who're on average becoming older all the time, and that's the problem.

I'm not the only person who'd like to see more younger people staying in the town, but the opportunities on the whole are very few. One of my great interests is our church and we want to keep that lively and thriving. I'm on the appointments board there, and we recently appointed as our new minister a young woman who's come to us straight from Yale Divinity School. Some people might think she's an unusual person to find in a church in a small community like this, her being a woman and so on. But she's made a very good impression and is greatly liked. On a Sunday in her sermon she talks to us for 20 minutes and then stops, whether she's saved us or not. Speaking personally I was astounded that she should agree to come here. Among all the candidates we saw, she was quite outstanding, and it was very much our good fortune to get her. My hope is she'll stay long enough with us to make quite a noticeable mark on people's ideas.

I think I've nothing much more to say; like most of us at my age I could recount endless rambling anecdotes from my past: I'd prefer to summarise it and say my time's been one of enjoyment, probably much more so than I've deserved.

C. J. Jacobsen

She perched on a packing case in the silent printing works: tiny, grey-haired, wearing a denim trouser suit, her thick-framed glasses on a cord tied round her neck. Her look was perceptive and her voice sharp. She wouldn't say how old she was.

– Information about age not given, let's put it that way. You could say upwards of 60, that'd be OK: upwards of 70 too, there's nothing wrong with that. Upwards of 80 even, but that's as precise as you'll get. I'm plenty old, so leave it there.

I'm the editor and reporter of the local newspaper: it's been in the family over three generations, and I came to Bird 56 years ago to join it, so I guess that makes me pretty much a local person by now. I used to say my blood was printing ink, but now with all this new technology and stuff you can't use that phrase any longer. Nowadays we don't even print the paper here, my stepson takes it to Deerfield: all we use our own machinery here for now is the commercial printing side of the business, business notepaper headings, wedding invitations or whatever.

In the time I've been here I wouldn't say much has greatly changed in the town. I've seen a few new businesses established and grow, a few old established ones fade away. Some storms and tempests and pestilences, the farm economy going up and down, the oil revenue coming in and beginning to go out again, wheat prices fluctuating. Those are the main things. I've seen everything change and yet nothing's changed, and as far as I could I've done what I've always wanted to, which was if it happened, report it in the newspaper. We have a column in it called 'A Hundred Years Ago', which I put together from pieces that were printed in it one hundred years back to the week exactly. It's very popular, folk really like to read it, specially if it's something that has in it the name of one of their own ancestors. I'd sure like to think that another hundred years from now someone'll be doing the same with things I've written myself, but whether there'll even be a newspaper here by then is something there's no way to tell. Maybe folks'll get their news entirely from television screens, just press a button and you'll not only read what was going on a hundred years back, you'll see it with live pictures too.

I was born in Colorado, then my family moved to live in south east Kansas some place, and that's where I went to High School. We had a neighbour friend who was a newspaper man, and several of us kids used to go to his house after school now and again: he had his own little printing place there around the side of his house in a building, and he'd let us roam about and pick things up, and if we asked him he'd show us how they worked. To me it was like another world, and I never wanted to live and breathe in any other. At school I talked them into letting me bring out a school newspaper, then when I graduated I edited and printed a community newspaper. I did different jobs here and there, always to do with printing or newspapers, and then when I came here I was just in my element and never wanted to go anywhere else or do anything else ever since.

I like writing, but I don't call myself a writer, I'm a journalist. That's first and foremost to me someone who puts the news first and tries to give it objectively in the way it's reported. A writer on the other hand, at least to my way of thinking, deals more with opinions. I give mine in the paper, but I put them in the editorial column. It's my job if anything at all happens in the town, the everyday news, to get the story of it from the people concerned. It might be a regular thing like the meetings of the City Commissioners or the Chamber of Commerce, a function at the school, an occasion of a club or sorority, a matter to do with one of the churches: whichever it is, I try to put in a straight report of it. I can't be everywhere all at the same time and I don't get around as good as I used to, so for things like that I'm reliant on people calling me up on the telephone to tell me what's happened. This way the newspaper's a record of what goes on week by week in the ordinary life of the town.

Then there's the special items, maybe a fire or an accident of some kind, or a special ceremony or some sports event, or the annual Fair: those are the things I make sure I get to and cover them with a proper story. I reckon I get to know about pretty near everything that goes on, because I make it my business to find out. Whatever it is, if it's happening people know before long I'm sure to appear and start asking questions of everyone. I don't think they mind me doing it, it's my recognised position to be the town's newsgatherer: they know I'm not doing it just for the sake of poking my nose in and trying to find some scandal. I know everyone, and everyone knows me: 'Here comes old CJ' they say and they make a joke of it to each other: 'Mind what you say now, else she'll quote you in the newspaper.' They don't really mean that, I know: sometimes someone's more hurt when what they've said isn't printed in the paper than when it is.

I try to make the newspaper as far as possible a mirror of the community, to keep them in touch with one another and with the town if they move away from it and ask for the paper to be sent to them regularly, like a whole lot of folk do. Something that's had continuous publication every week for more than 100 years, that's a pretty good achievement for a small town newspaper: it makes it like a part of the town's own life, which I think is why the leavers like to have it, to keep them still in touch.

It doesn't have sensationalism in it for two good reasons. One is that we're not that sort of a newspaper and we don't go in for anything of that sort: and the other one is that it's not very often anyway that we have any sensationalism in Bird. Nor not in Kansas either. About the only thing of that kind I ever remember in the whole state was those murders over at the farm place in Holcomb: *In Cold Blood*, that book Truman Capote wrote about it, did you ever read that? I don't want to print things about people that are matters in their private lives, like breakups of marriages and stuff like that. Everyone has problems in their lives which they have the right to keep to themselves, and the way I see it the local newspaper should deal with local news and not local gossip. We all live together and mostly in harmony I hope: I wouldn't like to think I was contributing to dividing people and setting one against another, I'd sooner contribute what I could to their sense of being a community with shared interests and lives.

Max Bellinger

A big bear of a man with a shambling walk, he had a booming voice, and his talk was punctuated with long pauses and chuckles and wheezings. His house was small and low-roofed, and was set on a small piece of ground of its own, south of the Highway. He sat at his kitchen table, sleeves rolled up and an old baseball cap on the back of his head.

– I'm 74 and a happy man and shall I tell you for why? Because I've got my lady wife who looks after me, and we've two children all both growed and doing well for themselves, and I work every day and have myself a full and an active life which is the secret of staying young. What do I work at, well I'll tell you. First and most importantest is I drive the school bus. I take it out at seven in the morning, in the winter and summer, whether it's blizzard or sun, and I go west. I go west to Garland and out beyond there, then I turn south and over the Interstate, through on to Deerfield and back to the school, picking up the youngsters all along the way. Then at ten of four in the afternoon I set out with them all backwards again to take them home. It's thirty-four and one half miles exactly each way, and I've been driving exactly that same rowt twice every day now for near on 25 years since I retired from farming.

When I started out, I had myself a little piece of land over at Hammond, which I'd saved all my money for and rented from a man. Only 240 acres, but it was my own. All my life before that I'd worked for others, so when I first went out on my own it was with a great feeling of pride. My wife and me, we owned a bunch of cattle and a bunch of hogs, 70 head of cows and 40 head of pigs. We'd take them when they were young in the spring and fatten them till maybe November, then take them into Deerfield or Hammond and sell them at the auction ring in the community sale. And our other thing we had there on the farm was a few acres of milo and a few acres of wheat. Never concentrate everything in the same place, that was the way I worked: if the crops weren't so good one year I could always manage a living from the cows, and then the next year it might have to be the other way round. I wasn't one of those cattle barons you read about nor the sort could go out and look at the wheat from one horizon to the other that was all mine. I was a small man, and happy to be one. When our children grewed and went, then I went smaller still because I didn't any longer have to work so hard.

So then I went to be Deputy Sheriff for a while, and I worked out of the Sheriff's Department at the courthouse. Did that for a few years, then ten years ago I retired from there and became the Court Bailiff instead, and that's what I still am now. I have the voice for it, that's what they like you see. 'Hear ye, Hear ye, Hear ye! Auburn County Court is now in session. Bring up the people and the Judge!' They say when I give it my best shot, you can hear it right down the east end of Main.

When they have a jury, it's my work as well to take care of them. When they retire to consider their verdict, I lock them in their room and then bring them out again when they indicate to me they're ready. Or I take them to the restaurant by the stop light there if they need to eat during their deliberations, and see no one approaches them to try and speak with them, and then after that bring them back to court. Or sometimes it happens they want to look at some property somewhere, what they call inspect the scene of the crime. That case, I go get the school bus for them and drive them there. I've delivered prisoners too to the Big House a few times: that's the penitentiary at Lansing. Once had to take a man there and he was facing from 10 to 25 years, and he never said a word to me all the whole near 300 miles of the journey. Until we got to within less than 100 yards of the place, then he asked could we stop a moment, which our driver did. And he said to me 'Tell me honest what you think now, will I ever come out?' 'Sure you will,' I said, 'sure you will. One way or another.' And he gave me a look, and then he gave me a laugh, and he couldn't stop: and we were laughing all the way in through the gate. And the guards there, they looked at us and one of them said, 'Heh, you guys sure you come to the right place?'

School bus driver, Deputy Sheriff, Court Baliff and small farmer: that's not a bad record for a man to say he's been all of those. I like to have kept myself busy and be involved with folk: and school kids or felons, they're all part of our human race the same, that's the way I look at it. And there's one more thing I do too that I've still to tell you, which is a very important position indeed. Some folks would say it was the most important of all. Come Christmas time, for three weeks every December I'm Bird's official Santa Claus. I attend parties where I'm wanted, I visit the old folks and distribute near on 200 plants in pots, and the last week we have a little wooden Santa's house which we set down near the Post Office, and for a couple of hours every evening I'm in there for the mothers to bring their kids to meet me, so's they can tell me what they want me to bring them for Christmas. Some of them little ones though they're mighty cute: there's no way you can fool them, no matter how many whiskers you put on your face and keep your head back inside your hood. They say, 'I know who you are, you're not Santa Claus, you're Max, you drive the school bus.' It's all just a bit of fun for the town, no more than that. And it's fun for me to do it, I tell you, it sure is.

I was born and brought up here in this town, been here all my life and wouldn't want to live any other place in the world. Everyone here, they're nice folks and kind people: I'm not saying there's not nice folks and kind people any place else, I'm sure there is. But I like to be where I know everybody and everybody knows me. I walk down the street and someone says to me, 'Got your suit of clothes on today Max, must be a court day heh?' All the things I do, everyone knows what they are: and I know most folks what they do too. Like that nice lady Mrs Oberlin in the library as an example: I'm in the library the other day and she shows me a new book they've had just come in about fishing for bass. She says, 'Here you are Mr Bellinger, this'll interest you.' She knows my interests you see: and believe me that's real nice.

Arnie Marsh

It was raining, so he wasn't out as usual in his wheelchair on his porch. Inside in his sitting room he sat with a dark-red plaid blanket over his knees, his hands folded together on top of it. White-haired and blue-eyed with steel-rimmed glasses, and a quiet firm voice.

– It's my greatest pleasure in life when folks stop by to talk. If I'm sitting out there and they're not in too much of a hurry, even if they have only a few minutes to spare they usually take the trouble to exchange some words. They don't know it, but I have kind of a photographic memory for faces and people: pretty near everyone, I can recall without even seeming to need to think about it. Where they went last year for their vacation, if they've grown-up children where they are and what they're doing, the names of their wives and their kids, how old they all are, everything. More than that even: I remember what their hobbies and interests are, what sort of thing they like to talk about, something they might have said to me about something maybe last year or come to that five years before. I don't do it to impress someone, just now and again a kind of a jog to a conversation between us. You have to be just a little bit careful sometimes though with some folk, they think you've maybe got a tape recorder under your blanket and as soon as they've gone you bring out your card index file on them and update it. I can't help being that way, it's just a piece of good fortune I've had in being given it, like someone who has an automobile say, that never breaks down. With me it's my mind, it takes in and keeps everything on file.

I've been in this wheelchair of mine now for coming up to 32 years. I'm 64 so it's half my life exactly, and next year it'll be more than half. I was an engineer with an oil company in Baxter, and one day there was this accident and I was crushed from the waist down. The doctors told me I'd never walk again: and you know, for something like the first ten years or more, I didn't believe them. I used to think to myself, 'Once you believe that Arnie, it'll be true, you never will walk again. So don't you let yourself ever believe it, not for one minute.' Only it wasn't belief, it was fact: I'd had every test that could be done, every X-ray picture from every angle you could imagine and some you couldn't. A fact: there it was, so one day I woke up to it, that you can believe things if you want to but that doesn't necessarily make it they'll be true. The funny thing is it made me much happier after that, I don't know if you can understand that.

Money's been tight, I won't pretend it hasn't: I've a pension from the company plus some accident insurance I carried, and a little bit from investment of money my father left me. On the one side Marlene my wife was a teacher, and when she's worked that's helped things out: on the other side I've been hospitalised a lot and that's mighty expensive here in our United States. We've just about broke even always, but without a whole lot to spare. We've one child, our son Martin who's married and lives in Wyoming and he's OK: but when he was a youngster and our responsibility, there were times aplenty when we wondered about how things'd be about putting him through college and the rest of it. We should be thankful things have come out as they did.

Religion's not come into my life at all, so I won't say to you that I thank the Almighty for the life I've had, and making it such a happy one, because I don't. Sure, it's been a happy one OK, and the person I thank most for that's been my wife. When I was talking a while back about fighting against the idea that I'd never again walk, I didn't know she'd accepted it a whole lot earlier than me. And what it made her do was make up her mind about something: which was that I might not walk again ever with my legs, but that didn't mean I couldn't walk in my mind. I wasn't at first aware what she was doing every week, when she'd go off down town and come back with some books for me from the library. But week in week out, she kept coming home with books: books books books, and not books of romantic stories but factual books, biographies, histories, political books, books of theories about ideas, geography books, economics and all other subjects in the world. Anything I got interested in, she'd take notice of it: and next week or next month there'd be another book she'd bring home in the same subject area, pushing my knowledge of it a bit further and a bit further like that.

She went on doing it, she's still doing it: opening up paths for me to follow, I can best put it to you like that. The assimilation of facts and the assimilation of ideas, equal to each other both: and there's been more than once that she's said to me, 'Oh Arnie,' she's said, 'you don't know how much I envy you that you've got so much time to read.' Now isn't that a clever person who could think to put it to a person like that? And she's succeeded with it: because I say to you honestly I do, I don't think of myself as a person who's handicapped, but as one who's had a big chance given him: someone who's a lucky sort of person in many ways, because he can do what lots of folks would like to do but never can, which is sit just nice and quiet most of the day and read.

Let me tell you something else too. I've never travelled far from here in my whole life: only to Wyoming once a few years back to see our son, and another time to Miami on vacation which I didn't like. That's been the extent of my travelling entirely almost, if what we're talking about is moving your body around. But inside my head here, well now that's something different again: there's not hardly a country in the world I haven't been to and know a little bit about. Your country England for example: you'll meet folks I'm sure who've been there as tourists a time or two. They've seen Buckingham Palace and the Tower of London, Windsor Castle and taken in a couple of days in Stratford-upon-Avon, and been north to Scotland. Well you'd like to know some of the places I've been in my reading? The west of England, the most westerly part, Cornwall, right along there as far as the Land's End. And I'll tell you what you see if you stand at the edge of it and look to sea. Right in front of you in the sea among those rocks you see the Longships Lighthouse OK? And then on beyond there if you could see about 40 miles south west, the next land you'd come to would be the Islands of Scilly right? I've seen pictures and I've read books: and there's many many other parts of your country, if I was to wake up tomorrow and find me there I'd feel I wasn't a stranger to it at all.

There's a thousand places or more I've been to all round the world: and a thousand men and women I've met, living or dead, in biographies I've read about them. The privilege of reading, that's what I've always thought it was: to have the interest in it and the time to do it, folks can envy it and they do, just like my wife says. Only it can make you a little bit too introspective too, if you let it. That's why if I can, I always like to sit out there and see folks go by, and have them visit with me and talk about themselves. That helps you more than anything else does, stops you living just inside of yourself. Yes sir.

19 *Monday afternoon*

Debbie, Sharon, Kim
Charlie, Karl, Mark

DEBBIE: OK so today we go on with our subjects for discussion list and the next one's religion and what we think about it. You'd like to go to bat first on this one Charlie?

CHARLIE: I had the idea last time you didn't say too much yourself about the different things, you kept asking everyone what they thought but you didn't say what you thought. Why not you go ahead?

DEBBIE: I don't mind. Well my view is religion's very important. In my home it is, I've been brought up to be a Christian and to go to church. It gives you something to believe in, and something as well to fall back on if you're having difficulties in your life. There's times in everyone's life when they have difficulties so you need religious faith for that.

SHARON: I agree with that, I think it's important to have belief. I don't agree with the church part of it though, you can still be a Christian but not go to church all that much. You can believe in God and everything in your heart or your home life or whatever, but there's no need you have to make a show out of it.

KIM: I don't think that, I think if you're a Christian you should show it. We go to our church not every single week, but something near it. You get the fellowship there with other people who think the same way you do, and that's important. And I think anyway Sunday should be put aside for religion, or part of Sunday should: and the best way to do that's to go to church.

KARL: It doesn't mean you don't believe in Christianity if you don't go to church. I think going to church can get to be very boring sometimes, specially if you've been made to go. My mom used to be very religious that way: she's not too bad now, but it got to where she almost made me and my sister feel if we didn't go to church, something terrible would happen to us. My dad backed us, he's not religious himself but he told her if she kept on making us go, that was one sure way to be certain we didn't go no more when we could please ourselves about it. She came round to his way of thinking in the end and it's better now.

MARK: I'm a regular churchgoer, all my family are. We go to church every Sunday, sometimes twice. My dad is very strict about it.

SHARON: When you go to college after you graduate, do you think you'll still go to church like that, I mean regularly?

MARK: I think so, I don't see why not.

CHARLIE: It depends on who your buddies are, what they do, that's what'll decide that for you.

DEBBIE: Charlie, you haven't told us your ideas about religion yet, what're they?

CHARLIE: Well I guess I'm a blank. I don't go to church, I don't know that I specially believe in religion and Christianity. I'd have to say I'm one who doesn't know. Maybe when I get older I'll either decide it all means something, or I'll decide it all means nothing. Right now I'm in a state of indecision. My mom is religious and my dad isn't: but she never puts pressure on me, she says I must work it out for myself. About all she's ever said was she hoped one day I'd come around to having some religious belief, because of the comfort angle. I think that's what a lot of it's about mostly.

DEBBIE: That was what I said at the beginning, if you've got faith it helps you.

KIM: Yes I think if you go to church at times like that, you get strength from knowing there are other people there who are alongside you.

SHARON: I don't know we've talked much about religion, I don't think we have, it's been more about going to church or not.

DEBBIE: So anyone want to say anything else? No OK then the next subject we have is sex. I'll talk first one about this subject too. It's not something that's much talked about seriously in school and I don't think that's good. You get it between the kids, making jokes, that sort of thing: but it's not discussed in lessons, relationships between people and so on, and I think it'd be good if now and again we had something like that.

KARL: All I ever heard about sex here was in my Freshman year, somewhere around 15 minutes' talk we had one day in biology class. All the girls were sent out some place to do something else, then the teacher he gave us this talk. The guy was just so embarrassed about it he gabbled away like it was something he'd learned by heart out of a textbook, then after that the subject wasn't mentioned ever again. He didn't take questions, nothing.

KIM: I think most of what you learn, you learn from your friends. We don't have talks about it here in school, but I'd never talk with my parents about it at home, they'd be too embarrassed. I couldn't ask them questions. If there was something I wanted to know I'd ask my friends. Anyway if you ask your parents about something, they might start getting suspicious and start asking you why you wanted to know.

DEBBIE: You're talking about birth control right?

KIM: Well yes that'd be one thing yes. With my ma that's the first thing she'd say, why was I asking her?

SHARON: My mom and me, we've talked about it plenty. I think I understand the whole scene pretty well. This all came up, you know, last year at the time **** and **** had their babies. She said she knew if I was going to do something, no way could anyone stop me: but at least I should know about birth control and she was going to tell me, which she did.

MARK: I think we should all have had talks about it here at school at that time.

DEBBIE: I guess they couldn't because it would have caused a whole lot of trouble with some parents: they'd have said the school was giving out information to the pupils that was going to help them be promiscuous.

CHARLIE: If they'd started in on it then, yeah: I think they ought to have done it a whole lot sooner. Then if they had, maybe that thing wouldn't have happened. I mean it's just as much the guy's concern right, only who tells you that? Not your parents, not the school, no one.

DEBBIE: This is another part of this small town problem, everyone knowing everyone. I have a friend she's at college now and she's sleeping with her boy friend and she's on the pill. She went to see a doctor in Baxter about it, she wouldn't go to her own doctor here because he's a friend with her pa, she thought he might tell him about it.

CHARLIE: Well this is the same with guys too. If you're going to have sex you don't go and buy rubbers at the pharmacy here because he knows who you are: and his clerk, she knows your ma, and that's how it is. So you go to Baxter to a drug store or a machine there, where no one knows you.

SHARON: Can I just say something here? The idea was we should talk about sex, standards of behaviour and things like that as well. So far up to now all we're talking about is birth control. It's not just that.

DEBBIE: Yes, sure, that's right. What do we think about boy and girl relationships?

CHARLIE: I'm in favour of them.

DEBBIE: OK, so how far?

CHARLIE: How far what? Oh you mean the relationship, should it go to the full relationship right? Well that's for you and the girl, how seriously you're going to take it.

KIM: That's what the guys want, they all want that same one thing.

KARL: Not always they don't. I think that's what girls think they want, but not always they don't. It depends what you think of the girl and what she thinks of you.

SHARON: I think it's important you should have a steady boy friend: if you don't, if you date with two different boys, you get yourself a reputation. And your parents come into it too, they expect you to have a regular date you bring home, go partying with, that kind of thing.

CHARLIE: My ma, she'd kill me for sure if she thought I was playing around too far with a girl. She's got very strict ideas that something like that shouldn't happen outside marriage. A guy who was a friend of mine, he was a senior here, now he's at Baxter and I went to see him for the weekend. He's got this girl and they're rooming together. But I didn't dare tell my ma that.

DEBBIE: No because here in Bird, the idea that anybody might live together when they weren't married, that's a great big no-no: it's just unthinkable you should do that.

KARL: It's not so unthinkable people don't do it.

DEBBIE: If they do they do it some place else though, not out in the open here in Bird.

CHARLIE: Well mostly they don't. I wouldn't here in Bird.

KIM: Your parents would say you were bringing shame on them.

DEBBIE: I don't think we did too good on that subject, was it because we were mostly too shy or what?

KIM: I think like we said at the beginning, you know, we don't talk about the subject much in school, not girls and boys together like this.

DEBBIE: I think maybe a lot of us don't have our ideas sorted out too. OK so now the last thing is this one, what we feel about being American and how we think America looks to other people.

KARL: I think how I feel about being American is I can't imagine what it would be like to be something else. I'm glad I'm American: I think it's a good country to live in, it has lots of freedom, there are opportunities for people to make a decent life for themselves, and it's a good country.

MARK: I'd go along with that, but you see a lot on the TV and read in the newspapers about how other countries criticise America, and I don't understand that.

SHARON: You mean you don't think they should criticise America?

MARK: No I mean I don't understand why they do. I wish they'd explain more to us in the media why they do.

CHARLIE: I think America wants to be liked and respected in the world. We lend money to other countries, we trade with them and try to help them with their poverty: but a lot of these countries they don't give us any thanks for that, they look at it we're trying to interfere in the way they run things.

SHARON: I think some of that's true though, we do interfere. If their government isn't one that's just how we think it should be, we try and get them to change it. We say we want them to be more like us.

KIM: I don't know that I can properly explain this that I'm going to say but I'll try to. There was a time, maybe around a hundred years ago or somewhere like that, where everyone in the world, they had it as their ambition that they wanted to come to America. I've seen movies about it, you had these boatloads of people sailing into New York harbour, the Statue of Liberty with those words on it 'Give me your poor and oppressed' and whatever. Only now two things have changed: number one is not so many folk want to come here, and the other thing is the immigration laws have been tightened up so not so many people can come in. But I'm not sure I know why this has happened.

DEBBIE: Nearly all of us have ancestors from Europe somewhere who came over here to start new lives for themselves and their families. Most of them it was either economic, they couldn't make a good living in the country they were in, or it was because they were having religious persecution. But I think these days it's not like that in Europe so much as it used to be.

MARK: You still get the Russian dissidents, they want to come here.

CHARLIE: Yeah that's right but you don't get German dissidents or French or Scandinavian dissidents. And I don't think there's the opportunities here either that there used to be, you're talking about a time when the pioneers came west and they all took land for themselves, a dollar an acre or something. You can't do that now.

SHARON: A problem for us here is that we don't properly know too much about what it says, 'How we think other people see us', because we've not had much chance yet to find out. Not many of us have been to other countries and we don't often meet people from other countries who come here.

KARL: There was a time once when America was I think it was called an 'isolationist' country, I think it was that: and it meant America kept out of other countries' affairs. Now it seems to have turned right around and gone the other way: you had the two big wars in Korea and Vietnam which America was in. We didn't win either of them, and I think it harmed America because other countries saw us as interfering all over the place.

CHARLIE: That was to try to be stopping the spread of communism, or that was what we were told it was for.

DEBBIE: I think it's crazy we should do things like that, lose thousands of American lives halfway round the world like that. I think it's our leaders who get these ideas, they think it's got something to do with national pride or something. I think a lot of people would get a better idea if they didn't pay all that attention to what our government says but just came here and met ordinary American people for themselves.

SHARON: And we ought to go to other countries too a lot more than we do and meet their ordinary people.

DEBBIE: OK. So now we've got just under five minutes until the end of this lesson period, and maybe we can put in here what else you asked us to do. This was tell you about some of the books we'd been reading out of school, and which we liked. We chose one each, and I've written it down like it was all in one piece, and I'll read it out.

One of us said the best book he'd read this year was one called *Jonathan Livingstone Seagull*. He said it was kind of a dumb book really, because it was about a seagull that talked and went to a seagull Heaven. But he said he liked it because it was unusual, and the way it was written was good, it was kind of a simple story but it made you think, and it was a book he'd remember. Then someone else said the book they'd liked this year was called *The Circle of Children*. This one was one that two of us had read, and we both liked it and thought it was good. We can't remember the name of the person who wrote it, but it's about a day-care centre for mentally retarded kids. There's one particular girl there who was very wild and out of control: she was always smashing things up and some of the people were a bit frightened of her, but she was treated with kindness all the time. There wasn't any kind of end to the story, but we both thought it was a real good book and very interesting to read, because it kind of took you into a world you wouldn't know much about unless you could read about it. Another of us mentioned *The President's Lady*, which was about the wife of President Andrew Jackson: it was kind of historical and about someone she'd never heard of before, which was why she liked it. Another one was called *Portrait of Jenny*: this was described by the person who read it as a strange book about a painter and a little girl. He had a kind of fascination with her, and at first you thought it was going to be kind of a weird book, but it turned out everything was OK. Me, I think that's a kind of a weird description of a book too, but it's all that was given me. And last was one titled *Daddy's Girl* which was about a young girl who was sexually abused by her father. Parts of it were pretty gross, but it was a good story about the kind of thing that doesn't often get written about, and it showed her unhappiness very well, and how mixed up she was about things, until in end she was able to get away.

Those were some of the books we'd read and remembered this year.

– Like we agreed, we'll have another session with you next week where we ask you things we'd like you to talk to us about to do with England. Everyone wrote their questions down, then we talked them through and put them together in one list. There's no special order for them. We'd appreciate it if you answered them for us, as well as say anything else you wanted to. We think it would be very interesting for us to hear what you say. These are our questions for you:

Do you think people are ruder in America than they are in England? A lot of people say English people are always very polite about saying things, even when they don't mean it, and very often you don't know what an English person really thinks about something because they think it would be rude to tell you. Is this true?

This sounds like a funny question but it isn't meant to be. Do people in England throw their arms about when they talk to other people, and touch them, as much as people do in America? This is something we got mostly from the TV, that English people seem to stand still when they're talking, while Americans throw themselves around, put their arms round your shoulders and things like that.

If you want to go to college or university in England, do you need to have a lot of money to go there, or are there scholarships and things like we have, to help people? Can someone who is poor go to college in England?

In your country is it an honour to go to Cambridge University? Are people who go there a certain type of person from the aristocracy or the children of people in the Government, or can an ordinary person go there?

Where you live in England, could a boy and a girl who were say 20 or 21, could they set up home together and live together and tell people they weren't going to get married yet a while, or would it be a big scandal? Someone said they read somewhere in a magazine this happened a lot and it didn't cause any ripples in the water, is this correct?

Is there much poverty in England, and what happens to people if they can't get work? Is there as much unemployment in England as there is in America? Do you have construction schemes that the Government finances to give work for people?

When American tourists come to England, what do people think of them? Do they think Americans are noisy and make a big show of spending their money, and demand to be served right away in hotels and places? Or do the English laugh behind their backs at them?

Is it true what someone told us, that there's no place in England more than 100 miles from the ocean? Does this mean that England is crowded with people everywhere and there are no open spaces?

What is the English weather like? Is it always rainy or foggy and cold, or do you have it warm sometimes?

Would you like to live in the USA? I think that's a pretty dumb question because it doesn't say where in the USA. I think it means here in Bird, would you like to live here?

If you had to say one main difference between English people and American people you've met, what would you say the biggest difference was?

20 *Kids at School*

Scott Blaney, Freshman, 14

He was small, dark-haired and blue-eyed: wearing jeans and a navy T-shirt, he sat swinging his legs on a desk in an empty classroom, popping bubbles of gum out of his mouth.

– What they call a Freshman like me is someone in his first year in High School. You're the lowest form of life there is, so one of the things seniors do is put you in a trash can and tie up its lid with rope and kick you around in it. It's pretty good: you learn how to curl yourself up inside of it, and put your arms around your head like this: that way you don't get hurt. It's just a joke, usually no one gets hurt, it's only for fun. All the freshmen get it done to them: when I get to be a senior I'll do it to freshmen myself because then it'll be my turn.

I think this school's OK. I don't go a lot at all on lessons and stuff, I'm more a man for sport. My favourite is I like to wrassle: they teach us some, and I hope to make Junior Team next year and wrassle for the school in contests with other areas. Wrassling's pretty good: a lot of people think it's strength that matters but it's not. A quick-thinking little guy can beat a slow-thinking big guy any time: so because I'm small I have to be a quick-thinking one, and I give a few surprises. I like to play football and baseball, and track is something I'd like to be better at: I'm a middle-distance runner. Lessons, well there's nothing I like too much: geography and American history I guess, they're the ones most interest me. Maybe when I'm older I'll get into something, right now most of that stuff seems pretty dull though.

What the school's mostly good for is your friends you have. They're the best part. Girls I don't have too much to do with, I like to run around with my friends. If you have a steady girl friend she always wants you to be with her and I don't want to do that, I like to do whatever I want. You can't do that if you've gotten yourself a steady girl, you have to keep asking her what she wants to do. Some of my friends, I've seen it that when they've got themselves a girl friend, it seems like they can't enjoy things with the other guys any more. I sure don't want to get that way myself: least not yet a while. I'd sooner have fun. My mom's always saying it to me, it's the best age to be when you're the age I am, you should enjoy yourself while you still got the chance. I don't do crazy things like take dope or alcohol, none of that: some of my friends do, but I gave my mom a promise.

She's a very nice person, a real good mom for a guy to have: she comes and watches me wrassle, she cooks good, and I think she's like every mom should be like. We have a nice home on South Adams, I have my own room with my own television and everything, and I'd say it's real neat. I'm the eldest, then there's my mom and my stepfather and they've two kids younger, a boy and a girl, and we all get along pretty good. My mom and my pa, they divorced when I was five, and my pa lives north of here at Hammond on his farm with Dana, that's his second wife, my stepmother. She's a real nice person and they have two kids too, and I go see my pa every Saturday and Sunday, and him and me get along great.

I have two hogs on his farm, he keeps them and feeds them, and the deal is I pay him back the cost of their keep when I sell them. I bought them from him last year, and I'm paying out to him for them over two years, then they're mine. If I want to sell them before that, I have to pay him off first and what he's spent out on them for me on top: then the rest of it's profit which I keep. The way we've figured it, I should make around 100 dollars, so then I'll put that in my savings account at the Bank. I have a checking account too, which my pocket money goes into each month: I use that for the things I want to buy, and I transfer a regular sum into savings. Right now I'm considering whether to buy a third pig but I don't have enough capital yet for that. But if I could get me a job through the summer in the vacation, then maybe I would. Pa says he might have work for me on the farm but I don't like farming too good, that's why he looks after the hogs for me: they're just a way of making profit that's all. If I could in the vacation, I'd sooner get a job with a garage, I'm happier hanging around automobiles than on a farm.

I'm saving up my money for when I graduate from High School. I don't have any idea right now of going to college: what I want to do if I have enough money saved up by then, is I want to move out and go to one of the big cities, Denver or Chicago or someplace, and get a business job. I think a real neat job to do would be selling things, what they call a sales person. You can make a lot of money that way if you get yourself a job with good commission and work hard, and I think I'd like doing that. It'd be like a chance to travel around, get your own automobile, your expenses paid and stuff like that, and you have a pretty good life. Then as you get higher up you have a bigger territory, and other guys working for you. By the time you're say 25 you can be doing pretty good. One of my uncles has told me about it: he's an air conditioning salesman working out of Detroit, they came to see us last year at the farm. He's got a trailer home, it's almost longer than the whole side of our barn. Him and his wife, they go around in that for two months vacation every year: he says he can choose his work time himself. That sure seemed to me a good life, a lot better than my pa does with his farm, which is mostly hard work and no money. You get yourself a job like my uncle, you can go anywhere you want, which I think's pretty good.

To describe myself, I'd say I was a happy person. The only thing I'd like different would be if my pa and my ma could get back together with each other one day.

Jody Stone, Freshman, 15

She wore a light blue casual jacket with her dark blue tracksuit trousers, and thick-soled running shoes. Short curly brown hair, brown eyes: an easy manner and a near-adult self-confidence.

– As of now I'd say when I graduate I'll go on to college and do business studies. To do what then I don't know, don't ask me: I've no great ambition further than that. Being 18, that seems to me a long long time ahead you know? I might even be married and have kids then, I don't know: I mean a lot of girls do, that's all some of my friends ever seem to think about. They talk like if you're not married at 20 your life's a wreck.

You've talked to my father I know, he'll have told you I'm adopted. I don't know how I feel about my real mother, they say some kids when they grow up, they can't rest till they know who their real parents are. I'm not like that, least not so far. I have a sister Bobbie who's five years younger than me: she's adopted too and she feels the same way like I do. Maybe it's because of having John and Magda, who're our adoptive parents, the way they are I mean. They're real good, they've always levelled with both of us about our backgrounds as much as they know them. John's always said if I ever wanted to he's a lawyer and he knows all the possibilities, and he'd give me all the help he could to trace my ma. Maybe I'll feel different when I'm older: it's not that I hate her or anything, but I can only put it like I'm happy the way things are, no one could have been more real good parents than John and Magda to me. Sometimes I wonder if it could be I'm a bit scared of doing anything to disturb that, I don't know if that makes sense for you.

Go on, sure yeah. One time at school there was a chance we might have a German teacher. All we can learn now here is Spanish, and I know Magda has her grandma and grandpa in Germany still: so I thought well, if I learned German some, that would be kind of useful if we went to Europe. When I told Magda she said go ahead, but I could tell from the way she looked she was feeling kind of funny about it, you know? We always talk about things, we don't have secrets from each other, so I asked her what it was. She put her arms round me, she said it really choked her up I should feel like I wanted to know about her ancestors when she wasn't really my proper ma. She is though, I mean to me she is and she's always been that to me. It was like all these years she'd not known if I really wanted her and'd sooner had my own.

Out of school the things I like best are riding around in my boy friend's car, going out to the reservoir in the summer, and things like that. He's my regular boy friend yeah, and he's a couple of years older than me. You've met him, he's one of the guys you had in your group to talk to: he told me all about that, it sounded real interesting, I'd have liked it if I could have come along too. One time he was going to ask you about it, if I could: but then we had a big quarrel and he didn't, because for two weeks we weren't speaking to one another. It's all OK now, we're back together again. Oh, what it was about was this other girl, I was real dumb about it. Someone told me he'd asked her if he could date her: I should have fronted him up, asked him straight out if he had done that, but I didn't. I accused him of doing it and told him to go jump in the river, I didn't give him a chance to say he hadn't. I was real gross I can tell you, it's not something I feel good about.

This girl's not long been here at school, she's come until just the summer: she has family problems or something. She's not especially pretty or anything but she's got a reputation: they say she's an easy girl, the talk is pretty near every boy in school's after her and she picks and chooses. My boy friend he made some remark to me that was just a joke about her: and a couple of days after, I blew my top when this person told me he'd been trying to date her. Only it's OK now: he's a nice guy my boy friend, he forgave me for it and said he didn't mind I'd treated him so bad, he guessed it showed I was serious about him.

Was I or wasn't I, well I don't know really: I mean I guess at 15 you don't get too serious about a guy, not if you're sensible. Him and me, we have a good relationship and we like being with each other: but I think you change a lot between my age and say 20. I told you I thought when I graduated I'd go to college and do business studies, right? But I think you say things like that without thinking too much about it: that's the current idea, but then something else comes up and you think that's what you'll do instead. I truly have no idea what it might be yet, I have an idea or two in my mind, but there's nothing grabs me so I can say definitely: I get crazy notions once in a while, but that's all.

One of the crazy notions? OK right I'll tell you. Bird's a little place, right? It's a nice place but it's a little place: there's a whole big world out there that I don't know anything about except what I've read in books. So a girl in a place like this, how can she tell what she might want to do unless she's gone see some other places first? Big cities, small towns, other states, other countries: some way you ought to get yourself some ideas about them, before you marry the first guy that asks you and start having a family and things. So my crazy notion would be that when I graduate, instead of going right on to college like kids usually do, I might ask John and Magda that if I saved up 500 dollars, would they stake me another 500 dollars on top? Then I'd take off west for maybe six months, California and New Mexico say, and see what I saw and where I got to. These days girls do that sort of thing more than they used to: I wouldn't do it till I was 18, but then at that age I reckon I'd be able to look after myself OK.

So I'd do either that or go to Australia. My boy friend, they had to do a project each all about different places in class this last year, and he chose Australia. He showed it me, I thought it sounded a neat place to live. We're talking in a couple of years, maybe, we might go there: the way he sees it, we get married and go start a new life. I'd go with him so we can look at the place, but I don't want to commit myself to marriage with him, then get there and I don't like it.

I guess I must sound a pretty mixed up person talking all this kind of stuff. But I'm not, I'm a happy person and I like my home and I like my family and everything: but I like to play around with ideas too. You know?

Charlie Gibbs, Sophomore, 15

He was short and squat, with cropped bristly fair hair. He talked with his head down, shyly in a low voice, with frequent long pauses between sentences.

– I'm 15 and in tenth grade, I'm what's called a sophomore: that's a Greek word, it means a second-year student at college or school. Our teacher told us it's made up of two words: the first part from Sophocles who was wise, and the second part moron, which means dumb. So a sophomore's someone who's halfway between a wise man and an idiot. That's how she told it us, I guess she uses it every year with each new class and thinks it's funny.

My mom's a clerk in the women's wear shop on Main, Moderna Modes, and we came to live in Bird here four years ago from Alliance. I have a brother older than me, he's married and he's with a team of custom crop-cutters: this year he's not around this part of Kansas and I guess we'll not see him till the fall sometime. He's quite a good guy, him and me we get on OK but I know my mom misses seeing him. I told her this summer she should take a trip to Nebraska or some place he'll be, give herself a break: but she says she doesn't have the money for it.

I haven't seen my pa for 14 years, he left my mom when I was two and I don't remember nothing about him really. I don't know where he is, once a few years back we heard he was in Denver and thought we'd maybe go there and try and see him, me and my brother who wasn't married then. But mom didn't want us to, so we gave it a miss. He don't send her money or anything, so she's always had to work to bring us up: I guess she feels pretty bitter about that and didn't want us seeing him. I kind of feel some day I'd like to know more about him though, see if he's really the heel she's always made him out. When I get older maybe, when I've graduated from school which could be next year I hope.

What I'd like to do then is I don't want to go to college or nothing like that, I want to be a pro footballer with the Chicago Bears. I run pretty good and I keep myself in good shape, so that'd be an ideal life for me. Mom don't want me to do it though, she says you get hurt too easy and then you're no good for nothing after that. The way I see it, that's the risk you take: and if you do OK and you make it at football, you can earn yourself big money. I don't know no other way someone like me'd earn the kind of money footballers do. What I'd do if I had money is buy a big house for my mom so she wouldn't need to work.

Out of school I don't do much partying or running around. Afternoons before I go home I work a couple of hours each day at Gover's: that brings me in around 65 dollars a week and it helps out at home. Mom works long hours and she's always had money problems: we have an apartment and we just about get by with my money and hers. Weekends I don't work, they have more people than they need at Gover's then: Gerry Meister's a good guy, and if I stop by an hour or so Saturday to help them with a delivery they've had, he always gives me extra for it even though he's got enough helpers there anyway.

Most times at weekends I go around with my girl: we go to Lake Morrow or Baxter to a movie if we've got enough money. She's got a car, she's a senior here, she's two years older than me and when we date we always pay equal. Next year she's going to K State University: she wants for me to go get a job somewhere around there so we can still be together but I don't know, that would mean leaving my mom. She'd be very lonesome: and if my girl's at college and not here, I'll be lonesome. So this is a kind of a problem. My girl friend, she's my only friend: I can talk with her about anything and she listens, she understands the way I feel about things like no one else does. I don't talk to people much except her.

I'd say the best thing she understands is that I'm a very moody person: somedays I won't speak to her at all, we just ride around and I don't speak. That's no fun for her, but when that's the way I feel I don't see no point to pretend about it. Afterwards sometimes I get scared, I think she won't want to have me around because I've been like I was. But up to now she's never told me anything like that: all she tells me is if I don't feel like talking that's OK, don't talk. It worries me as well that when she goes to college, she'll maybe find some other guy there who'll be more fun to be around with. We've been dating a year now and she says there's no one else for her: she'd like for us to get married or live together at least, which is what we could do when she goes to college. She sure is a nice girl, I'm lucky that I have a girl friend like she is, and my mom likes her a lot too: so maybe something'll work out.

The thing I get moody about the most often is the world situation. I have bad dreams at night, about nuclear war starting and everywhere being destroyed. I worry about that: most every night on TV, you switch it on and there's a war somewhere, or the big countries in the world like America and Russia are threatening what they're going to do to each other. I don't think Russians are bad people and I don't think they want war any more than America wants war. I'd like it if they got together on things, do things together like space research and that stuff. Making it like they do into a competition all the time, I think that's a real dumb way to behave.

It all kind of makes you feel, well it makes me feel, we're all unimportant people: no matter what we want to do with our lives, we don't have much say about it whether we're going to be still alive in the future or what. You get some crazy idiot presses a button to start a war with someone, just because he thinks that's the right way to behave. He doesn't ask anyone, he just goes ahead and blows up the world. That's something that makes me moody a lot, is that.

Tandy Watkins, Junior, 16

She talked rapidly, now and again emphasising a point by tapping her clenched fist in the palm of her other hand. She was small and fair-haired, with bright blue eyes.

– I'm fourth grade, 16 going on 17 and next year I'll be a senior. After I graduate? Go to college somewhere, maybe Baxter: what I want to do is study for some kind of help work, with disabled or disadvantaged kids. This is an idea I've had since my freshman year: I've got one big qualification for it that gives me a head start, and one big qualification that puts me way back on the track behind all the other runners. It's the same thing, the qualification and the handicap. I'm what they call dyslexic, so that makes the whole study scene pretty tough: like it takes me three weeks to read something someone else reads in an hour. Writing's not too bad, there's ways round that, you can speak your essays onto a tape recorder: but reading, there's no let-out there.

So the qualification it gives me is I know what it's like to be handicapped, to be not to be able to do things other kids have no trouble with at all, and have them sit there laughing at you for it. We have special teaching: but there's only three of us dyslexic in the whole school. The main thing they try and teach us is we shouldn't feel ashamed of it, we should talk about it and laugh along with the others. It's some help but only some: you still wish you weren't like that and were the same like everyone else. I'd say the guys are worse about it than the girls are when it comes to teasing: they pass you a note and there's something vulgar written on it. They know you can't read it, so they all have a good laugh while you're trying to decide whether to ask someone else to read it for you. Some guys really are real funny guys.

I like sports, especially basketball and track, and I try and make up as an athlete for what I can't do in class. Only like you can see I'm not very big, I have problems with that in basketball. And I've got a hot temper which I shouldn't have: but I do get aggressive with it. You know, I might be an athlete but I'm not a sportswoman, believe me. That's another thing about boys, they think a girl should be all like candy, sweet and polite all the time. I might not be able to write them down too good, but I know all the swear words: a lot of boys tease me, just to see what they can get me to say when I lose my temper. Are all guys like that?

Right now, I'll tell you, I'm between boy friends. A lot of girls think that's terrible if you don't have a regular boy you date with. There's one boy who's a Senior, I guess he's my boy friend really. Only we have problems with our relationship: he wants me to be just his girl and not date anyone else, and I don't want to, not the way I feel right now which is I want to please myself.

My best friend says I should stay that way, she's like that too. Her and me, we're big buddies: the best thing about her is she always calls me 'Tandy' and I like that. Yeah, I'll tell you what I mean, I've got a big hang-up here about this. My dad, he's very well known in the town and his Christian name's 'Donald', right? Everyone around him calls him Don though. So that's OK: but where it gets to me is that everyone calls me 'Don's daughter'. I don't like that, and not only I don't like it, let me tell you I hate it. We had a teacher last year, she came in the gym one day looking for me and she called out, 'Is Don's daughter here?' That really made me mad, so I turned my back and started doing some beam work. She came over and she said, 'Heh Tandy, didn't you hear me asking for you?' I said, 'No I didn't, I heard you asking for Don's daughter you schmuck.' You're not supposed to talk to teachers that way, but like I told you I've got this big temper see. She was pretty mad at me and reported me to our Head, Bernie Westerman. He was mad too, he made me apologise to this teacher in front of the whole class.

I guess this is a psychological thing with me about my dad. I'm an only child, and he's not unkind or anything: but my ma once told me when I was born he was very disappointed because he'd hoped I'd be a boy. I don't know properly what, but something wasn't like it should be and they couldn't have any more kids, and my dad wouldn't adopt. He's a real old-fashioned type, and he's got very rigid ideas about what women should be like: he doesn't like me wearing jeans around the house, and he won't have that women cop show *Cagney and Lacey* on TV because he says women shouldn't do what they do, and definitely they shouldn't talk the way they do. I think he likes it I'm called 'Don's daughter' around town and not by my own name. Don't get me wrong, I'm not saying he isn't a regular guy and a good parent, he is: but this thing about my name is one big problem thing. I've tried to talk to my mom about it, but she and me we're not very close about anything, she always tells me just forget it, it's only a little thing not worth making waves about.

I'd say I'll probably be happier with myself when I go to college. Sometimes in Bird you feel you can't breathe: maybe I'm too old inside of me for the age I am outside, but I feel I want to get away and try and grow up a little. You can't always see forward to what comes after things though.

The biggest fault with a small town like this is it's gossipy, there's nothing you can do without people get to hear about it and tell other people. Last year I had a boy friend who was just that, that's all: he was a friend, only he was 22. He was married, and him and his wife they were separated and going to divorce. I knew him because he was a friend of friends, and one time he took me out to Milton Reservoir, and we sat in his car and talked. No more, nothing else, he didn't kiss me or even try to, all he wanted to do was talk about his wife. We were out there one hour, then we came back to town. By the time I got home, my dad already knew about it, would you believe that? He was stomping up and down shouting and yelling like I was a tart or something. I never did find out who'd seen us and come straight back and told him. Only that's the kind of thing doesn't make you happy at living in a place: you feel everywhere there are eyes, and big mouths whispering too. I felt it was pretty sneaky, I really did.

Well I guess that's it for what I'd wanted to say. I hope you don't think I'm a bad person because of things I've said about my dad. I like him a lot basically.

Arlene Stephenson, Senior, 17

A tall handsome girl, she sat astride a turned-round chair with her chin on her arms along its back. She wore a yellow blouse and a long black skirt: she had ropes of beads round her neck, four or five bracelets on her wrists, and rings on most of her fingers.

– To start at the beginning about me, I came here four months ago Friday, and I'll be leaving here two weeks Thursday which is my seventeenth birthday. I could say I'm from Columbus Ohio: that's where I was born, but I've lived in Amarillo Texas, Los Angeles California, New York City, Cleveland Ohio, Louisville Kentucky, Norfolk Virginia, Atlanta Georgia, Pine Bluff Arkansas, St Louis Missouri, St Paul Minnesota, and somewhere around 35 other places. That's for starters: I'm what they call a much travelled lady.

Right now I'm in Bird staying with my aunt, which was a condition of the six months' probation I got in Kansas City. The terms of it were I should live with her and go to school: and be a good girl, which is just what I've done. A little place like this isn't much my scene, I wouldn't have bet money on me staying here a week when I first came. But I've gotten along OK: my aunt's a real nice person, she came all the way over to Kansas City to speak for me and make the offer of giving me a home. She and her husband have three daughters of their own already: they're all younger than me, but they're real cute kids and they've treated me like I was their real sister. So you could say it was a success story. I don't want to sound ungrateful or anything, but I'll sure be glad when the 29th comes and I can go back to New York City and get into the mainstream again.

I'm supposed to be a bad girl, only that's not the way I see it myself. I see it I'm a person who's got ideas and ambitions, wants to do something in life but so far I don't know what. Some days I want to be a singer with a band, other times I'd like to be a theatre director, another day a painter designing and making scenery. All I know is it's got to be something in theatre and entertainment, it doesn't matter exactly what. I have talent, I have energy, I'm young and fairly good-looking: that's a lot of pluses. All I'm missing on is I don't organise myself. I think it's the problem a lot of people have: I talked about it with a psychiatrist when I was in a place in Washington one time for delinquent girls. I wasn't there for punishment, only assessment: she said I wasn't a bad girl, I was one who hadn't found her sense of direction yet, and I guess she was pretty well right on that.

I've been in trouble mostly for all the usual things, from the age of about nine on, somewhere there. Out of control, absconding, stealing, in need of care, assault, possession of marijuana: nothing serious ever, and most times it's been my mother who's turned me in, not that I've got caught doing anything. My mother, all I can say is if I sat here telling you till school started again in the fall about her, that'd only be like the introduction to the book, we'd have gotten no further than that.

I'll see if I can précis it for you OK? Well it starts where my dad left my ma when I was five. I have the idea they got married because she was pregnant with me, then things between them turned sour almost immediately. That's not surprising, I mean if a kid coming's the reason for marrying that's not exactly a good foundation for marriage. I don't recall much about him: he used to give me piggyback rides, I remember him taking me to the zoo once and buying me an ice-cream, things like that. I think he was bright, my ma wouldn't have married him if he hadn't been in the same league as her intellectually. She's a university lecturer, her speciality's modern literature: that's the one thing she's put her mark on me with, reading. Wherever we've lived all over the place, that never changed, always before anything else was done we had to unpack the books. Everything my ma knows is out of books, she lives out of her head if you know how I mean.

I'll tell you something: even if I hate her, and I do hate her without the even to it, I recognise she's always had problems with her men. There've been plenty of guys she's had that've treated her like shit, knocked her around and stuff: and there've been guys that've gone off with other women and only come back to her for money. And you know what, I've never seen her cry over any of them for it. The only time I've ever ever seen her cry is reading a book, Carson McCullers or Mary McCarthy. She sits there tears running down her cheeks, and I ask her what's the matter and she says, 'Oh, this is so sad.' She's a strange lady, let me tell you.

I used to try to understand her. I used to want to understand her, I thought if I did it might help me like her. Not now though: I don't like her and I don't want to understand her. She's no problem to me anymore, I've cracked it. It's the only thing we've ever agreed on: we don't ever see each other anymore. My aunt's her sister: we've talked some about this since I came, and she says she thinks it's sad but it's true, my mother and me get along worse than any two other people she's known. I never knew what I wanted from her: they say love don't they, that's what you want from your parents? In my case though it doesn't apply. Love's something I don't like, not hers, not anyone's, because I can't respond to it with love for them. I don't know that I've ever felt it, if I have I didn't recognise it as that. Crushes, you know, for a guy here and there, now and then: having the hots for someone, I know what that is. But loving I don't.

Around the school here, I know there's some people say I'm an easy girl: that's the reputation I have. But I'm not: no way am I an easy girl, I won't go with a guy just because he makes a play. The guys here anyway, they're most of them kids. They take you to a McDonald's, buy you a hamburger and a coffee, you know, spend out on you real big, five dollars or something. Comes the end of the evening, and what they want back is 50 dollars' worth. I don't go on that, if I don't like the guy it's no. I don't string anyone along though, I'm honest about it from the beginning: a boy asks me out, if he's not my sort I say, 'Let's get something straight first. Take me out if you want to: but I don't screw, OK?' Then we don't get misunderstandings.

It's been nice talking with you.

Danny Luckman, Senior, 17

Tall and thin, he had fair hair and hazel-brown eyes, and sat at the kitchen table of his home, formal and upright for the first five minutes. Then, relaxing, he pulled up another chair and sat back with his legs up on it.

– I'm a senior at the High School and when I graduate next year I'm going to Kansas State University to take a master's in engineering. Least that's what I hope it'll be, I want to get a job in aviation if I can, like my brother. He works for a company in Wichita and he's doing pretty good: he and his wife have two kids and a nice home, and that would be my own ambition if I'm clever enough.

I was born and brought up here in Bird: my dad's in farm insurance and my ma, well right now she's a homemaker and says that's what she likes being best. She says when I'm gone from home like my brother Mike, we should all watch out then: she's going to strike out and fulfil herself she says, and we'll all be real surprised at what she's going to do. A few weeks back I asked her to let me in the secret: she said OK so long as I didn't tell anyone else, what she's going to do is be Chief of

Police. I guess really what she might do is she might take a part-time job as a clerk in one of the stores.

My dad and ma, I'd say they're a pretty good example of a happy couple. They've been married I think it's 30 years, and through all my life I don't recall I ever heard them raise their voices with each other in a quarrel. I figure you can't be married to someone so long as that without there being a few things here and there you disagree about: but I don't remember no bad vibes in the air like they weren't talking to each other, nothing like that. You hear a lot these days about divorces, sometimes you think marrying someone must be like digging yourself a grave. But that's not the feeling I've ever gotten from my dad and ma. I talked about it with Mike once: he said the same as me, we both reckoned we'd been brought up pretty good and had a real good home.

This house is neither the largest in town nor the smallest: just around average, so I'd say that makes us a typical mid-west American family. That first or second night you were here, when you gave that programme at the library, I remember you said the idea you had of America was what you saw on your television in England: I think you said *Dallas* and *The Colbys* and *Dynasty* and maybe *Miami Vice*. I guess by now you'll have a different picture, least I hope so. Programmes like that, they give a real misleading impression: everybody always ripping everybody else off, trying to get their money or their wives, and everybody envious and full of jealousy. I think most ordinary American folk, in real life they just want to have a good home and a nice family, see that their kids are educated and well fed, and be friendly with their neighbours. I think this community we have here in Bird's as good an example of that as any, and I hope it's always going to stay that way. In my family all my life, as I remember it, we've been brought up to think about the other person as well as yourself. Whether it's your family, at school, when you work or wherever you go, think of the other person as well. I think that's a good way to try and live: it's how I'd like to be when I have my own family, and behave towards them the same way my dad and ma always have towards me. I don't say there aren't folk like those people in television serials: but I do say there aren't too many of them around. If it means most of us are just dull and dumb, OK I'll go for that.

I hope none of this I'm saying doesn't sound like I think there aren't any things are wrong and shouldn't be put right. The number one of those I think in America and the world everywhere, is that there are too many poor people, and I think it's up to rich countries like ours to do something to try and change this.

A place you might have been is Garland, where even in America there are people living who have a hard time. The way folk talk about Garland around here, they say they're all drug addicts living on welfare and don't want to work. Well we have a guy in our class, he lives there, but for a long time he'd never invite me home to meet his folks. When he did, he was living in a place with his ma and three kids, and he hadn't wanted I should know what a hard time they had. It wasn't his ma's fault they had no money and a home nothing like as good as I've got: his pa'd gone off with someone two years back, which was why they were so poor now. I don't know if I'm getting this over as I'd like to: what I'm trying to say is I don't see other people should blame people like that, they've had a tough deal.

One other thing I'd like to say about it is the world situation generally, I mean in international affairs. I think America must give an impression sometimes to other people which is very bad: I mean I don't know how it looks out there, but I sometimes think it must look we want to tell everyone else in the world how to run their lives. A lot of it's only propaganda from the American government leaders. I'd say to people just like I wouldn't want them to base their ideas on *Dallas* and *Dynasty* for the domestic scene, in the same way I hope they wouldn't think all Americans can't sleep in their beds at night because they're scared of the Russians.

I don't believe it's like that. I think most ordinary Americans are like me and my family. We don't hate anybody, we don't want to be at war with anybody, we just wish the world leaders would all get together and agree we should all live together with one another in peace.

21 *Trying to see forward*

Gene Dyson

– My age is 20, and I'm a student at Fort Baxter University where I'm in my second year of studying business administration and general studies. I'm halfway through roughly I guess, and I haven't decided for sure what I'm going to do after this. Where I am now, I'm trying to see forward: but that isn't too easy a thing to do right now.

My parents have a farm out of town on Route 12, and I know my dad hopes that along with my elder brother I'll take on the running of the place. But from what I've figured the last few years, my calculation is the farm'll support one person, or rather one family like my brother and his wife and children when they have some: but not two. The farm economy right now is bad, and my opinion is it'll get worse. I think the US is going into a recession, and if the only thing you can do is farming, you'll probably suffer more than most.

I have a regular girl friend at college, and she comes from south east Kansas. Her father's in Law and she's studying to be a teacher, and in another year she'll have her diploma. We've talked this through together, and I understand how she feels exactly when she says farming's not for her: she wants to be a brain work person and not someone who works with their hands. We have to get this sorted between us, because we're hoping we'll get married next year.

There's been pressure on me from my dad and also to some extent from my brother about this. They're keen for me to what they call carry on the family tradition: but if that means accepting what I've seen my dad accept all his life, an uncertain financial situation at the mercy of outside things you can't control, then I'm not too happy about it. This is why I'm talking anonymously and without description, because I haven't properly yet made up my mind about it and if I did decide to stay here in Bird it might be awkward later.

I actually don't happen to like too much the idea of living the rest of my life in a small community like this. Not just from the hard work and no money situation, but also because of what you might call the atmosphere. I'd like to see something of the world, and Marlene and I have talked about when we leave college, while we're still young and without ties we might take a year maybe and go to India or some place like that, to get to know a bit more about the world. There's a kind of tradition in America that if you take a trip you go to Hawaii or Alaska, one of the United States where you're still in your own country. You ask folk here where they've been to a foreign country, and for most of them foreign parts usually extend to Mexico but nowhere much else besides.

Another thing I don't have is the great American dream too much: that's the idea of being my own boss and having my own business, which is behind why a lot of people are farmers. I'd be happy to work for someone else as a company representative or sales person, so long as it was a good company I was with and it could offer security and prospects. Folk who heard me talk this way would say the spirit of my pioneer ancestors has faded. I guess they might say too that I'm one of the lucky ones, having a family farm to part inherit, and that a whole lot of young people my age would be very glad and proud to have it: also that with Marlene having her teacher's qualification, that's an extra kind of source of income to fall back on if things get hard. I can see their argument, but I don't know that I'm convinced by it. One way and another it's kind of a tough decision to make: you want to do what's the right thing by your own family, but I think equally you want to think about your own family.

That must sound kind of dumb: I'll try and say it again for you, right? Number one is you think about your family that you come from, your dad and what he did with his life. He had plenty of hard times, I've heard him tell about the things that happened to his father too, what they called the dust storms and all that. Himself, he didn't have much chance of an education: and I think he must have had to work hard and go short on things, him and ma, so they could make sure my brother and me went to college. So that's the one side of it, the family tradition side of things. My brother and me, we represent to him what you might call the outcome of his efforts and endeavours. I guess it must be kind of tough when you do all that for a person, and then they turn around and tell you they don't really want to do what all through the years you hoped they'd do, which is pick up and carry on where you left off.

But the other side of it, the number two thing, is that before long now I'll be starting my own family. I'd like it if it was with Marlene because that's the way we plan it to be: but even if it doesn't turn out that way, my life's still ahead of me and I'd want to marry and have children and all the rest. But I think what I'm fairly certain of is I wouldn't want a family of mine, through the whole of their lives while they were growing up, to be thinking when the time came they too'd be carrying on my pa's and my family's tradition as well. I'd say I'd try and make darn certain they didn't do that, but went into some other way of life than farming. Somewhere along the line someone's got to make the break, because like I said I don't see that farming's got much going for it. I'm talking about the small individual farmer, the one or two man family outfit: the future's going to be all these big conglomerate companies, not small concerns, they're too under-productive to survive.

I still don't feel I've spelled this out too good for you about how I see things and how I feel. You won't need for me to say I'm still confused in my mind about it all.

Kathy Keys

She wore a red skirt and matching waistcoat, and a crisp lemon high-collared blouse. On her finger was a small diamond engagement ring, and there was a gold watch on her wrist. She talked easily, sometimes putting up her hands and unselfconsciously ruffling them through her short curly hair.

– Oh I'm very very old, I'm all of 23 and I've lived every year of my life here and never been away from home, isn't that a terrible thing to say? You don't think life's passed me by? Sometimes I do, yeah. I've three sisters older than me and they're all married: my mom keeps asking,

'What's the matter with you, Kathy, how much longer've me and pa to go on keeping you?' Only she means it nice, you know? Her and me we're real good friends, she's like another sister really, not like my mom at all. And they don't keep me, I keep them: least that's what I say to them. I have a good job, I mean by that the pay's good, at the office of one of the town's attorneys: I'm the receptionist, I like it, it's real interesting work and all the people I work with are real nice.

I have plans of marrying, as you see from my engagement ring. My boy friend Rick, he's at college in Baxter and we've been dating now six years since I was 17. Another year and he gets his bachelor's in chemistry and economics, and then we'll get married: leastways that's our plan. We've got to do some pretty hard figuring first though about it, about the economic side of it I mean. The main problem is that where I am here, I have a good job and I earn good: but there'd be no work for him here though, so that makes things difficult. He'll be looking for a position with some company or other in Baxter, or maybe Wichita or Kansas City even. That'd mean I'd have to give up my job and try to get another one some place else where he was, which I wouldn't like too good I know because of me being so happy in the one I'm in here. The other thing is I know I'd miss my mom, that sounds like a kid talking, but it's true and it scares me.

I guess this must make me sound like a girl who wants to keep a hold on everything she's got, but it's not that way entirely, least I hope it's not. The first thing for me is Rick: he's the only guy there is and the only guy there's ever been for me. He's a local boy and we first met when we were at school. He's three years older, and he was a senior while I was still a junior. I fell in love with him the very first time I saw him, and for me it's been that way ever since. When he left Bird and went to Baxter to college, like all girls I was scared he'd meet someone else once he got there: you know, someone a lot prettier, a lot less dumb, more like his own age and all the rest. I don't know whether he did or he didn't: he's a very good-looking guy and I can't imagine some of the girls there when he went didn't make a play for him. I think maybe he did play around a little with a couple maybe: I don't ask too much about it. But the last nearly three years now, I know he hasn't: he tells me I'm the only one for him and all he wants is for us to get married, and I believe him. As a regular thing now, either he comes to Bird or I go to Baxter: every weekend, we've never missed once in three years, so I guess that must mean something. I said to you I'd miss my mom if I went some place else to live and I sure would: but if I stayed here and didn't have Rick, there wouldn't be any comparison with how much I'd miss him. Every week, comes Wednesday and I'll tell you, I'm looking at my watch to see how long it is to Friday.

I'm not a girl who's got ideas very much of a career for herself, and I think I'd be happy being a wife and a homemaker with Rick, and bringing up kids which we'd both like to have. The money I earn at my job here is important, and my mom and pa'd miss having it: my pa doesn't work, he's sick, so there's not a lot of money there. That's one of the reasons why I'd like it if I could go on working a while first after I got married, so I could send some money home to my folks now and again.

Now I'll tell you what my one big main worry is, OK? It's this. It really does scare me that two people like Rick and me can love each other very much like we do, and they can get married and have a couple of kids maybe: and then wham, divorce. This does, this idea really really scares me. I told you I'd three sisters older than me and they're all married, right? Well, they are: but the youngest one of the three, that's the next oldest one to me above me, she and her husband have broken up and they're in the process of getting a divorce. I know this is a kind of a crazy thing to say, but it's a fact that in the United States every one marriage in two ends in divorce. My sister she's only one out of three: but if I got married, well then I'd be the other one in line OK? That's a crazy way of thinking but that's it, there's the way I think.

There's no way I can see how you can tell possibly at all if your marriage to someone is going to work out unless you try it first. By that I mean absolutely yes, I think you have to live together for a while to find out. I'm not just saying from the sexual side: you can have a very very good sexual relationship, but that's not the same thing as waking up every morning with the other person next you in the bed. It could be something very small you discover you don't like: maybe he picks his teeth after he's eaten pomegranate pie, or you like to take off your brasseer when you come home from work, something of that sort. Whatever floats your boat, you've been doing it all your life or he has and neither of you knew it about each other. And just as crazy, the other one can't live with it. So that's what I think you ought to do, absolutely and definitely, live together a while first and find out.

You can imagine though if you did that in Bird. I mean wow, you can imagine. Or if I told my mom I was going to Baxter and I was going to live with Rick. My mom I say, but that's nothing to how it'd be with my pa. He has a heart condition and it would, I guarantee, he'd just give one last breath and go like that. I talked about it with Rick once, I mean this idea we should live together first awhile. You know what he said to me? He said 'You know we couldn't, we just couldn't ever do that to your mom and your pa.' I mean honest, I was so mad with him about it: he doesn't know this but it's true, if he'd gone on just a few more words and said he was going to make an honest woman of me, I'd have walked out on him then and there.

Oh, so, so I guess I'll get it sorted in the end. They say you do, right?

Jacqueline Smithson

Eighteen, pretty, tall and slender and dark. She wore black trousers and an open-necked white and red striped shirt, hanging like a blouse outside them.

– I've got the whole of my life to look forward to, and even earlier than last week when I graduated from High School I'd been starting to plan out what I want to do. Nothing's fixed or absolutely definite about it, and I'd say the only thing I knew for sure was I didn't see any future here in Bird. I've two brothers and a sister older than me: they've all gone away like most young people have to, and when I do the same too, it'll be something my ma and pa won't be surprised at. They're sensible reasonable people, they've always treated all of us kids the same: that it was our lives ahead of us, we were the ones who'd decide what we wanted to do with them. We're not a farming or business family: Pa's a teacher at the High School over at Alliance, which is a long way for him to travel each day, but he enjoys his job and he wants his children to enjoy theirs.

He's keen on us having an education, naturally: he's told me like he told my brothers and sisters, that if I want to go to college he'll see to it

I go to college. I got good grades and I'm a slightly better than average student, and I'm going to K State University to study music and drama. I have scholarships which will help some: but I don't want to take more money from my parents than I have to, so through the summer I've got me a job waitressing at a diner over at near Deerfield. It doesn't pay all that good, but I reckon I'll be able to save some by the fall when I go to college. I'll be sharing accommodation there with three other girls all the same age as me, and I'd like a little money of my own so I can contribute whatever fair share will make me on the same level as them. That's the plan as of now.

I say as of now because my personal affairs are a bit unsure. I have a boy friend 24 who's a graduate engineer: he's not from Bird, he comes from Hammond. He works with the government, and he has the chance he might next year be offered a position in Washington State, in Tacoma near Seattle. It'd be a big step up the scale for him: and if it comes out that way, then we'd get married and I'd go with him. I'd like to have a family, so that would mean forgetting my studies a while, then coming back to them when I'm older. I know your education is important, but if you're a woman you put your husband first. My speciality in music is piano and I'd like to be a teacher of it. Whether I could do that as well as run a home and have kids too I don't know, it might not work out or it might. I'm a restless sort of a person, and I figure I'd need to keep my mind occupied with some sort of activity for myself outside the home always.

This is one of the big drawbacks with Bird, that it's a culturally dry place totally. When you talk of a concert, that's a school concert: if you want to hear some classical music ever, you're talking of going to Wichita at least or Kansas City. A 400 miles round trip, or maybe even a 600 mile one, that's sure a long way to go to listen to someone playing Scarlatti. I don't want you to think I'm going crazy here, mentally starving to death, it's not as bad as that: I know we have a good library and they'll get you any book you want. But sometimes you don't know what you want, except that you need to browse around and come across something you didn't know about. That's not too easy here. If my boy friend, or my husband as he'd be then, if he went to Tacoma that's near Seattle, which is one big city if you want art galleries and concerts and books.

My pa, he always says there's nowhere else he'd like to live than here. It's fine for him: but he doesn't try and apply that to his children, because for them he knows it's not. He's 46 now, and I kind of lose track of people when they get up to that age. He's happy and so's my ma, the life suits them. But I don't see myself being here in Bird when I'm as old as they are. When they look back and say there's nowhere else they want to be, I think older folks have often forgotten what they felt like when they were young. Or maybe when they were young, they felt differently from the way I feel, I don't know. If they never wanted to go any place else but Bird in the first place, naturally they'd feel like that still when they were older. You could say they were very sensible, they knew what life was all about, they were happy with what they'd got and so on: but from another way of seeing it, I think you could say of some of them they weren't very venturesome, they weren't that type of person and never have been. In my pa's case, I know because he'd never made a secret of it, when he was around my age he wasn't happy with his life and there were a lot of troubles in his family: his parents divorced, he was brought up by a relative, and a whole lot of other things like that. When he and ma married, it was only at that time he began to get himself together, be educated, get work teaching which was what he enjoyed. Then their four lovely kids started to come along, least that's the way he describes it: so OK, yes you can see how he's had his share of unhappinesses and is glad now to settle for some tranquillity.

I go along with him all the way on that for him, step by step I do. Where I depart is from the folk who are older still, the next generation up further from him: that's when they start into all this stuff about what's the matter with young people these days, society's crumbling, no one's got any respect for tradition any more. I mean tradition, all that means sometimes is don't let's have any change: not in ideas, not in ways of thinking, not in anything ever. But I'd say even just as an American, that's no way for the people of any country to be: if you want to grow, you've got to look for horizons and decide which one you're going to head for, like the pioneers did.

Darrell Greaves

Open and friendly in manner, he sat in the kitchen of his family home, a large old-fashioned room in a freshly painted farmhouse five miles north of town. His voice was quiet and thoughtful.

– I'm in my second year at college, and I'm studying agriculture and business studies. I'm 21, and when I've done another year of study or maybe a little more, I shall come back and work here with my two uncles and my ma who own this place. My father was killed in an accident on the highway two miles south of here: it was winter and there was a lot of ice around, and his car went out of control and collided with a truck. I was 16 then and at High School, and I shall take over his interest in the property, which he owned with his brothers, when the time comes. I have one brother older than me by two years: he was at K State and now he's in Denver Colorado with an oil company. He's a businessman, he prefers that to farming and has done all along. The family all knew, including my pa, that he didn't want to come into farming: so there was no kind of bad feeling about it between him and the rest of us, nothing like that. He never felt even when pa was alive the same way about living here like I do.

I was born here and I went to Junior School and High School here. Ever since I can remember at school I just hung around waiting for vacation so's I could get on with work here, which was chiefly with the livestock. I liked the cattle and the hogs more than anything, though I can't tell you properly why: all I can say is I'm a person who's happiest when he's on the back of a horse. I didn't like the book work and studies at school, and I'll be honest with you and say I still don't like them at college. I know I won't do anything at all brilliant there, but my ma reckons, and I do too, that these days if you're in farming you need to know about a whole lot of extra technical knowledge so I'm studying up on it.

The other aspect that's very important to study is the business management and financial side. Anyone'll tell you, there's been far too many farmers who've loved farming but not been able to do their sums: they've gone into things without doing the figuring first, and as a result of that they've overstretched themselves, gotten into financial difficulties and couldn't get out again. I've known of farmers who've gone to a bank or a credit firm to ask for a loan, and all they've had is some sums they've done in pencil on the back of an envelope: that's all they've taken to show the person they were asking the money from. He could take one look and see they'd forgotten to put in this item and that item, they'd taken last year's prices and not this year's prices, and when it came to grants and subsidies they'd guessed at what they hoped for rather than put down what they needed. So they didn't get their loan, or if they did it wasn't on terms they could manage.

No guy's going to lend you money if you make yourself out to be a dumb idiot. I don't know if the story's true or not, but I heard of one farmer not far from here, when the manager asked him what collateral he could give for security, he said his wife had some valuable jewellery which would cover it. So when the bank manager said that was OK but he'd have to have it valued, the guy said no he didn't want that to happen because he didn't want his wife to know about it. So what d'you know, he didn't get his loan. If you go with a good proposition which shows you can handle yourself and the situation, you'll always find someone'll back you: that's their business, that's how they make their money, they're not looking to turn business away. But they're sure not looking to pour their money down the gulley either.

What made me decide, after my pa died that I wanted to carry on with my uncles in the farm wasn't really one thing. I'd say it was three things. The first was he'd always said that was how he hoped it would be: he respected Rod's decision to go some other way in his life, but he hoped my feelings would stay the same as it had been from when I was a kid. So it gives me pleasure to know he'd have approved of my decision to stay. But when it comes to the bottom line, it was still my own decision, and I'd have taken it even if he'd said he wanted me to look around at other things. But I think farming suits me: there'd be no point to doing something unless you were sure you were going to be more happy doing it.

I know the future of the farm economy right now is uncertain. I had to take a decision a couple of years back: it could be one day I'll regret it, but I don't think so, and I don't hope so. It came about that my uncles and my ma had what seemed like a good offer to sell the farm: they had the chance to dispose of everything and move out. I thought it was a fine thing that they sat down around this table here with me, and we all discussed it together like we was equals, as to what would be the best thing to do. If they'd sold, it would have given my uncles enough money so they could stop working and retire. Ma and me, we couldn't anywhere near raise the capital to buy them out. Well we all talked around it, they asked me whether I was sure I wanted to stay there for the future: and when I said yes, that decided them not to sell. I've thought several times if they'd been thinking only about themselves, they could have gone over my ma's head and looked after their own interests. They didn't, but I'll gradually over time buy them out.

The third thing, a very important one, is this is my home and I like to feel I belong here in what you might say was my family succession. I have a girl friend and she's a farmer's daughter herself: she says there's nothing she'd like better than to be the wife of one too and come in here along with me. She and my ma get along real good, so when we marry we'll all live here together. No one's ever said to me farming was an easy way to make a living, but I reckon I'll be happy to stay right here and farm and have a family and raise kids just like my folk before me. I think it's right for a man to lead his own life and be independent by his own efforts and rely on himself. If I could keep the farm running as a viable concern, not land up myself and my family in debt, then I think that would be a good lifetime's prospect for anyone.

22 *Two Lives (4)*

Achievement: Gordon Ronson

– Thank you Tina. Anyone calls I'm in a meeting but I'll call them back in an hour. Oh except Berkman: Berkman I need to talk to, OK?

A near-replica of a Barbie doll in her off-the-shoulder floral summer dress, his auburn-haired secretary nodded, gave a big blue-eyed smile and went gracefully out of his office again, closing the door behind her. He gestured invitingly towards the silver tray she'd left on his desk: on it were two white china beakers of coffee with an ear of corn design in gold on them, two plastic stirrers and a cut-glass dish with envelopes of sugar and sweetening powder, and little plastic tubs of cream. His spacious, light and airy and thickly carpeted glass-partitioned office was at the rear of a huge showroom full of gleaming new automobiles.

He took a black coffee himself and stretched back in his high-backed leather swivel chair, lifting his arms and clasping his hands behind his head. Slim and fit-looking, smart in a white shirt with a silver thread, he had a dark-blue tie with a small gold emblem on it of a spoked steering wheel.

– Tony my friend, welcome to my office here. You don't know this, but it's a particular welcome for you today, because you've come to visit with me on my birthday. A guy couldn't want nicer than that as a birthday present. I've never had the pleasure of seeing your country yet, but I'm a sincere admirer of it: your Mrs Thatcher is a wonderful woman and I absolutely mean that. She's a great leader, the world could do with more like her: an example to the free world, in the mould of Winston Churchill. Yes indeedy. Is the coffee OK for you or isn't it to your liking? I can have Tina bring you in some iced tea if you prefer? You're sure, you only need say the word?

Since we talked about talking like this, I've thought about it a lot: it's been occupying my mind because appropriately I'm in a kind of a way today at a milestone in my life. I'm 45, and this is a marker, a three-quarters marker: not three-quarters the way through, but somehow so far my life's divided up into three separate periods, each one of them exactly 15 years long each.

From when I was born through until I was 15 or 16, when I look back on it, that wasn't a very happy period of my life. No sirree. I had three sisters older than me, and what I recall is they were always fighting among themselves, shouting and yelling and everything: not the conventional behaviour of young ladies, let me tell you. On top of that, my ma and pa, they were always yelling at one another too. We all lived together on an old rundown beatup farm sort of place, out to the north of town here: but my pa, he wasn't no farmer, if you want the truth he wasn't much of anything except a drunk. We never had money: my ma had always to be going off to work for other people as a domestic in their homes. I don't blame her and I never have: I admire her, she had to do it to get some money. I think maybe she thought with three daughters they'd do the things women mostly do in the house, you know like cook and wash and clean. Maybe that's what my fine sisters were mostly argumentifying about among themselves all day, which one wasn't going to do what. To be fair about it I suppose you could say my pa should have taken control: whether he tried or not I never did know, but mostly I remember him not being there. I saw him once drunk in the town one day: I still have this picture in my mind of him standing there on the sidewalk, swaying from one side to the other like this, looking at me like he kind of recognised me from some place. But he didn't say he did, just went on standing and swaying there while I went right on by.

That was my life that I had for the first 15 of my years. Things couldn't go on that way, they just could not: so then they changed. For the first 15 years they'd been bad: for the next 15 after that, they were terrible.

I've never exactly discovered what happened properly, except that one day I came home from school and Elvira who was my eldest sister told me that Ma had died. She said Pa was selling up the farm and they three girls were going off on their various ways, while I was to be sent to live with my aunt in Idaho. I've still the idea in my head somehow it wasn't true, about my ma being dead I mean. There was no funeral I remember being held or anything of that sort. I have the notion that one day she'd had enough, or maybe met some man who was better to her than my pa had been and went with him, or something of that kind. All I do know is from that day forward she was out of my life for evermore, and so was my pa. Ten years back now a certain person told me he'd died: but he'd never been much to me but a shadowy figure in my life, or maybe a shadow on my life would be truer to say.

My sisters, well Elvira the eldest she'd gotten herself a man by that time, a husband: she went with him to Washington State and prospered, or so she says. We exchange a Christmas letter each year with news of our respective families, but contact between us hasn't been all that great. My two other sisters, the younger girls, I understand through her they're both in their different ways married and settled down. I believe they're in Vermont, living not far away from each other. I'd say to them it's 30 years now since we've spoken or communicated with each other, and I wish them well. I'm not greatly into the psychology of these things, but I reckon we could qualify as what might be called altogether a fairly broken-up family, right?

So at 15 or thereabouts, that then left me as the person most concerned with me, except the good lady who was my aunt in Idaho. The first thing she and her husband greeted me with when I arrived at their farm was a very serious dissertation: about how great my good fortune had been that they, out of the kindness of their hearts, were prepared to take me into their home and feed me and clothe me and give me shelter. Then next they made clear was that since for some reason they'd no children of their own, there was an eventual possibility but no more than that, that at some future unspecified date I might be considered for the great honour of being officially adopted by them. Only in the meantime and for all forseeable time to come, I was to consider myself on probation. The terms of the probation, though they didn't say so in so many words, were that meantime I should work for them as an unpaid hand on their farm: every day 365 days a year, from the rising of the sun until the setting of it, obediently and without complaint.

If I sound kind of a little bitter about this, it's because I am. Say from around then until I was 20 about, I had the idea in my mind life'd given me a raw deal. I wasn't a bright kid and it wasn't like I had my hopes dashed or anything: it was more I hadn't any hopes, but I couldn't escape the feeling there was surely more in life than I'd up till then had.

A couple of times I ran away. That's more an expression you talk of regarding a 12-year-old kid, rather than a 20-year-old young man which was what I was. But that's just how it was, I was a kid in a man's body. I'd no idea where I was going or what I was going to do in life: all I had for ambition was that someone different would take me on as a hired hand. Then maybe I'd get some money together and go some place else besides Idaho. I don't think my thinking went any further than that, only it never worked out. After a few weeks I'd be back to my aunt and uncle's saying I was sorry and would they take me in again.

Around where they lived, which was a place 120 miles north of Boise about, it was mostly timber country. One day one place I went, there was a sawmill there owned by a man with two daughters. One of them was a real pretty girl: when I first saw her she was 16. Her and me, any time I was passing and I stopped by, we both seemed to have the same idea: if we could get to some place else, to the big city like Boise maybe, then life'd have more meaning for us. Looking back now, I'd say I don't think we were in love with each other so much as we were both in love with the same idea: which was that our futures lay in escaping, because in her case she was almost as unhappy as me. And eventually one way and another, somehow we achieved what we both wanted, which was out. It took us near on a year to arrange it: but one day we met up by arrangement, we went to Boise, we got married, and we set off together into the sunset for a new life. I don't know why it is in all those movies it ends that way, the hero and the heroine riding off into the sunset together. How come no one ever stands up and says when the music swells, 'Heh hold on here, what comes after sunset, isn't it night?'

That's how it was with us. Two kids, I guess that's all I can say: me a dumb ox and her a pretty little thing like a feather, without so much as a single idea what life was about in her head. We made it to Boise, sure: but we never made it in Boise, that's even more sure. I was a pump attendant, a labouring man on a hydroelectric project, a cattle herder, a potato truck driver, pretty near anything you can think to mention. And she was a store clerk, a waitress, a drive-in movie hop, oh everything else too. Also she was a couple of times pregnant and both times miscarried, and she was very very sick. How things would have been for us if she'd had the babies, or only one of them, I don't know. Maybe it would have kept us together and we'd eventually have found an equilibrium: or maybe anyway we'd still have gotten apart, and I'd be like a lot of other men, a father with kids he never sees. I incline to the view that all together, the way it was is the way was best. About all I know for sure Tony is we became two mighty unhappy people, with our lives and with ourselves both.

I'll tell you from there on in how it went: in one word, it didn't. Towards the last two years of it I'd got me a commission job in a small town I'd sooner not name, in the south of the state: I was selling farming tools and equipment to people who didn't want it, and if they had have, they'd have got it less expensive some place else. I worked out of a shack on an old lot, run by a guy who'd take anyone on, on the principle he'd make himself a dollar if they sold something and save himself a dollar if they didn't. Anything like a promising lead came up, he'd follow it through himself and move you over to scouting for new business.

Maybe there's a lot of other guys who've experienced that feeling, when they're at the age of 30 their life's over: they've reached a milestone and they've achieved nothing, so draw the line, that's it. I did. When my lady wife then told me she'd met a guy and was taking off with him to the other end of the rainbow where they'd find a pot of gold, I couldn't think of two arguments to put together why she shouldn't. One of them could've been we loved each other, but we didn't: and another could've been we ought to give it one more try, only we'd already been through that routine, a dozen times or more. I said, 'OK then honey, goodbye, nice knowing you,' and that was about the extent of it. I had no feeling about it, nor she did. Or maybe we both had the same, the one that's called relief. Still does something to your self-esteem though, when your wife leaves you for another guy, yes sir.

Well, 45 today: and 15 years back, at the age of 30, I was where and what? Nowhere: a no hope, with no past roots and no kind of future to look forward to, that would be about the size of it. Nowhere to go, nowhere I wanted to go, no one to go to. I see it now as God's plan for me: but I didn't see it as that then. It was though, and it's as simple as that. There wasn't no thunder clap or flash of lightning from Heaven, no voice calling me, no revelation, nothing of that kind: a turning, but not one I could see. As far as I was concerned all I was was a spare-parts salesman at the bottom of the heap, and to be truthful not with a lot of ambition to work my way up.

It'd round the thing off nice and clean if I could tell you that was the moment I let God into my life, and He turned it around for me. But that's not how it was Tony. That wonderful thing didn't happen to me till a while later, almost gradual you might say. It'd be neat and clean too if I could tell you things changed because at that point I met Larissa who's now my wife: but that wouldn't be right either. I can't say to you it was because of it, that one thing, not if I'm being honest which I'm trying to be.

But I'll set out the simple facts for you, and it went along something in this fashion. Idaho had nothing to hold me: I'd been born in Kansas, and though for sure I'd not even been happy, if there was anywhere I belonged it could only be here. My health was good, and there weren't many kinds of places I couldn't go to and ask for work in, and not be able to say I'd had some experience of doing it or something very like. I'd no ties and no great financial needs: my wife had left me for a man with more money, or at least more prospects of more money, so she wasn't either getting or expecting financial support. So what did I do, I started to move south: at my own pace, but all the while keeping my thoughts on Kansas where I was eventually hoping to arrive. Idaho, Oregon, Wyoming, South Dakota, Nebraska: over I guess around 18 months I was moving, staying a few weeks to earn me a little money, moving on again, until I finally made it right back to Kansas and here. It was 15 years since I'd been in this part, and I didn't need more than a couple of days hereabouts to realise I'd be better placed for finding work somewhere with more population.

So where I came to rest, made my journey's end, but I didn't know then that it was that, was Conway City. That's 19 miles east of here right? A June evening, late and hot: the clock on City Hall was showing six o'clock I remember. I was walking along the west side of Main: I was looking for a room for myself for the night. And there was an automobile showroom, about one third the way along, with this handwritten card in the window. It said on it just three words: 'Auto Salesman Wanted'. I thought to myself well next morning I'd maybe stop by and ask if there were prospects for an out-of-town bum who'd never sold anything bigger than a magneto for a tractor.

I went in there at eight the next morning, and what do you know, there were. The guy who's salesroom it was, his partner who ran the front of house side of the business'd dropped dead a couple of days before, and he wanted someone temporary to help him out. He didn't care too much I knew nothing about automobiles, the only word I told him which interested him was I'd experience of selling. If I wanted it, he said, the post was mine. The only little detail about it though, which he said there hadn't been space for him to write it on the card, was there was no salary: it was strictly commission only. I didn't tell him I'd had experience of that too, I said 'Sure, that's OK by me.' I figured I couldn't lose: ten per cent of nothing was still nothing, so how was I going to be any worse off?

What happened next, here's where if you want to talk of God moving in mysterious ways, you could. No more than at most ten whole minutes later, after he'd finished telling me which of his eight automobiles he was desperate to unload at any price so's he could service his bank loan that month, and which was the one which was so bad he'd give it free to the first enquirer, who comes walking in but a lady in deep distress. She'd just half an hour earlier let her husband's sedan roll off of a clifftop where she'd parked it, and into a ravine, where it had bounced on from there into a lake. Naturally she thought he wasn't going to be pleased about this: and then lo and behold, what should she see when she's walking down Main but the identical model of the identical automobile in the same identical colour for sale. If it was OK by me, please could she have it there and then: only would I hold it five minutes, while she went over to the Bank and brought the money back in cash?

Which she did, and went off delighted. When the proprietor came back I altered the story slightly, building up my struggle to clinch the sale. But I think what impressed him most was that having handed over the money to him then and there in cash, I asked him to please give me my commission the same way, then and there in cash too: and when he did, I went straight over to the other side of the street and bought myself a new suit. I kind of impressed myself with that too: the first time in my life I'd had the feeling of being proud to be a salesman.

From that day to this Tony, like I said a milestone measuring out another 15 years, what's happened since I can sum it all up in maybe not much more than a few sentences. I just went on selling automobiles. I worked hard, real hard: selling came first second third and last: long hours, I was ready to sell to a customer any time of day or night. And in all honesty I can say this: I never sold someone something they didn't want or shouldn't have tried to afford to have. To me it's not just a phrase to say I want every one of my customers to regard me as a friend: it's a fundamental creed. Every night you should be able to look yourself in the face in the mirror and say 'I know I didn't make myself any enemies today: and I hope I made a friend.' The proof of that's right there in our sales documentation: you'll see the same person coming back four five times in a row to us for their new vehicle. Another thing I always do is a little exercise: 48 hours after a sale, I want to know how the buyer's feeling. So what do I do? I call up the gentleman or the lady on the telephone and I tell them I want to ask them a question. Just one: are they happy? Always, but always, they say 'Yes': and they remember that, and pass it on around their friends.

Five years back now, I bought into the business as a partner. We have this sales room and offices here in Conway City, two others at Baxter and at Deerfield, and one at Hammond. We have the franchise for Goey for the county, we employ total sales and servicing staff of 24, who we pay good wages to and additionally reward with incentives and bonuses. I don't myself do a great deal of actual direct to customer selling now: I'm responsible for overall area sales management and the development of fleet leasing. As an innovative and competitive sales force we reckon we're way out in front of the rest of the field in the whole of this part of Kansas.

Seeing how it's all grown so swiftly and knowing the growth comes from strong foundations and sound business principles, it's a good feeling. We believe what we do's worthwhile as well as profitable. You'll have heard the old saying, the business of America is business: well I think we stand as an example of excellence in that. I tell any new trainee salesman he should look on it that what he's selling isn't only merely a thing called a consumer durable: it's something much more important than that, we're selling happiness, the great American ideal of freedom to roam. I believe that, and if they're to excel they must believe it too. The other thing they have to know is you can't sell happiness if you do it by fraud or less than total honesty. You have to sell honestly and proudly, that's the only way there is.

These are simple fundamental principles: to work by and to live by, both. To me they're no different fundamentally to the basic principles of Christian belief. This is something we're very keen for our employees to have in themselves too. When I said to you earlier I'd let God into my life, I meant both my working life and my domestic one. I only wish more folk could have the experience of that, finding out as I do myself daily how very much God can do for you.

My wife Larissa and I, I can safely say this, we're liked and respected members of the community of Bird. You've been to our home on North Adams Street so you've seen the standard at which we live: comfortable, but not I hope in any way ostentatious. We have our two lovely children you've met, Alan eleven and Ann Margaret nine, both of them now at Junior School and making favourable progress. I guess we like to think of ourselves as Mr and Mrs Average American: over the very happy years of solid family life we've established together, to be that's been our aim. I don't have any shame to say I'm proud of being it, and after such a hard-time journey, of my achievement.

Failure: Stanley Fricke

No, he said, he preferred it this way, it made it easier to talk in somewhere impersonal like this, away from home where his wife wouldn't even know he'd been *talking: only please be careful about exact details like dates and precise sums of money, otherwise he'd be too easily identifiable.*

A thin, good-looking man in his late thirties, with a pale complexion and thinning fair hair, he clasped and unclasped his hands constantly. He talked quietly and unemotionally and bravely. One of the overhead strip lights in the bare room flickered and clicked erratically all the time, nearing the end of its life.

– I'm married and I've two children, a boy 15 and a girl 13. I was born and brought up here, our farm's three miles north, halfway between here and Hammond. You can see it if you're on the road, it's set back two-thirds of a mile up the track, edging on a group of pines. It was my father's before me and my grandfather's before that. My father was an only son, I'm an only son: and Boris, my son, it looks like he's in the same tradition. We had a boy older than him, Marshall: but he was killed in a tractor accident when he was four. Now and again you look back at something and you think that's when the bad luck started: that's when it began, and it's been following me around step by step, all the time in my footprints right behind me ever since. Your thoughts can soon get morbid that way.

There'd be other people besides me in this town would tell you I've had my share of misfortune more than most, maybe around enough for three or four. There'd be others though who'd say I'd been born lucky, and grown up a small fool first and then on into a bigger one. I'll tell you how I see it was, then it's for you to make your own judgement. I won't excuse myself saying I don't know how it happened, because I do know that, in every detail. I was there when it happened, and it was all the time happening to me: I can't make a lot of sense out of it but I can sure make a lot of no sense out of it, because that's the way my life's become for me, to put it in a word. Sure: the word's failure.

My father wasn't an educated man, and when he was young they didn't set so much importance on education. If you were born on a farm and it was going to be yours, one you were going to inherit, what you needed then was experience not education. That was the way it'd been for him. It didn't stop him being an intelligent man though: he could see the way things were going in farming, how more and more new ideas and aspects were coming in. So he reckoned that for his son, having experience on the farm wouldn't be enough, it'd be handy if he had some book learning and knowledge in his head too. My High School grades were good, so an early plan was made for me: one way or another, money'd be got together for me to go on after graduation to college.

He saved and he gave me a few acres of land of my own to raise money on. I worked hard at High School, and in my senior year I got together a package of scholarships, and everything was going along sweet. So it was a big blow when he suddenly died right after I finished at High School: literally just a few weeks after, that's all. There was talk between me and my mother about whether maybe I shouldn't give up the college idea and stay on at the farm, taking over the running of it. But she persuaded me to carry on with Pa's plan: we were both pretty certain what he'd have liked was for me to do that.

Financially we could about manage. Even though I was away at college a deal of the time, I came home whenever I could, while she kept control of things. She knew how the hands should work and where they should work and what they should do: she was a real farmer's wife and proud of it, and any farmer'd have been proud to have her as a wife too. And around that time while I was still at college, I started testing out a few ideas about the business side of farming they were teaching us, particularly to do with buying and selling of land. If I saw an adjoining parcel to us for sale at a good price, I'd sell off some other part to buy it instead. All told I did pretty good, I seemed to have an eye and a nose for it.

By the time I'd finished college and got my Bachelor's in agriculture, our farm had close on half a million dollars' worth of land. Not all of it was paid for: some of it was financed by banks and credit associations. But I knew what I was doing, and they knew I did: I put up to them carefully budgeted schemes, the land itself was collateral, and they wouldn't have backed me if they hadn't seen it looked they were supporting a sound business venture. Everything looked good to them and to me. The other thing I brought back home from college to the farm with me was a wife: Janie and I'd met in my final year and we seemed to click together straight off. She was studying to be a teacher, but made a choice instead for marriage. She was a girl from north of Hammond, so she was local too, and we'd known each other at the High School. She liked my mother and Ma liked her, so no problem there either.

We went along that way a year or two, and we had our first child, the boy. And I'd say without precisely working out the date on paper, this was when the whole farm economy started to go on the slide, right across the state. I wasn't the only one who didn't recognise what was happening: I'd say there was very few anywhere who did. Land prices going down? They'd gone down before: all it meant was if you had the money, it was a good opportunity to buy. If you had to borrow more money to do it, you estimated what your crop sales were going to be, then you went along to the finance company: here's what I need, here's my last five years' figures, on this basis how much'll you lend me and what rate at? You get seduced into it, you seduce yourself into it: it's always worked before, why shouldn't it go on that way? You had faith in yourself and so did the money people: that was the business they were in, to make loans. They'd always covered themselves five different ways though, naturally they were first of all careful about that.

I bought: and by the time things were at their height, I was in for close around a million dollars, more or less double where I'd been four years before. But the land prices stayed depressed and stayed going down: and I guess I still might even, if I'd known how to lay my hands on more money, gone on into one and one half million, maybe even two. You stop thinking real numbers any more. But as well wheat prices were falling too. Slowly the equity, that's the difference between what you own and what you owe, slowly that was all the time being eroded. The finance companies and the banks, they start getting uneasy about where they've put their money: and when you can't service the loans, pay the interest on them at least even if you're not reducing the outstanding amount, that's when they start getting worried even more.

Then the other things start to come in, like hail damage. You'll have one storm that in ten minutes ruins the whole year's crop. OK, every good farmer's got hail insurance, always has had. It's pretty damn expensive, but at least you don't see hundreds and thousands of dollars wiped out of existence in less time than it takes you to read up your policy. Only wait a minute, what did you do for the first time ever in your life this year? You'd had all these years paying out the big bucks in hail insurance and nothing ever happened: so this year you'd some pressing debts demanding immediate service, so for once you passed on the hail insurance. Then next year you can't really afford hail insurance anyway: so you think well last year was the first time I was ever caught, it can't happen two years after each other. Least this year it *will* be safe to give hail insurance a miss. What happens again? You got it: hail.

That's a simple example but it can be multiplied and multiplied, several times all within one individual's economy. He contracts for a high price for a custom cutter to come and get his harvest in for him one year, and that year the harvest's poor. The next year he decides the hell with it, he'll cut it himself. It's a good year, a big harvest: and too big for him to handle. So he's got no contract with a cutter, he's got to pay double what he should have to hire men and machinery to help him because everyone else is wanting them too: result, he either loses half his crop, or what it costs him to get it in takes away darn near all his profit. Or he doesn't spray for bugs: so he gets bugs. Or he has a bad year for wheat, so he decides next year he'll go into milo. He does: and the next year's good for wheat and bad for milo. OK so he's had enough by now of all the time choosing the wrong choice: the year after he reduces on crops and goes into cattle instead, because meat prices have got to rise, they can't go lower than they are now, everyone says that. What's the sure thing says they do go lower still? This guy goes into cattle, that's what. Guys who bad luck follows around step by step: they're who I was telling you about, right? Meet one.

You could say I overreached myself, overstretched myself, went bigger and bigger when I should have consolidated and stayed satisfied with what I'd got. You could say that, and some people in town do: but it's those same people who back in the good years were shaking me by the hand, telling me how good I was doing and how proud my father'd have been of me if he'd lived to see it, all that stuff. Your own home town, where everyone knows you and's known you from a child, where you were born and brought up: it can be the cruellest place to be in the world when you walk down the street and you know everyone's looking after you, everyone's seen you make all your mistakes, one by one. You feel you've got like some contagious disease or something sometimes. People won't stop to shake your hand in the street no more: they pass you by in a hurry like they was afraid of catching failure from you.

Once it all starts to go down hill, it gathers its own momentum: there's nothing you can do except stand by and watch. Your debts get so pressing you sell off some of your machinery to pay them: but that reduces some of your capability to produce and sell. You're driven to where you have to start to sell off pieces of your land: you bought it at a far higher price than you can get for it now, so your loan contract's high. That means you have to sell twice as much to get back half the price: and that reduces your holding, which is your collateral for future loans you need. That's the way it goes, down and down, on and on.

The one piece of luck I didn't have that might have helped me was that they didn't discover any oil, none at all anywhere under my land.

The line of the field where the big strikes were, that was about four miles south and three miles west, in a curve like that. Draw it on a map, and it looks like someone almost deliberately carefully cut me out. There's quite a few farmers I know, they don't have anything dramatic from their oil: just a small few thousand dollars a month in royalties coming in. And it's the difference between not having to worry about their grocery bills for their families, and farmers without any oil who've got to feed their families first out of what they produce, before they can start to even think about reducing their debts.

So what I have to do now is I can't work on my own farm any more: instead, I've got me a job driving a truck for a haulage company in town. It's one less mouth to feed out of farm income, one bit more we can pay towards the debts, one bit of sure money we know every week'll be there. It's not enough nor anything near it: but it decreases the rate my indebtedness is growing at. Only a part solution would be to sell up completely: what I'm worth wouldn't clear my debts even if I sold everything I'd got. Like I told you, 12 years ago I was in for one million: what I have now, everything put together, it wouldn't fetch more than one quarter of a million. I'd say I'd be fortunate even if it brought that: it'd leave me somewhere around another quarter million adrift, that I'd still have to find to free myself of debt.

It's no surprise news to the town I'm in this situation: I'm fairly well known as the example of the man who got it wrong. But what I don't like is when folk you thought might give you sympathy if nothing else, and recognise it just might have been them who were somehow fixed the same way: when such people come to you knowing the pressure you're under, and it's only to see if they can get a bargain off you in machinery or a parcel of land. They know you're so desperate for money you'll take almost any price. So they stop you on Main and ask you can they put a proposition. I used to think at first it was going to be an idea intended to help, that's the way they'd put it. But it's only one person it's going to help and it's them, not you: all it's going to do for you is drive you further each time into the ground.

My wife and the kids they know it's bad, my mother still lives with us too, there's no way of pretending to her. She's seen our land going smaller and smaller over her lifetime, right in front of her eyes. Like me, she knows nothing but farming: and we both see no way out. The children are old enough now for my wife to think she might finish her teaching studies and get the necessary certificates for her to work. But what I'll do as my contribution to the family's fortune I've wasted, I don't know, that's for sure: I truly don't know.

23 *Visitors from another planet*

Kelly Road from Washington DC

Her dark straight black hair was stylishly cut. She wore a cream linen jacket with a high buttoned collar, and a lavender skirt.

– Well that gives me a kind of a funny feeling you know, because it was only yesterday I was asking myself that very question, could I ever come back here to live? That's real weird isn't it?

Every year now the last 12 years, in the spring I bring the kids here to stay with their grandparents, then in the fall I come again with them and my husband for another maybe four weeks. They think it's great: all this space, going out to the reservoir every day fishing or water skiing, taking Grandpa's camper and going into the prairie a couple of nights. It's sure different from Washington for them, and for me and Tom too. The whole pace of life here's totally different, and the way people talk to you. I guess Ma and Pa have been telling folks weeks ahead that we're coming so they're looking out for us: but it still gives you a very pleasant surprise every time you walk down Main and they call out 'Hi there Kelly, how're you doing, good to see you.' And the kids too: they come running in the house saying, 'Heh Ma guess what, we were in Dorothy's having an ice-cream and six people in ten minutes came over where we were sitting and said hello to us. And Ma, they all knew our names!'

In Washington the traffic, the streets, the noise, the crowds, standing in line for everything, just the whole kind of frenetic energy you need to keep up every day to carry on your ordinary life: it all puts you in the frame of mind you live in. You've got to be at a certain time in a certain place always, whether it's picking up the kids from school, meeting someone you're working on a project with, going to friends for dinner, shopping and cooking for them coming to you. But you come back home to Bird and after a few days suddenly something inside you's unscrewed itself, wound down, gone completely relaxed: you think you're going to stay here for ever, you're never again going back to the big city. That's a wonderful feeling.

Yeah I said 'come back home to Bird' didn't I, and that's the way I do think of it, yeah. This year I'm 41, and except for the biannual visits I've been away now 20 years. Only it's still home, this is where I come from. Yet I don't suppose that truly I'm even really a Kansan any more. Like everyone else, it gets so it's more that I'm putting on an act. The other day I read an article in a magazine and I thought what it said was largely true, that everyone everywhere in America likes to pretend to be a character: the big slow drawling Texan, the sophisticated New Yorker, the plains farmer chewing on a toothpick, the West Coast intellectual. I know I do it myself: people in Washington ask me where I'm from, I say Kansas and straight off I'm dropping the speed of my speech a gear.

Then when I get back home to Washington again – and there, I've said that too haven't I, 'home to Washington' – and I'm immediately the quicker-talking much more sophisticated person, politically aware of things, and kind of slightly European international in flavour. I drop it when I'm here as much as I can, but sometimes I notice my parents give me a look when I say in passing what a heel Nixon was, or talk about the inexcusable slaughter in the Vietnam war. I used that phrase over supper when we were eating the other night, and my pa said to me reproachfully, 'Kelly, that wasn't inexcusable slaughter, they were all brave boys dying for their country.' I said, 'Pa, what I meant was the hundreds of thousands of women, children and the elderly Vietnamese who were killed right there in their own country.' Pa and Ma they just sighed and looked resigned, it wasn't worth talking about it even, I was a lost soul: I mean would you believe she even votes Democrat?

After High School here I went first to K State University, and that wasn't what you'd call a hotbed of radical thinking. But not long after, I went on to the University of Michigan in Ann Arbor, and that was entirely something else. All-night discussions: not just anti-war, but things too like sexual freedom, women's liberation, freedom of information, civil rights, no oppression for gays and lesbians, the whole bag. When you came back to Bird from there, you were a visitor from another planet. People'd never heard such ideas existed, never mind them openly expressed. That little girl of theirs they remembered running around the yard in pigtails or later being a pompom cheer leader with the school football team, now here she was coming out with ideas of her own. And they were anti-American ideas, they were commie ideas! She even said she'd got gays as friends, oh please Lord help us, help!

It's been like that ever since, and Tom and I's whole way of living, it's totally incomprehensible to them. Last year for example I said to Ma something one day in the kitchen when we were talking, something about a couple who are our best friends more or less: they come over to us twice a week, we go the same to them. She asked me what he did so I told her college lecturer, which he is: then not thinking and because it's what she does, I said she works for a black activist movement. Ma said 'Oh they're coloured people?' No I said, she was black but he was white. Ma thought for a little while to let that sink in, then doing her best to keep up the conversation she said, 'Do mixed marriages work better in Washington?' Mark the 'better'. I said, as I would have without thinking anything of it in Washington, 'Some do, some don't: you know, like non-mixed marriages, Washington or anywhere else.' And then I went on conversationally, still not thinking, 'But they're not married anyway.' I'm not exaggerating, honest to God, Ma went pale and walked out of the kitchen. A white man and a black woman, living together and not even married: and here was her daughter mentioning it like it was no more than a trip to the candy store.

But you know yes, I guess it's as much to do being a different generation to my parents as it is to living in such different places. I'm sure if they came and lived in Washington DC a while, I'm sure their ideas'd loosen up a little, they'd have to. But I don't think if I came back here to live for good mine'd harden up and regress to quite the same extent: I don't think your mind can go backwards that way.

I don't want to give you a complete picture of someone who finds small town attitudes suffocating, because I don't. There's a lot here that's good and valuable, and that I think in the cities we've lost. I'd say it's most of all to do with the nature of the people. In Bird, you've mostly had to work hard all your life, and where you've got to doesn't depend on how many strokes you've pulled or deals you've tricked, it depends on how you worked and were thrifty and how you and not anyone else handled your life. Washingtonians, you sometimes feel they're slightly arrogant in their pride in themselves: where in Kansas, the pride Kansans have is different, it's a pride in their roots and keeping in close to them. I've moved a long way from that, and every time I come back I'm aware that I'm now very very different: both to the person I was, and to the people I've come back for a while to be among. I'm no longer a pigtailed schoolgirl, with all the good implications and all the not so good ones as well.

But it doesn't stop me still having a profound feeling of deep love and respect for my parents and everyone else, for being the people who they are. I'm sure I'll never lose that: I hope not, I think I'd be a lesser person if I did. And most of all I want my children to grow up having it too.

Marilyn Ryman from LA

A small plump fair-haired woman in her forties: she wore a lime-green trouser suit and had green-framed glasses. She spoke rapidly in a crisply confident voice.

– I'm here just on a week's visit: my aunt, that's my pa's sister died, so I came for her funeral. My mother died a few years back now, Pa's by himself so I felt maybe he could use some support, you know how it is. I don't come back here a lot, we don't get on too good my pa and me to be truthful about it. He liked my first husband, a man from around these parts: but then we divorced and I went to California, you know the usual story. He didn't approve of my second husband, said it was him'd broken up the marriage and stops him seeing his grandchildren. They're both teenagers, they've made a duty visit or two but they don't like it a lot here, they're westerners and here's kind of a lot different for them from home.

They've never really known anything different from Los Angeles, the kids: for me, I spent half my life here and then the other half there, so yes I can compare one with the other even if I don't see Kansas too often now. My last time here was six years ago: and this is what I find the most striking thing about it, not the difference but that it's so much the same. It's incredible: I walk down Main Street and it's like you know, a museum almost, the same stores, the same everything. My pa says 'Old so and so, I'm afraid you won't see him no more, he's passed away': or 'You remember the leather goods store you used to go to so often, at the corner of Jefferson? Well don't take it hard Marilyn but they're closed down.' I don't even remember old so and so whoever he was, I don't recall the leather goods store. To me it all looks the same: there's still the stop light at the junction of Main and Washington, the clock by the bank still blinks at you the time then the temperature, the stores still open 8.00 am till 7.00 pm, folk still go out for picnics to Milton Reservoir or Lake Morrow: if you ask for a Teflon cake tray in East West Hardware you'll still be told you'll more likely find that kind of thing in Baxter. The only way I can put it is it's like seeing an old movie you've seen ten times already.

Coming back, what strikes more I suppose are the good things. You go out and you remember you didn't lock up at home, and you think well what the hell it doesn't matter: you're going to lock up your automobile and you realise you don't have to, things like that. Yesterday, I left my purse in Gover's, and when I got home I said to Pa I should call them. He said, 'You don't need, they've already called to say they've got it for you safe.' It didn't even have my address here in it, but everyone knew I was Pa's daughter so this was where I'd be. Everywhere, everyone, the people are all real friendly like they always were, even if the way they see it was I did take off 20 years ago with a guy who wasn't my husband.

The people where I live in LA, they're not unfriendly but they're much less direct with you somehow: they don't ask you how you are every time they see you, they don't have the same concern for you, they treat you altogether different somehow, especially if you're a woman. Let me try and explain it for you like this: in LA every guy you meet, you have to keep a part of you on guard. You know what he's got, I won't say he's got only in his mind, but always for sure in some part of his mind. Is there the chance of a screw here? Not all men, but it's there with most of them and it's a difference: here you don't have to watch out so much in conversation at road junctions, you know what I mean?

In LA, a few mischosen words and you're way along a track you didn't intend. 'So long Larry, see you,' and he comes right back with 'Sure, when?' But here it's 'Sure, see you' and that's it.

What else can I tell you strikes me when I think about it, oh yes sure I know, the blacks. LA, you've got a much bigger population mix. Have you been down at Nicodemus yet, the black settlement ten miles south and east of here? There's black people there and there's poverty there: I'm not saying it's been deliberately kept out of Bird, but you could sure stop here a long time and people'd not even mention it to you less you mention it first. Folk turn their faces in the other direction from something they'd sooner not think about, and they don't much like you talking about either. 'It's not really any concern of ours,' I think that's most people's attitude. Or starting even further back from there: 'We don't have no colour problem here because we don't have no coloureds. So long as the Nicodemus folk mostly stay where they are, what's the problem?'

And the local newspaper, that's another good guide. I was looking through it the other day, it's something hasn't changed a line in itself since I remember it as a child. The same people graduate from High School, the same people marry, the same people die. They're not the same people of course, but they sound like they are. Baseball and football, the school team's lost some and won some: people've got speeding tickets, the Chamber of Commerce has discussed this, there's been a function to raise money for that. You feel they have the stories all set up ready in type, and slot in new names when they need them. If something sad happens in the family of well-known folk in town, that's a misfortune everyone's asked to share: if it's something not very creditable, mention it but pass on quick and let's turn our faces and look some place else. If it happened here in Bird, gee that's worrying, whatever it is. If it happened 360 miles away in Kansas City Missouri, what's that to do with us? And if it happened in New York NY, gosh where's that?

Going alongside of that you get the attitudes, particularly regarding women, that when you hear them you think they've come out of the history books. Then it comes in on you, no they haven't, they really believe it. I asked a neighbour's wife the other day, she was a woman I was at High School with so she's the same age I am, I said had things turned out for her the way she hoped. First off I thought she was having me on, because she said 'Oh better than I hoped Marilyn, I've two lovely children and I've always been a good wife to my husband.' Then I thought, God she means it: and there was a little thing in there too for me you know, like she'd not gone off with some other guy, she'd stayed faithful right down the line. But even leaving that out, she was still telling me the way she looked at life. That was all there was: doing nothing, never being no different from anyone else, that was your goal and if you make it, well who wants more, and what more is there?

My mind's run on, I've said more than I meant, I think. They're basically good people here and I don't want to sound like I'm patronising them for it. I think America could do with a lot more of people like this, who don't have all these fancy liberal ideas you get nowadays: they know right's right and wrong's wrong, and they don't complicate it. They're good kind people, they help one another and if you're one of them, they help you. There's a lot to be said for that: never mind how you've gotten in a mess, we'll help you out of it, and the world could do with a lot more of that. I said earlier I thought sometimes they had their ideas and everything preserved in a museum: maybe they have in a lot of ways, but that's not to say it's all bad. Some of it's very good, museums preserve old things because they're valuable to us.

Michael Dormer from New York NY

A short chubby man, bald-headed and in his fifties, he wore an open-necked shirt and trousers patterned with a large check. He laughed often, talking in a deep rumbling voice.

– Oh sure, you'll find me out in the boondocks here quite a lot, three four times a year. This time it's just a short vacation for a few days to see my ma: I work on an in-house magazine and I'm doing a piece on a company in Lincoln Nebraska, which as you'll know isn't far away. Last time I was here was with my family, we came down for Thanksgiving. Dad died ten years back so Ma comes to New York State fairly often too, we keep pretty close in touch.

I left Bird now what, 30 years ago almost for the first time, but there hasn't been a year since when I haven't been back twice at least. When they were younger we used to bring the kids for vacations, now it's usually just my wife and me. Coming back regularly you don't notice the changes so much, not like you would if there'd been a long gap between when you were last here, know how I mean? I guess like a lot of other folk the thing I notice most is how much things haven't changed, more than how much they have. Some of that I like, it gives you a nice feeling there are still places you can be where you're treated like an individual human being and not just a faceless number.

Often it can be something very trivial, you know a small incident like the other day when I was driving on Main: I was looking through the windshield into the sun, I was trying to see what temperature the Bank's digital clock was giving. And you do that sometimes, you get the sun in your eyes and you miss seeing the stop light's against you. There was only one other driver in sight on the whole of Main: and he was the cop, in his vehicle waiting right there on the other side the junction. He couldn't miss seeing what I'd done: but so all he did was just wagged his finger at me as I went past. He knew it was me because of my NY tags. Later on in the morning I'm in Dorothy's having a coffee and he comes in for a coffee too, and comes over and sits right at my table. Well how are you Michael, how're things, how's your ma, how's the Big Apple, all the usual chit chat. In a while I ask him so where's my ticket for running the stop light, isn't that what he's giving me? Oh that, he says, you get the sun in your eyes there looking up for the clock, you can easy miss it, I've done it myself a time or two. It couldn't happen in New York: and I don't mean at a busy intersection, I mean not anywhere at all. Running a light means only one thing to a policeman: you're a fugitive in a hurry to get away, and he'll have you out with your hands up and search you for your piece before you've time to draw breath.

Small sorts of things like that, they're what's good about Bird. Of course there are other sorts of small things not so good, that could irritate you too if you let them. The number one to me would be the way people who've got religion push it at you. Like some folk who live just over the other side of the street there: they're good friends with my ma, and when Peggy and I come to stay, or like now when I'm here a few days on my own, they always invite us in for a meal with them one evening. Very generous, very hospitable: they always take a lot of trouble with the preparations and everything. But they're very devoutly religious people, or way over the top on piousness, depends on your viewpoint. Peggy and I are both agnostics: they must know that by now after all these years. But that doesn't stop them when we're sitting around the table before we eat, we must all join hands and bow our heads while the husband says grace. And such a grace, you wouldn't believe it: not just thanks God for food to come and eaten in the past, but a kind of a shopping list for Him to remember to tick off. Give Peg and me a safe journey back home when we go, keep an eye out for our kids while we're not there to do it ourselves, it goes on ten minutes or more. I think out of politeness to us they could cut it to their own essentials: but the way they put it over when we're there, such earnestness and such length, it's like somehow they hope some of the fallout from their fervour will irradiate us back into religion.

Maybe that's exactly what they do hope: because you couldn't hardly say the religion you get in these parts has what you'd call a high intellectual content. Back home we have Catholic friends, friends who are orthodox Jews, converts to Buddhism, even a few ordinary straightforward Christians in there somewhere too, if that's not a contradiction in terms. More often than not you'd spend a whole evening with all of them together, and not know at the end of it which one of them was what. Here though that kind of a conversation couldn't happen, or not with most people it couldn't. They'd all be too anxious not to let the chance pass to tell you how important their own particular religion is to them.

But you have to remind yourself though that those people are only a small number: they're a minority in this community, like pretty well anywhere else. A few years ago now, just for my own amusement through a summer vacation we took here, I asked each of the church ministers separately how many church members they had. They all gave those kind of estimates called 'guesstimates': and it'll no more surprise you than it did me to learn the totals they gave me added up to over the entire population of Bird. They don't have here a bigger percentage of regular churchgoers than most other places: say the usual between 10 and at most 20 per cent. Hearing all the talk goes on though, you'd get the impression anybody not going to church was an oddball old loner.

I guess talking like this it sounds sort of strange to say how much I like coming back here and I hope to keep on coming back. That Robert Browning poem, 'God's in His Heaven, All's right with the world': I often think that's the attitude of most of the folk who live here. And when I'm here too, because everything's so just as it should be, I get around to feeling the same way myself. There's things here people never worry about for the simple reason they never think about them in the first place. Like the idea of America being invaded: sure, they get a scare about Russia from watching too much television once in a while, but deep down in their psyche they don't really believe it could ever happen. America be invaded? How could it be? It never has been, it'd be against the laws of nature. The fact that it *has* been, you say that to them and you see the look of blank incomprehension on their faces. You go on, you say oh yes it's been invaded near a hundred times: by the Spaniards, the Portuguese, the French, the British, to name only a handful. And you you say, you're invaders yourself, least your ancestors from Europe were. That kind of idea's beyond them altogether, they won't think about it: they look at me and say to themselves this is one of those smartass easterners talking.

That said though, I'll still say this too: home is where the heart is, and this is my home town: I love it and wouldn't want no other. There's bad goodness and there's good goodness, and this is that one. I don't want to see it change, I want for it to stay like it is, for me to keep coming back to it.

Christine Peach from Houston Texas

Slim and lightweight, under five feet in height, she roved round the barely-furnished room while she talked, pausing to sit for a few brief moments occasionally on the bench at the big wooden table. Her short black hair was a mass of curls, and she had deep dark smiling eyes. Bare-footed, she wore scarlet jeans and a black T-shirt.

– I never miss out on my annual trip here to Nicodemus, it's become so important to me for so many different reasons. Dinah loans me this old house of hers she doesn't use any more for just so long as I like: when I come, I've left all the world far behind me and it's great. I spend six weeks all at once or more if I can take the time. I have my camp bed through there, there's no phone, no television, I see no newspapers and I write no letters, and I go work in the fields with the men or read books, and it's wonderful. I'm a new person when I go back: I've done this every year for six years and I hope I'll be doing it for the rest of my life.

I'm 34, a history professor at the University of Texas, and I'm in charge of a small team of students and graduates who're working on an extended project about the architecture and history of this and other Negro settlements. When we first came six years back I felt it was very important to try and get the people who live here to feel they weren't just objects for study to us: Nicodemus has had more than its share of that, people coming and looking and then going away again. I was enormously lucky, because when I came I don't know how or why, but I seemed to rediscover part of myself here. It was almost like members of whole families were my own folk. In the same way a lot of them seemed to take to me too, like I was a daughter or niece of theirs: they soon began to ask me to stay with them in their homes. I do that a lot now, as well as stop here on my own according to how I feel.

I'm at university and educationally I've done well in their eyes. But that's no big deal any more, they've gotten past all that. Instead they tell me I'm skinny and I need feeding up, and it's that sort of nice inner-family relationship. It goes on throughout the year, while I'm away I write regularly to them and them to me: and if I have the chance of a break for a couple of days I bring my husband up, it's that kind of continuous thing. At the beginning there was some small degree of resistance to me as a person in a few houses: to some families it still hasn't gone completely. It won't ever, because to their way of thinking I've chosen to make my way in white man's America and not stay in theirs. That's how they'd feel about anyone who was their own daughter and chose to live some place else rather than stay here and marry a Nicodemus man and live and work on a farm. It's a deep-seated feeling, and not one can be devalued just as old-fashioned.

The other side to it is many black people, most black people probably, like to see a black person succeeding in the white man's world. It pleases them I'm in a position where I have white students: a black woman teaching white men things, think of that. That kind of attitude exists quite strongly in some people. It's very complex, this interplay between black and white. Fear comes into it a lot on both sides, and I don't see it being eradicated for a long while. But another problem is how much a lot of blacks want white approval and acceptance, and how important it is to them. It limits the way they can behave: those who've made it and achieved a degree of upward social mobility, they're often the ones who're the most scornful and look down the most on other blacks who haven't had the same success. They say 'Integration can happen, look at me. Why don't you lazy bums work like I did for it?' They conveniently overlook the fact that for a lot of black people, you can work your tail off the whole of your life and still stay poor.

One of the things now and again I do miss here is the chance to talk along these lines. I have to remind myself that for me the point of my coming back here regularly is to relax, recharge myself by rediscovering the simple things in life. Live a while in a world that's entirely peaceful and calm, where every day ends with the gentle setting of the sun and a slow drift into sleep. But I know in some respects it's a cop out: I've stepped into a society that's a deliberate cop out itself from most of the rest of America. They've made it into a calm peaceful haven for themselves: and I'm not sure they'd be too enthusiastic about some woman from university coming preaching dissatisfaction and sounding like she was trying to stir up revolution. There are some radicals here, one or two, and I'll be happy to introduce you: but of course you'll meet some too who'll play the jovial white-haired old negro for you, because they'll think that's what you want.

I don't know how you've found the people in Bird with regard to Nicodemus: a white experience of whites can't be the same as a black person's, but for myself when I go there, maybe once or twice in a week to the library, I feel there's a very definite, almost so positive kind of indifference you almost touch it. We may be only ten miles apart along the road, but very few people there seem to have any sense we're neighbouring communities. Nicodemus could be 1,000 miles and 1,000 years away for all the thought they give it.

In a way I find that infinitely depressing. Bird turns its back on Nicodemus and pretends it isn't there and it isn't happening, the same as it does with a lot of other things. That's small town typical, I guess. And Nicodemus turns its back on Bird too, you have to say that, here's just as much an inward-looking community. Only if you happen to believe like I do, that the only solution to the problem of race relations is complete integration – the opposite being complete and total separation, which like in South Africa becomes total dynamite – well then it's hard to see how and when and where this coming together is to occur. There's not a sign even the thought of it exists, not in a place like Bird: and how you'd begin with it is not something you can even see starting to happen. Now that *is* depressing: in the heartland of America there's no sign of progress at all in such a vitally important area of human relationships.

24 *Down at Nicodemus*

Lucas Barton

He sat in a rocking chair on the little veranda round the back of his small wooden house, fanning himself against the heat with a folded newspaper: he had thick curly snow-white hair and a trimmed white beard, and a rolling bass voice.

– Sure I'll tell you, I'll be glad to: not many folks know the truth of it and they'll give you fairy tales rather than admit they don't know the truth. But this that I'm going to tell you, now this is the truth, the facts of history as they say. Our township here, Nicodemus, is named after a man: a man who's in the Bible with his name and everything all about him there, for everyone to read. This Nicodemus, he was one of Jesus's disciples, and from all I've heard of him, one of Jesus's own favourites. He was an educated man and he could read many languages, and turn them into other languages: he was what they call a translator, and he devoted all his life to translating for God. He translated the books of the Bible, every one into many different languages, so that all men could read them.

A translator you see, now he is someone who stands between one person and another who cannot speak the same language, and he makes it possible for there to be understanding between them. So that is the true story of who Nicodemus was, and this township was named after him because of the inhabitants of it, who also translate for God. They take their position between God and man, and they make it possible for us to understand Him, and Him to understand us. Not many people know the history: but they are the true facts of it, and I was told them by my granddaddy when I was a little boy, and I'm glad to pass them on to you because you had the interest to ask.

Now as for myself, I'm 82 years of age, and I was born right here in this little wooden house. My mammy and my daddy they had 11 children, and they bore and raised them here every single one. My granddaddy, he was born in Kentucky and he was a slave, but after the great American Civil War them slaves they were turned loose to run like rats wherever they chose. Him and his brothers, they didn't know whether to go north south east or west: but then this man came, and he told them if they came to Kansas, they could homestead. That meant they bought a piece of land for five dollars and they lived on it and farmed it for one year, and then it was theirs. That's what they did, and you can still see their land there just north of the highway.

My daddy, he stayed here the whole of his life because he hoped one day that piece of land would be his: and so did I, I stayed here all my life with the same hope too. But sometime around what they called the depression years, things got so bad we had to sell our land to the big landowners in Kansas City Missoura: and ever since then, all we've had was the renting of it to work on but never again to own. That landowner he was a white man, of course he was: and in that story is the story of how things have always been between the white man and the black man.

I'm a hard-working man and I have been all my life: I'm as poor as Job's turkey but so long as I can work I'm happy, and I've four of my children living here in Demus working the land. I go along every day I can do and I work with them too. One of my boys he works the land I was telling you of, another one works for a farmer in Conway City: and my two daughters, they're married to men who make their living out of farming too. We've had times that were hard, and times that were very very hard: but we're none of us educated people so we'll never be anything but poor. I had my beautiful wife Laura who died seven years back, and she was a wonderful partner to me: a hard-working woman who saw to it her children were fed and looked after, even if it meant we had to go without sometimes ourselves. She was so good a woman the Lord took her away before me to join Him in Heaven, because He was impatient for to have her there. He's letting me stay on here on this earth a little longer, but when the time comes that Laura's getting lonesome and tells Him she wants me up there beside her, she has a persuasive way with her and I'm sure the Lord'll do for her what she asks.

The only thing I've not done in my whole life I'd have liked to have done, is that I'd like to have done some travel. Well, the place I'd like to have gone to most is either to Brazil, or in Europe to Spain. The reason for that is because my mammy once told me she was of Spanish origin somewhere way back down the line. So I'm not really a black man, I'm what they call an Hispanic, and that's what I'd like to go to one of them countries for, to look at the people there and see if I belonged with them. All the way on from the very early part of my life, I've always known there was something about me that was that little bit different from most black people: it's that I've always been a little bit quicker than most others, for example in mental things. At the country school I went to, in such things as reading and writing and arithmetic, I could understand faster than other black children could: and I've kept those mental facilities longer than most black people do. There's black men in Nicodemus who're 20 years and more younger than I am, and they can't hardly talk two sentences together any more. But I've kept my teeth and I've kept my brains, and that must mean that in some way I've been specially favoured I feel. It's my Hispanic origin: I don't go around boasting of it and it's not a thing I talk much to people about, but it's there.

I guess I'm too old to think of travel though now at my age. I'd like to have been able to say least I'd been one time out of Kansas, but I can't. On the television you see some mighty fine places: you say to yourself you'd like to visit them if you had the money you could afford it. But I think if you think too much like that, after a while you only make yourself unhappy. So I remind myself of all the blessings I've had in my life, and all the happinesses the Good Lord has showered on me: my mammy and daddy, our good home, my pretty wife Laura, our children, everything. It's been more than any one man deserves: but like it tells you in the Bible, if you're a servant to God and carry out His will and don't complain, He'll be storing up treasure for you in Heaven, and when you go to Him there, you'll get your reward.

Willard Murphy

A small smiling man, wearing a check shirt and dungarees, he sat in his kitchen with his bedroom-slippered feet on the table, gulping a can of iced beer and smoking a cheroot.

– Glad to have you visit with me: I knew last week you'd been visiting with Lucas, and wondering what talk he'd been giving you, all those wild tales and romantic notions. Did he tell you his account how Nicodemus came to be named? Yes, he tells that to anyone who'll listen, he's told it so many times I think he now believes it himself he does. You want to know the true version? Well I'll tell it you, it's very simply this: Nicodemus is named after an early slave settler who came here at the finish of the Civil War. Lots of those negro people, they were given those old Bible names of that sort by their owners. There's no more to the story than that, take my word. Still, I don't want to speak too harsh of Lucas: he's an old man who likes to pass his days dreaming, and talking with the Lord. But you know, sometimes I think His patience must be sorely tried: when He hears the voice I think of Him saying under His breath, 'Lucas, Lucas, give me a rest, go talk at someone else.'

Perhaps I'll be that way myself when I'm more than 80: but that's a good while yet, up to now I've only got to 65. I'm no more an educated man than Lucas is if you talk about book learning: but I've had a different sort of life from him, and seen more of things. I came here from Louisiana: I was born in Mississippi in the first place, but there was always poverty in our family and I left my home like the rest of my brothers and sisters, just as soon as I was old enough to go find myself work. When I was 15 I went to Chicago in a meat packing factory: then to North Carolina, South Carolina, Georgia, Alabama and across home to Mississippi again. If you was a strong black young man you could always find someone that'd give you work, and that's what I did. Never made a fortune for myself but I wasn't looking to do that, only to have enough to eat and keep moving, and wherever I was, my aim was to have myself a good time. And that I did I can tell you, all through my life I've had good times aplenty, I certainly have.

When the World War Two began, I knew I'd be one of those who'd be drafted so I don't wait till they came for me, I went to them. I could offer certain skills I'd picked up like a knowledge of automobiles, and before long found myself chauffeur to a General, which was a very fine job. He was one of those who carried on the war from his desk in the Pentagon most of the time, and was very very careful not to do anything foolish like letting himself be sent either across the Atlantic or across the Pacific near where any fighting was. He was an able man, and a wise one was that General: and I was happy to chauffeur him anywhere he wanted to go across the continent of North America. It was an arrangement suited me like it suited him. Doing that sort of an occupation you know, that meant I did, I continued to have some very good times.

After that, after the war was over, let's see now what did I do then? Oh yes, I recall: I got married. I met a very nice black lady who had a restaurant in Santa Monica and she had money and all the things that you can get with it. I made her happy, and she made me happy, because with all the money she had there was no need for me to work. But these good things they all come to an end, so after a while the time came again for me to move on. This was the west coast where I was this time: I stayed in California a while, I've never liked the big cities too much. There's always too many people there who want to take your money off you. I worked mostly on the fruit farms, and that was an ideal existence, with many more happy times. One of my daughters, by then she'd come to live here in Nicodemus: she was married to a man whose family's roots was here, and she came with him to farm. One day I came to visit her: and that was how I met the lady who was my wife. She had this very same house here, one of the biggest in the township: and she was a widow who was lonely, and was glad a man should come courting her as I did. It's 15 years now since we married and we were very happy for eight of those years until she died. And I'm speaking the simple truth when I say this now that I do: if that lady hadn't died when she did, you know I think it's possible she would have been and remained the very last woman in my life.

There have been a number, oh yes there certainly have. That's nothing to be ashamed of for a man. Some of them I married and some of them I did not, but we lived together happily as if we were man and wife. I've never objected to marrying a woman if that's what she wanted and I was free to do so at the time. It's a difficult question for me to answer as to how many exactly there've been: but if we're talking of wives official, or those who've lived with me in the position of wives, I would say the number would be in the region of a total of ten possibly, or perhaps a little more. But at the most no more than say perhaps 15 or 16. There were others too that were shorter and more trivial encounters, but I've never been a man greatly attracted to that kind of living. I prefer a more permanent way, and I've always been happy to continue it until the time to move on.

And children yes certainly as well: there were many of those, and they were always a great joy. More wives and children than I can exactly remember you know. There are nine children of mine I know of who come regularly to visit their daddy, and always I'm very happy to see them. Five of them live here in Nicodemus, three girls and two boys: they've all grown into fine people, four of them now married themselves. And there's not one of them whose home I'm not welcome in: now that's a proud thing for a man to be able to say, in these times when you're hearing so much everywhere about the breaking up of families and divorce.

I thank the Lord for giving me such a good and happy life. All my pleasures have been the simple delights of loving and laughing, most particularly with the ladies: I've had so many good times, I really have, times beyond number most every place I've been.

Luther Brown

A tall powerfully built man in his forties, he sat on the steps at the back of his house at the end of the day, waiting to eat the meal someone inside the house was making. His working clothes were ragged and dusty and his voice was tired. Chewing tobacco, from time to time he paused to think and spit on the ground.

– I was born here: not in this house no, in that old falling down one the other side of the street here. My mom and dad, they'd been Nicodemus people all their lives and they had seven children and I was their eldest. Two of my brothers died when they was kids, two of my sisters went away, and the other two got married and still live here, one at the corner there and the other one in the house by the church.

If you're born in Nicodemus you can stay here and stay poor, or you can go away and try to get less poor. That was what I did: I went to High School in Deerfield, but I didn't graduate from there: I left when I was 15 because a man offered me a job at a garage. I thought it was a chance for me to break away from working on a farm all my life like my father had done, and staying poor all my life the way he'd been too.

There was a black girl at school, and her and me we set up home together and then when we was both 18 we got married. She had a job, she was a bright girl, a clerk in a store in Baxter. So we had a time at first when we had money and rented our own house and everything. We weren't rich folk, but it looked like I'd done the right thing moving away from Nicodemus. But I guess when you're a country boy from some little place like this, to go live in somewhere like Baxter isn't always too good an idea. There's young men there in the big town who are the same age as you, and they like to show you how clever they are. So if you're young and impressionable like I was, you can soon find yourself imitating their ways and wanting to be just like they are. That's what I did: and before long I was finding myself in all kinds of trouble. I never did no big crimes, we weren't the Chicago black gangs roaming the streets robbing and terrorising people, nothing of that sort: but we was breaking into houses and stealing television sets, joy-riding in stolen cars, drinking and smoking and dumb little crimes like that.

I wasn't one of the successful ones except in one thing, that I never got caught for anything serious. The result was I was always the one got fined or put to the Probation Officer. The other result was I lost my job: and if you don't have no work to earn money to pay your fines with, then there's only one way you can get some, and that's go and do more crime. So that's what I did. The girl who was my wife, she wasn't in to that kind of living at all, and she didn't like it that I was: she had a family who was interfering, her mother was all the time telling her I was a no good sort of a man and she should leave me, and that's what she eventually did.

Things was shaping up pretty bad for me then. This was 20 years ago now, when I was 25. I was lucky I hadn't started me on a regular crime and prison career, that's about the true situation regarding that. But then just when it seemed my life was going that way for evermore, the Lord or whoever it was stepped in and took a hand. I'd not be sitting here on this stoop tonight talking with you if they hadn't, that's one thing that's sure. But what happened was I met a tall fine handsome-looking woman two years older than me: she had three small children of her own, and her husband who'd deserted her had gone off some place with a young girl. So there she was on her own and not knowing what to do.

So her and me, we set down and we had a talk, and we agreed we'd see if we could do something by way of living together. Me working to provide for her children, and her making us all a home. I told her she wasn't getting no great competition prize with someone like me: I told her everything I'd done, the crimes I'd been caught for and those that I hadn't, the fines and the probations, everything. And how it seemed before long I'd end up in a prison. She said so long as all that was past for me, then she'd look at it the same way too: we made it a promise to each other, that however poor we was and however hard it was, we'd never take anything belonging to someone else but only have what was ours that we had by right.

One of my sisters that was in Nicodemus here, she told us of this house we could have for next to nothing: the man who it had belonged to had died, his wife had gone back to Kentucky and she was more concerned not to have it to look after than to get a price for it. So we borrowed some money and bought it and we moved in, and we've been here ever since. From that day to this I've never had a good job with good money ever: but from that day to this also, I've never had one single day I was out of work. Each week we always had enough to get by on, or a little less, even if we never had a whole lot more. But the children have been fed and they've growed up into three fine young ladies: one of them's married and gone to California, one of them's married and living in Conway City, and the youngest one you can hear now cooking in the kitchen there for our supper.

There's one big sadness though: it's like there always is in life for everyone, joy and sorrow. Two years ago now my wife was taken into hospital with cancer: they found it too late to do anything that could save her, and she died two weeks to the day from when they took her in. Only still a young woman, 45 years of age: and if you'd have seen her she looked as young and as well as the day I first met her. It takes a time for a person to find a purpose in life again when someone's taken away as sudden as that. It's difficult to see how I will, especially when our baby here goes off as she will in her time. I'll go on working because that's the only way of life I know now, but I couldn't tell you at my age who it'd be for. I come home here after a day's work on a warm summer's evening like this, and it seems living's got no purpose to it any more. Maybe the Lord'll take a hand again, and step in again to show me a way.

Lucy Farmer

She sat in her darkened kitchen, the curtains drawn against the blistering heat keeping out even a hint of air and making the small shabby room inert and stifling. Her hair was ringleted and plaited tightly over her head.

– Sure mighty hot isn't it, do you have it like this where you come from in England? I imagine it there as always rain rain rain. Well you know it's nice having you visit with me, I don't recall in all my life I've ever had a white man sitting in my kitchen before. My daddy over the street there Mr Willard Murphy, he said he'd talked with you some. He's a very romantic man for the ladies you know: but the nice thing is as I've always seen it, most of his ladies they've all seemed to like him and there's never been no hard feelings for him after he's moved on. He never wanted to be tied too closely down, my daddy didn't: and his last wife, she was a very nice lady and all of us children, we were mighty sad about it when she died, because him and her they were getting along together just fine.

I was born in Mississippi but I didn't like living with my mother because of all her different men she had around the home all the time: so just as soon as I could I wrote to one of my sisters in California and went to live with her instead. Then I came here to Nicodemus to live with my aunt who was my daddy's sister, and here's where I've been ever since. I came when I was 19 and I married a Nicodemus man, and now I'm 44: we have three children and it should have been five, only two of them died. My husband too, he died: he was killed in a farm accident six years back, and since then times have been very hard. He wasn't a rich man but he was a good man, and if it wasn't for my sisters and their husbands who are living here, I don't know where we'd have turned next for our food. But we all help one another, that's what the Good Lord put us on earth for. Our daddy may not have been a good man in some people's eyes because of not always providing for all his children, but the one thing he taught us was we should all always help one another when there was need.

I go three days a week to Baxter where I work, and the money I earn there makes the difference for us between having to beg and having to borrow. The job I have is in a home for old people there, in the kitchens helping to prepare their meals: and I eat my food there, near enough sufficient for a whole week, and if there's something left over like some potatoes or meat, they let me bring that home. I do some cleaning there too, like pushing a mop around, and some washing of bed sheets for them as well. It's work that has to be done, and everyone's friendly enough: everyone who's one of those running the home that is, but some of the old people who live there, they're not that way at all. Because they pay all that money for it, they treat you like you wasn't a person but a slave around the place, and if you so much as give a cross look in their direction they complain of you. One old woman once she said to my face that I was a wicked black devil and I'd stolen money from her purse: then when it was found again she didn't say nothing to me that she was sorry for calling me that, only that she wasn't going to ever have her purse anywhere but in her hand.

Or another time there was an old man and he said I was a prostitute. He said all black women were prostitutes, and he didn't want me around him or touching the plate I was serving him his food on or anything. In front of everyone there in the dining room: and then the next day after that, when I'm on my own in the corridor he comes behind me and tries to grab hold of me, and asks me will I come to his bedroom with him if he gives me some money? I guess you've got to think some of those people there, they're old and feeble and their brains have gone and you should feel sorry for them. But I don't always do that sometimes, sometimes I get mad. I'd like it if I were able to go to the lady in charge and tell her I don't have to take that sort of treatment, I'll go work some place else. But I do have to take it: someone who's not got no education like me, they have to work and be thankful they have any kind of a job.

You'll hear tell these days there ain't prejudice against black people just on account of them being black, there ain't that kind of prejudice anywhere no more: because it's illegal and against the law. But you can't pass laws that are going to stop people being rude to you, and saying things against the colour of your skin like they do. My children, they all go to school in Deerfield, and they sure get plenty things said to them there. There's teachers who tell them they're lazy and slow with their work and say that's how all blacks are, and things of that sort. I tell them pay no attention and work hard, so that one day they'll maybe be like that Mrs Peach lady: they'll be the ones who're clever and they'll have white pupils who have to set listening to them.

It's sad there's all this prejudice still, one person not liking another and only for because they're black. I don't know why all people can't live on earth together friendly like the Lord said they should. Perhaps it'll come, but it needs for us to have another president one day like President Kennedy to pass laws to help black people and who'll unite people together. It was a very sad day when he died, for all people, not just the ones who were black.

My my, it's mighty hot today isn't it? When I have my two days here that I don't go to Baxter to work, I'm at my happiest: or when I come home in the evening too, and I can forget everything except my babies. It's leisurely and peaceful and calm here in my little house, and I think I've had good fortune to be here. We bought it with my sister, and I'm still paying my share of it to her. My husband and me, I'll tell you, we didn't have a very happy married life together: if you're a woman, you have to accept the Lord made men different in their ways and they're never going to change. My daddy was one who wanted more than one woman alone could give him: and my husband, he was about the same. When I was a young girl in Mississippi and lonely, without any friends and unhappy with my ma, there was many a time I laid on my bed, and all I did was cried and cried. I think sometimes if you have unhappiness as a child, that helps prepare you for what life does to you later: you're always going to have unhappiness and perhaps more still, but you know you've had it before and you've survived. That gives you a kind of comfort somehow, and a strength. It does for me.

Gina Dunne

– You're the man from England who's been coming to Nicodemus to visit with folk, right? I've seen you around. When I asked Christine about you, she told me who you were and everything. You going to come in my house and visit with me?

A big woman in a sleeveless blue dress, with plump arms and legs and a round face, she wore her long black hair loose and flowing down to her shoulders.

– I was named for a film star, I think she was Spanish or something: my mammy told me she was the most beautiful lady there'd ever been. I guess she thought if she gave me the name I might grow up to be beautiful like she was too. Well, she'd sure have been disappointed at the result. I think my mammy was some kind of crazy woman with her ideas: she had ten children living, and most of them by different men. From very little I went to live with my grandma in Tallahassee: she died when I was five, then I was sent to Georgia to live with my aunt, then to another aunt, and it went on all the time like that. When you're a child you soon pick up the idea you're an embarrassment and a nuisance to people, being passed on from one to another that way. I don't think I was troublesome or anything, it was just no one wanted me or knew what to do with me.

It stayed that way till I was 14, so that meant I never had much schooling. I was just going from one place to another, never long enough in one place to settle down to learning. And with no one to take much interest in me, as to whether I was in school one day or I wasn't. A young girl wandering around most the time, I had plenty of education though in other ways. Sometimes when I think about it, a lot of it I would have done better without. I was a pretty girl I guess, and I soon found out about men: I don't mean boys my own age, but men much older than me, how to get things from them in exchange for what they wanted. This'll make me sound hard I guess, and I guess I was. Was more than am: the older I've been, the more tolerant my way of looking at things seems to have grown. Now I'm too much the other way I think sometimes.

Today I'm a woman of 35. Twice married, once divorced and once separated. I have five children of my own, and one who's lived with me as though she was mine in the first place, since she was a baby a few weeks old. The eldest's my daughter April who's 17 and at High School, going on to college: and the youngest's my baby boy Ben who's five. I live here in this two-room house in Nicodemus where I came with my second husband ten years ago: he's a Nicodemus man and he brought us here to farm. Then he took up with a lady he liked more than hogs and chickens and children, and went off with her to live in Baxter instead. Sometimes he sends some money for his family and sometimes he doesn't.

I'll not say he's a bad man and I'll not say he's a foolish one: he's neither of those, and while we were together we had some happy times. When he married me I'd three children already, so I brought him nothing much but a burden of domestic things. I'd have lived with him without marriage if that's what he wanted, but it was his choice to be wed. There's nothing I'd say about him though that would compare him disfavourably to my first husband: now he was a cruelly violent man who beat his children, and most of all when he was drunk which was often he beat me. We were in fear of him all of us, we truly were.

Well those days they're gone: the bad times with my first husband and the better ones with my second. I wouldn't say I'm an unhappy woman though, that wouldn't be true at all: I've discovered there are other things in life than being a domestic servant and or a mistress to a man. I'd like it if I could say I discovered them before, I mean earlier in my life: if I'd done that I might have made more of it while I had the chance, insofar as educational things. I'd have read books, I'd have studied, I'd have travelled, I mean I really would. You know something, I've never in my life been out of Kansas, not even to Kansas City Missoura.

The place I'd wished I'd been to most in the world, oh that's easy, that's Paris, France. The reason is I read an article in one of those magazines, and it said Paris is where there's a group of women who call themselves the World Peace Corps. I'd have liked to have gone to join them and fight for peace in the world. It said how they go to different countries wherever there's war, and they work in schools and health clinics and things of that sort: they try to bring together the people who are fighting, and show them the way to live together in peace. That seems to me a fine fine thing: I wouldn't be able to teach people too many things like how to read and write, but I could sure work and sew blankets and feed children and things of that sort.

Us black people you know, we had a great leader of our own once upon a time for peace. You'll have heard tell of him, he was called the Reverend Martin Luther King and he was a perfect man: he went up on the mountain and he came down and preached to people and he told them he'd had a dream. His dream was that all people, black and white, they could live together in peace: they didn't all the time have to be fighting one another, he said to them it was wrong to do that and to kill other people so you could get what you want. He was a great man, a man of peace, what they call a pacifist: and he said there was no power on earth could resist the power of peace. I'd like to have gone there to Paris where those women are, all of different races and colours and who're keeping his memory alive: and I'd like to have said, 'Sisters, can I join you, can I work with you wherever you want me or can use me in the world, please let me do what I can for peace.' It's the biggest thing in the world, that all its peoples should live together without war: else one day I'm sure, we're all of us going to blow ourselves and our children to Kingdom Come.

Well like I said, I get these ideas from books and magazines. Every week me and the lady who lives over the street there, we're around the same age together and we're both of us on our own without our husbands: we go to Conway City to do our shopping, or to Bird. We don't go just in the supermarket to spend our food stamps, we go to the library too for an hour while we're waiting for the bus to bring us back. We look at books, we look at magazines, and we look at newspapers: her in one section and me in another, and then on our way home we tell each other what we've read. I wasn't going to say nothing to you about this part, but in Conway City there's an organisation for black women just started that's to do with what they call raising women's consciousness: and my friend and me, we're going to find out what we can and try to join it. That's sure a long way to go and a lot of things to do here in a place like Nicodemus, because everyone's so old. But we shall try.

It's been real nice visiting with you and talking about these things, and I hope you don't think I've been too pushing at you with my ideas though.

April Dunne

A small thin girl with wire-framed glasses: she sat on the edge of the old sagging settee, leaning forward with her hands hanging between her legs. She spoke in a low voice.

– Nicodemus is OK I guess, but when I graduate from High School at Conway City next year when I'm 18, I'd like to go to live in Baxter a while or some place like that. If my grades are good enough I'll maybe go to college but you need money for that, and that's something we don't have. Ma says we might go see one of my uncles in Arizona who she says is a kind man who's got money, and he might lend us some for me. But I don't know, you do something like that and you end up worse off than you began: it means if you want to leave college and get married or something you're kind of letting the person down who loaned the money for you to go there.

When the time comes I'll go see my granny over the road and ask her what she thinks. That's Mrs Dinah Johnson: she's not my real granny but everyone calls her that because she's like she's a granny to every young person in Nicodemus there is. I told her once I hated math at school so she used to give me extra lessons in it. She helped me a lot: only I'm sure she didn't have a great amount of schooling herself. Where she learned from how to do it I sure don't know, but she's pretty smart at figuring though.

My school's OK but some of the teachers there, they have a down on black kids: it makes it sometimes you feel you can't get away from it soon enough when you grow up. There's one they call your careers adviser: and every black girl goes to talk with her, she tells them all exactly the selfsame thing. She says there's lots of good jobs for smart black girls in supermarkets and restaurants if they work hard: she says the trouble with black folk is that they most of them don't want to work, so anyone who does they can do OK. White girls, she encourages them to think of going to college and learning for a proper career: but I've talked with my friends, and I've not known one black girl she's ever said to anything like that. If that's how she feels about black people I don't think she should be the person to advise them.

There's prejudice in school for sure, just like there is anywhere else.

There's around 20 black girls in our school and the same boys: altogether there's 550 pupils, so there's a lot more whites. The head teacher we've got now, he's OK: but the one before him, if you did something wrong and the teacher told him about you, he'd say things like you were letting all black people down because of how you were behaving. That used to make you feel real bad, because if you're a school kid and your head teacher tells you something, you think it must be true. But you get prejudice worse from the other pupils, specially where it's the boys. Right now there's a white boy there, he's a senior, and he's always telling everyone how he's scored with every one of the black girls there is in the school. It's not true and he gives black girls a bad reputation. He's all the time boasting, and then some of the other white boys come whispering behind your back and calling you black trash. I'd never go with no white boy myself ever, not now or the rest of my life. I think the whites should stay with the whites and the blacks with the blacks. There was a girl at our school and she and her white boy friend, they loved each other and wanted to get married: but the boy's ma and pa, they said they weren't having their son marrying no black girl, and they wouldn't let him take her to their home not once.

I don't see how white people and black people are ever going to get together in a country like America, where those who are white have all the things and keep them for themselves. I don't know what it's like in other places because I've not been nowhere else, but you see programmes on television about other countries: and wherever you look, you see black people who are poor. I read in a book from the library once there was an idea some black leaders had, that they ought to set up in America one state which was just for black people, so all those who wanted to could go there to live and that'd be their own negro state. Something like they have in that country Israel, where it was given to the Jews as their own land after they'd wandered the earth for thousands of years. If they did that with some place like Georgia or Alabama, I think that'd be a neat idea. It wouldn't mean white people couldn't go there, but they couldn't own houses or land. I guess if you tried to set up something like that though, you'd find the white folks already owned the land and there was no way they were going to let go their hold.

I'd like to know more about these things and I talk about them with my ma. She tells me I should read books and study good and learn everything I can, so when people are talking I know what they're saying and when they're right and when they're not. She says she's sorry she didn't have an education herself, and that's why she's so keen for me to go to college. She's not had a good life my ma, so she wants better for me. I've known times after our pa left us when she was crying because she didn't know what to do or how to feed us: there were times she got real down about it and sometimes she's said we'd have happier lives if she sent us to live with folk who could look after us. Because I'm the oldest one she's always talked about things most with me, nearly like we were sisters: I know she's always done her very best for us that she could.

If I did get good grades and I did get to go to Baxter or some place to college, I'd like to study to be a dancer. That's the thing I do best, and I think that way I could maybe earn more money than I could just if I was a teacher or in a bank or something: anyway I don't think really I'm clever enough with brains for that. But dancing I like: I'd like to be a dance teacher maybe, I'm not crazy enough to think of myself being a movie star or anything like that. What I'm most thinking about is I could go to college a couple of years maybe, then try and have a school of my own for kids who want to learn the latest dances. That way perhaps I could do something I like doing, and at the same time be sending money home. I'd like to do that because I think my ma, she'll have a tough time on her own when I'm gone.

25 *Two Lives (5)*

Dinah Johnson

In her two-roomed apartment in the small single-storeyed low-rent accommodation block, she sat erect in her high-backed chair with her hands on top of her stick and an embroidered shawl round her shoulders. White-haired, blind in one eye and with the sight going in the other, she spoke in a deep rich voice, often laughing at herself and at her memories.

– The little lady from Texas, she told me you'd like to visit with me, I'm pleased you did. Now isn't she something, that young lady? They say she's a very clever person, teaches in a university. I can't believe that, not someone as young as she is: she's surely at school herself still I'd have thought. When you're my age though you think everyone's getting younger every day: and my sight gives some trouble too, I can't tell just how old folk are or properly read a newspaper now without my magnifying glass.

How old I am, well I'll tell you: I'm 87 and I've lived here in Demus since I was 19, which is 68 years. Before that I was born and raised in a sod house in a field just east of the highway here: my daddy came to homestead and he had 11 children, and I was his oldest one. I went to the little country school there was there those days, then I went to work for a family who had a big mansion out near Milton Reservoir. I was nursemaid, I was parlourmaid, I was cook: and I had to work very hard. In return they gave me my keep and a roof over my head but no more, that was how it was in those days. If I wanted to see my brothers and sisters and my daddy and my mammy, I had to walk six miles home and six miles back, and I did that sometimes just to spend there no more than an hour.

I stayed working with that family until I was 18, and then I met a man I became pregnant by, and he married me and brought me with him here to Nicodemus township and we built our house together, the big one down the road where the little Texas lady is. Him and me we built that house of wood, which we chopped and sawed and cut with our own hands: he was a fine good man, and we were married for 66 years 5 months and 11 days until the good Lord took him away. We had six fine children, three girls and three boys: I can't exactly remember the dates they were born for you unless I get out my old Bible where I have them all written down. And then from them I have 21 grandchildren and 28 great-grandchildren, and I can tell you they still keep coming, yes they surely do. It's got now sometimes I can hardly remember some of their names when they come to see me: I have to ask them to tell me because like I say I can't see their faces too good now with my eyes. One little fellow, just last week he stood there and I gave him some lemon candy I'd made and I asked him, 'Now tell me young man,' I said, 'Because I can't see you too good, which one of my great-grandchildren are you?' You know what he said? He said, 'Mrs Johnson,' he said, 'I ain't none of your great-grandchildren, I've come 'cos someone told me you gave out candy to children.' Imagine that! He's a young man'll go far I reckon, don't you?

My own six children, I can say without telling no lies that they've all grown to be fine people every one of them, and good upright citizens of the United States: that's true of each and every one of them, from my eldest who's married a doctor in Arkansas and has five lovely daughters of her own, to my baby boy who's in the US Army in Phoenix Arizona. There's not one of them ever in their lives been mixed up with drugs or alcohol or crime in any way, and that's something for black people to be proud of in these times when there's so many temptations in everybody's way.

But my dear husband and me, we gave them a good solid family home to start from and I think that's what counts. We never had money in abundance or anything of that sort: we had a piece of land we rented to farm on, and we all worked hard, the children when they were old enough same as everyone else. They was brought up strict, and when they came home from school each one of them had a chore to do: this one and this one for working in the house, that one to help me prepare the meal, another to feed the chickens and turkeys, and another one to tend to the hogs. They had to do their work, otherwise they was sent to bed: but not hit, none of them was hit, we didn't hold with that.

And another thing in our home was very important, least to my way of thinking it was, and I'll tell you it. We all loved one another and because we did that, we were happy and all of us was laughing many many times. I don't know there was anything was specially funny we had to laugh about: but you know the way things are, if you can share laughter in your home then that gives you something that no matter how much money you had, you could never go out and buy. I remember a time once when it was harvest and we hired two horses to help us with our work: we thought that was a real smart idea, because the more of the crop and the quicker you got it in for the farmer, the more you'd be paid. Well that husband of mine, he'd no more idea of how to handle horses than I had: and if he couldn't handle one, he twice as much couldn't handle two. So instead of us getting the crop in faster'n anyone else, we was the slowest by far: we were so slow all the other folk had finished their work while we hadn't begun.

That night I remember all of us sitting around the table in the kitchen in our big house there and wondering what we should do. In those days we had I think it was four of our children then: so late in the evening we took them with us into the field, and we roped them up to the haycart and we used them for practising. And there was a Reverend came by, he was the pastor just come new to our church: and when he saw us driving around the field with the waggon and these children all roped up to it and hooting and hollering, he threw up his hands in horror and came running after us and begging us for mercy, and this Reverend man he rolled up his sleeves and he told my husband he was going to give him a hiding which he richly deserved. It was only finally settled when all those children of ours, they just couldn't keep their faces straight no longer and they all burst out laughing right there in front of the poor man.

You look back on those times like that you know, and you've a store of memories through your life that you can think on. So however much we didn't have in material things, and we never had much ever, we made up for it other ways. It was a hard life for them as so it was for us: there was years when the crop was all hailed and we had nothing, and there was years when the sows ate more in food than they produced in meat. But we had hens to give us eggs, and we grew our own vegetables in the garden so we always had sufficient to eat. I canned and I sewed and I made them the children's clothes, and we shared our troubles like we shared our joys, and there's none of them since have ever told me they wished it'd been different.

The chief thing was they were taught they should share with one another what they had, and they should respect their parents. I always used to tell my husband, I'd say to him if we wanted them to respect us then we had to be worthy of that respect and not just demand it should be given us as a right. So sometimes if he came home and he'd taken a little to drink, and something in the house upset him and he wanted to swear as men sometimes do, then we had the rule he had to go outside of the house in the garden or some place, and do his swearing there where none of his children could hear him. And in all our years, I recall there was only one time ever when I had to go push him out the door: other times he'd always go of himself without me telling him. So like I'm saying to you, this was the reason why our children grew so good.

But you know, now there's a great-grandson of mine, he's only a young boy around 21 or somewhere there: and he's not a bad boy, but he's one they say of that he's fallen in to bad company, and the result is now that he's serving a term in jail. From what I hear tell of it he'd done nothing of a very serious nature himself, just mostly gone along with the rest who were caught taking an automobile. He didn't have a good home life though at all you see, this young man: from an early age his mother was living with someone else who wasn't my grandson who she'd originally married. I don't think she ought to have done that: if she didn't like being married with my grandson, then it's sad but they should have done things properly and got themselves a divorce. I don't hold with all this what they call shacking, not when there's children to be considered.

And he came to see me did this young boy, last year while he was awaiting for the case to be heard against him in the court in Wichita. He sat there where you're sitting now, and he told me all about how his childhood had been, him being unhappy in his home life and everything: and he was trying to tell me how it was he'd come to start getting into trouble you know, he said as a result of that. Well you know, I said to him there was lots of young boys who had unhappy childhood lives: their daddies or their mammies, they went away and left them or they died and things like that. And I told him what I believe, which is that the Lord put these things upon you to test you, and it was up to you to see to it that when He did that, you didn't fail. The Lord would not be pleased with you if you did.

So then this young man after that, he began to say to me that well it might not all be the fault of the way he'd been brought up, but also there was in addition for him this burden that he was black. He had one great big chip on his shoulder the size of a pine log about this, he did: how the police was always very hard on young blacks, they'd not give you hassle if you were white and be always picking on you. That may be true for all I know, how would an old woman like me be able to tell if it's so or if it isn't so? But I said to him that about that, I thought two things. One was if it was so, then young black men should watch out more how for they behaved themselves, and should always be able to say they'd done nothing the police could pick on them for. I asked him was he one that could say that for himself? No he couldn't.

And the other thing I said was that if the police were truly hard on blacks, it didn't necessarily mean the courts were hard on blacks too. From what I've read, they have black judges most everywhere in the courts now: they put up black offenders in front of them specially, so that folks can't say it's the whites punishing the blacks. It's to make it clear if you do things outside the law and you get yourself caught, then you're in trouble whether you're black, white, or any colour in between.

He said I was too old to know what I was talking about, I'd never lived on the streets and I couldn't know what his life was like. And that may be true and he's right, that I'm an old woman that doesn't understand. But he'd come to talk with me, so all I could say to him was what I thought. He went away and he went to court and he went to jail: and a little while back he wrote me a letter. He said while he was in jail he'd been thinking about our talk and what I'd said to him, and he was going to think about it some more. I hope he does, and I had my daughter write back to him for me and say when he comes out of that jail, that's the time for him to make resolutions about himself, when he can put them into practice. He's not a bad boy, I think he just needs to straighten himself up and get back his pride. There was a time once when with my husband and our babies had flown away, him and me we were thinking we might adopt that particular young man for our own and take him to live with us. I didn't tell that to him when he came and was telling me about his childhood and his mother making him so unhappy and all the rest: but I can tell you, I did very near. You can't help thinking that you might have been able to give someone like him a better life than he had. I wasn't too sympathetic to him when he was telling me about his childhood, because that's all over and gone and nothing's going to change it now. But I did wonder about what we'd done for him and what we hadn't done: and my good husband, he might just have helped that boy. You don't like to see it that someone so young is growing up with so many problems, do you?

I think about it though, and you know the world is changing so much from what it was when I was a girl: the young people, they see and hear of all these wars everywhere, and I think they must sometimes wonder what sort of a world they've been brought into. I never had that sort of worry for a single day in my life, whether I'd be here the next day or the one after. I'd only my husband and our children and our home and work to contend with, and I was always happy with that. It didn't matter to me whether one foolish man in Washington and another foolish man in Moscow were quarrelling or whether they weren't, it had nothing to do with me. That's how I look at it still: at the time in life that I am it's easy to be not too concerned by the way things go. You get kind of selfish with yourself the older you get, and that's not too good a thing. It's maybe because I'm a widow now and have been for two years, with no one to bother with but myself, and no one to please but me.

Well I'll tell you, in answer to your question because you've asked me it: it's a kind of a private thing, but I'll tell it to you all the same. What are my plans you ask, where am I going to go from here? It's something, I can tell you, that just right now's exactly's on my mind. There's two gentlemen and they both want to marry me you see: in one single sentence, that's what it is. I've promised a decision to them, and it's one it's getting very near now that has to be made.

The first man, he came to see me here, it was exactly ten months to the day after my husband had died. He is a local man, and he knew that my husband had passed on: and he knocked at that door there, and he came in and he sat down in that other chair over there, and he said he'd come to speak to me about a serious matter. He's a very gentlemanly man in his ways, and lived most of his life here in Demus like me. He and his wife, they had ten children who'd all grown now and gone: and his wife, who everyone knew had been a very fine lady, she'd died too herself six years ago. He had been very lonely ever since, he said, as I'd understand: and I told him yes I did. And he said he didn't want an answer to it there and then, he didn't want an answer to it until I felt I was ready to give him one. But he would be very honoured, he said, and he used that very word – he would be honoured if I would give thought to a proposal of marriage from him.

Now he's a gentleman and I've known him since a boy here: I estimate him to be 75 perhaps, somewhere around 12 years younger than me. I saw him through that window the other day going by: and he's a little stiff in the way he walks, but otherwise a good-looking upstanding sort of man, who I know's always keep himself neatly dressed and clean. A good Christian man too, and a deacon of the church here: and I think we could both give each other happiness and companionship.

But now then there comes along this other man you see, one day in August time last year when he'd come to visit his daughter here. He's a gentleman from California and he has one of them big shiny automobiles which he drove me around in a time or two, asking me to show him the countryside. A well-spoken man and of some education I'd say. His wife too had died a time back, and he was another who was lonely too. Now he writes to me, and he says he'd like me to go see where his home in California is, close by the ocean: and he writes if I like it, and if I like him too, would I consider we should be married. He's more the age that I am, 85 I believe he said he was. His daughter, I've talked with her about him because he told me I should ask her if I wanted to know further information about him: and she says he's always been a good kind father to her, and she's sure I'd want for nothing if I was to go live in California.

So I'm puzzling it out in my mind. I've told each of them that I've had another proposal from someone else, because I think it's fair they should know that and not think I was the sort of woman who'd play them around. But I don't know, I don't know. The man from California, I'm sure he's a nice gentleman but I don't think to move away from where you've lived your life so long is good for a person when they start to get old. The local boy, he's been frank with me and told me he's little money except his pension the same as me, and he can't promise me much in material ways. But with a matter like marriage I don't believe money should come into it, and I'm not taking that into account.

I think though I'm inclining towards him, and staying here in Demus: but it's not the kind of decision anyone should be in a hurry to take, not for a thing like that. But I'm hesitating, you know: I believe like I've always believed that marriage is for a lifetime until death do you part: and I'd hate to be married to someone and then find I'd made a mistake. What I'll do yet awhile is I think I won't be hurried, I shall give it some more thought, that's what I'm thinking I'll do.

Mary Everton

Making a definite arrangement for a meeting was difficult. On the 'phone she was polite but evasive: yes, Christine had spoken with her about it. But she herself wasn't certain much purpose would be served. Maybe I should call next week when she'd had time to give it more thought.

Yes, she'd given it more thought, and spoken again with Christine: and OK then, if something could be arranged. Only right now it was difficult for her, she had a lot of things she had to do. If I could call again Thursday?

She'd thought she might be able to make it Friday, Fridays were usually OK, but unfortunately something had come up for this Friday, and oh now she came to look at her calendar, for next Friday too. Look, why didn't I call Monday to see how she was fixed?

'OK,' said Christine, 'I'll put it to her again. Only with Mary, well it's not that she doesn't mean to be difficult about it: she does. I've told her to say to you exactly what she likes, but she says you won't want to hear it. Leave it with me.'

A small woman in her early fifties with straight black hair cut short and beginning to go grey. She wore a black blouse and skirt, with a black bolero waistcoat and a small gold brooch. She sat sideways at her desk, one elbow on it and her folded hands held loosely in her lap. Her voice was level and soft and firm.

– I hate all white people. I won't say to you that it's not a thing against you personally, because that wouldn't be true. It is against you personally, as it is to any black man or black woman when a white person insults them or demeans them or mistreats them. This is something whites don't know, or don't choose to know: that when you strike at a person because of their race or the colour of their skin, you're doing it to them as an individual and they feel the hurt as an individual. They might protest it afterwards and say it was done to them because they were black: but that's to cover the hurt that's been done to them as a person. Unless you've had it happen to you, I don't think you could understand it. The black people are seen as being without individual personalities by whites but that's not how they see themselves.

It will take another great leader to teach them that: Dr Martin Luther King was beginning to help them feel they had worth and needn't for ever be slaves. But those who killed him, and I'm one of many many thousands who think his assassination was planned by a group of people and not the responsibility of one crazy man, they planted such bitterness by that in black people's hearts it'll take a hundred years or more for it to go. He was a great man: not faultless, but a man who had charisma, and without that no leader can lead. But what happened to him was an example to black people of what would happen to them if their movement for freedom and equality became too sweeping and too strong. The lesson of it for many black people will be this: that for their next leader, he'll take them further only if he offers them their rights not in some future dreamtime, but now. If he tells them they mustn't wait any longer for their rights to be given them but must take them now, that will be a time we've not so far seen the like of ever in America. There won't be just street riots and damage to property, there'll be killings and burnings and terrorising and worse things still, beyond imagining. I'm speaking now not of what I'm advocating but what I fear: difficult though it is to be, myself I'm a pacifist and I don't want to see black justice come through the injustice of force. But it's hard to see a successful alternative now, here and the same in South Africa.

I wasn't always a pacifist, no: not at all in fact until I began to listen to what Dr King was saying. Like many other black people I had a hope that a leader would emerge, and when I was at college, along with the rest of my friends, I talked wild and I thought wild: any black person could get our allegiance from the colour of his skin and his ability to make rousing speeches, more than from his ideas. I see that kind of time coming again, some kind of black Messiah appearing who's perhaps at heart a black Hitler: and if he gets a sufficient following he'll visit a holocaust on white people far more terrible than Hitler did on the Jews. I remember a speaker came to our campus once and he said being tolerant and patient hadn't helped black people anyway anywhere ever: they'd suffered and been put upon always, and now the time had come to do violence in return.

This was exciting to us as young people: he touched on a very deep and primitive part of you. And as well as exciting it was frightening, because you realised what violent forces and feelings there were inside you. I think the word I'm looking for is 'stirring': he could stir you and he did. OK he was a demagogue: but it's not wise to use that as a way of dismissing someone, that's something else that Hitler showed. When you see the lethargy of so many black people and how they accept their lot is always to be second best, you can't help it that you get to feeling only a demagogue will arouse black people.

All across the United States, and from what I've read it's the same in your country, black people get short-changed. They have the worst housing, the worst education, the worst jobs. They get conditioned right from when they're born to accept the situation's like that and can't be altered: so they retreat into a kind of apathy and it's horrifying. I've even had black people tell me they seriously believe white folks are smarter than black and they work harder, so nothing'll ever be able to make a difference. Their portrait of themselves is the one that white people have painted for them, a kind of brain washing into believing all they're good for is athleticism and dancing, activities which stress physical ability rather than brain power. And fostering this idea is one of the terrible things whites have done to the blacks: they've got them eating from their hands like they were tame animals.

This is all I have time for to talk about with you right now, I have someone outside my office waiting to see me. But if you like to come to my home in Nicodemus Wednesday evening next week, if you want to we can talk some more.

– I was born in Washington DC. Least I think I was, that's what I always say because living there is the first I remember. I don't know my mother or father: I was adopted from a young baby, and brought up with their other two children by a couple I've always thought of like my parents. They were both black: he was a school teacher and she'd been a teacher herself, but stopped home to bring up us kids. They had a good standard of living, I guess what could be called middle class, and we lived in a mixed neighbourhood. I went to a mixed school too, but the whites outnumbered the blacks. The thing I recall most of all there is as a child I had a very short fuse: anything annoyed me or upset me, I was ready to fight anyone, or if I didn't do that I did the opposite, which was burst into tears and run away and hide. I was unhappy and unsettled all the time as a child, but I can't recall particularly any reason why. It got me a nickname, you know how kids are: they called me 'The black cloud', and I can still hear them saying it like they used to in the playground, 'Watch out, here comes the black cloud.' That was the first time I realised the colour of my skin was something that was important to other people, and I recall I was ashamed about it and wished I was white.

I was a good student: a little rather serious-minded I'd say, which is something I've been most all my life. But I liked study, I was happier with books than I was with people: and of course I got encouragement at home from my parents. I went to college and the ambition of my life was to study law: but when I was somewhere around halfway through my studies my father died, and I came back home to get a job and earn money for my mother and younger sisters. I'm saying that as the reason for giving up law: but I guess I'd realised too I wasn't going to make it anyhow. I had boyfriends and so on at college, but the thing took up most of my time there was involving myself with civil rights for blacks and the rest of it, neglecting my studies as a result and finding I was falling way way behind.

I took some jobs: I taught some, I worked in a law office, I went to night school to keep up with my studies, one time even I thought I might be a writer and involved myself with a theatre group. There were a couple of love affairs but neither of them brought much happiness, and I guess I was mostly passing time: and time was passing me too. I had the sense I wanted to do something definite and positive with my life but I couldn't have told you what. Finally I took the choice a lot of women do: I married. I married, as though that was a kind of a something you decide to do with your life: 'I know what I'll do, I'll get married', it was like that.

He was a nice man and a good man, and that we were brought together like we were was kind of a joke, it must have been. He hadn't the education I'd had, he had very little in that way at all: I guess what we saw in each other was the things neither one of us had and hoped we'd get from each other. To him, I was an educated woman, a black who'd bettered herself: to me, he was a black man who'd stayed in touch with his roots and not been spoiled by his contact with the white man's sophisticated world. He had family here in Nicodemus: his mother, his brothers who farmed, and a whole lot of relatives and friends. I thought it was basic and real, and that what he had was something that was very valuable. It was too, I still think that was right: it would have been the ideal kind of a life for some woman, only not for me. I tried to make it so, but anyone but us could have seen where it would lead. Maybe if we'd had children it would have been different: but I think not, I think there'd then just have been more unhappy people in the world. I wasn't the sort to be a farmer's wife and I'd been a foolish person to think I might: it was dull drudgery and I didn't fit in with it, not any way at all.

The choice to be here had been mine: he was offered a farm to rent, south of the highway in with his brothers. The three of them worked hard at what they knew best and what they could do. I felt bad about being unhappy and dissatisfied, because I felt I'd brought the situation on myself. When I found I couldn't have children in one way I was glad about it, but in another way that seemed like another way out for me had been blocked off. The only choices left for me were to admit it had all been just a romantic idea and a failure and go back to Washington, or to do the best I could with staying here and getting a job.

That was what I chose. I went to a company in Conway City that manufactures and distributes fertilisers and agricultural chemical products: a big company that employs around 300 people, and they offered me the post of personnel manager: to set it up and deal with the expansion of their work force they were going to embark on. They paid for me to go on a training course for two months, and from then on the job was what I made it. That's where I still am: when I went to start with them 12 years ago I didn't have my own office like you saw, but in terms of work conditions they've always met all my requests for what I needed. I said I wanted a place where I could talk with people about their problems, I got it: secretarial help, I got it, and so on. In ways like that there's never been anything to complain of.

They're a white-owned company of course, a subsidiary of a big conglomerate that has operations all across the States. A modern forward-looking corporation they call themselves: and you look at it from the outside and you have to agree, as employers they're among the best. They look after their work force in the true traditions of enlightened paternalism, oh yeah: and I wonder sometimes if it's right of me that I should help them do it. In the Conway City plant there, 90 per cent of the workers are black: they're treated good so they don't give no trouble. If you asked them about it, I'm sure they'd say I was appointed to my position because who could be better to handle problems of black personnel than a black personnel officer? I'm never in a position where I'm asked to do things I don't agree with: but on the other side of it, I see my function as being what I don't think there can be argument about, which is to maintain the status quo. No black person from Conway City's ever going to go higher up the management structure of this company: there's no opportunity and the way things are arranged, I don't see there ever will be. Work hard, be good: we'll treat you kindly, but don't get any fancy ideas about yourself: it's the total white stroke black situation put clear.

You get to hear in the job all kinds of problems people have: they like to come and talk with you about things nothing to do with work but in their personal or family lives. All of that too reinforces the view you have of the life of black people and how they're disadvantaged. You'll have heard around these parts of oil being found? But on black man's land, the companies aren't even yet drilling looking for it. I've known of two cases in these parts where farmers were moved off land by the owners of it, and as soon as they went the explorations started: but I've not known of a single case where a black man's profited from oil, not anywhere near here at all. Such things as that, they all add to the picture of two classes of citizens, the first-class whites and the second-class blacks.

In my spare time two evenings a week I work at a youth club: there it's the same too, there you can see young black people already growing up and knowing they're not going to go anywhere in life.

They have poor schooling, which doesn't encourage them to have ambitions for themselves. A lot of them get in trouble with the police, and I don't excuse that: but I think it's the only way for some of them to be anyway different or better than their friends. Those with the records or reputations of criminal behaviour, that's all they have that gives them anything they can boast about, anything they can excel at in comparison with the rest. That doesn't promise good things for the future where whites are concerned, when young black people are thinking like that. I've thought a lot in my mind the last two years or so that maybe I ought to go back to Washington DC and involve myself more deeply in youth work or social work, if not there then some place else, some other urban area where there's need.

I maybe will next year, and I don't just say that. Since I separated with my husband last year he stays with his brothers at the farm where they are, and he's willing for me to stay here yet awhile. But this is his house, and when I move out he can maybe sell it, or move back in again and maybe marry too if he finds someone better suited for him. There's no animosity between us, nor towards me by his family, and I'm grateful to them for that: only I don't want it to go on like this where I'm a hindrance to plans he might have. Three nights a week now I stay in Conway City with a friend, and by the time it's year end I intend to be away from here completely.

Becoming restless is the feeling, that I'm not doing enough and life's not being used properly. Last time it was like that I took the wrong choice and decided to marry: this time I'll not make that mistake, I'll stay on my own and try to do more positive things.

26 *Land of the Free and Home of the Brave*

Oh! thus be it ever, when freemen shall stand
Between their loved homes and the war's desolation!
Blest with victory and peace, may the heaven-rescued land
Praise the Power that hath made and preserved us a nation.
Then conquer we must, for our cause it is just,
And this be our motto: 'In God is our trust'.
And the star-spangled banner in triumph shall wave
O'er the land of the free and the home of the brave.

Francis Scott Key (1799–1843)
Designated the American national anthem
by Congress in 1931

We Americans are the lavishest and showiest and most luxury-loving people on the earth: and at our masthead we fly one true and honest symbol, the gaudiest flag the world has ever seen.

S. L. Clemens (Mark Twain) (1835–1910)

– The way I see it? OK well I'll tell you. The way I see it is that America's just the greatest little country that there is. Whatever you want, America has it, right here. A fine, freedom-loving country, democracy, free speech, freedom of religion, everything. And you know what the greatest freedom of all is? Well let me tell you: it's freedom of opportunity. A man wants to improve himself, make his way in the world by his hard work and his efforts, and he'll do that: if he works hard and lives a decent kind of a life, there's no limit to where he can get to, right up to one day becoming the President of the United States if that's what he's got a mind to. You only need look back through the history books, and it's all there, how the ordinary men and the women too for that matter, if they worked and had the determination to succeed, then there wasn't no one could stop them. Now you tell me how many other countries in the world can say that? None, not one of them, not in my estimation can they truthfully say that they have it like we do here. If you ask me, there's far too many people in our country these days who have it too easy, they don't have no idea what it was like for folk before them, those pioneers who made our country the great place it is. They're for ever running their country down. Well like I say, it's the greatest country the world's ever seen, and if they don't think so then why don't they go live some place else?

Lester Gover, Mayor

– I'd give my life for my country tomorrow, it's as simple as that. I'm a patriotic American. That's not too fashionable a thing to say or to be these days, but that's what I am. 'My country right or wrong', straight down the line, and I think those who don't see it like that can't call theirselves real Americans and they shouldn't be allowed to. If they're not prepared to die for their country when the call comes, well then they shouldn't be allowed to partake of the benefits of that country which other people have fought and died for so they could have them. You hear these people on the television and in the newspapers and they're saying things like that America's not doing right here or what other foreign countries are saying that's criticising America: and those people, they're being paid thousands of dollars for saying unpatriotic things about the country. How crazy can you get? They're communists those people, they're people dedicated to destroying the American country and the American way of life – and they're getting paid by the lefties who run our news media to do it. And what does the great American public do? It sits there and lets them get away with it. Any other country in the world, they'd take them out and shoot them, or leastways they'd throw them in the sewers where they belong. 'America's my country, America's God's own country' – and if you can't lay your hand on your heart and swear that, then you're not an American, not to my mind you ain't.

Eldon Simmonds, VFW

– You know what I don't like most is the way so many other countries in the world, and I mean little countries like Arab countries and places like that who've got nothing to be proud of themselves in the way they run their own countries – they push us around all the time and think they can get away with it. If they had half the things we have in the way of civilisation, decent homes to live in, a good standard of living for everyone and stuff like that – if they had those things then maybe they would have a right to say what they thought was wrong with America. But until they get to be as good as us, then no way should they be let have an equal say in the running of the world. They should watch us and listen to us and learn from us, not be for always screeching and yammering about America throwing its weight around. Sure America throws its weight around: because it has a right to. We were a backward uncivilised country ourselves once. But what are we now, we're the greatest and most civilised nation in the world, and so we ought to be given respect for that. If it wasn't for America the whole world'd be overrun with communism: everyone knows that. We've got our troops all over the world on guard to prevent that, we've got our boys giving their lives like they have done, and ready to do it again every time it's necessary for world peace. But do these countries we're protecting appreciate what it's costing us? No they do not, and when they get the chance they stir up trouble for us. Sneaky, that's what they are.

Sandy Carlton

– My feeling about being American is most of all I'm proud. This is just sure one helluva country, the greatest that there is. I wouldn't say there's nothing wrong with it, what place on earth is there that isn't?

But when I think of our history, and I'd say it was our God-given history and I don't think we should forget that – when I think of it, I get that great big feeling of pride swelling right up inside of me here, and I think I belong to the finest and greatest and strongest and bestest country on the face of the earth. It's a land of freedom, a land of opportunity and a land where the good guys come out best. We've given a lot to the world, and the world hasn't always appreciated it. But I'd say America represents one of the finest examples to everyone the world over just what a country can achieve in only just a couple of hundred years, and all by the efforts of its own ordinary hard-working pioneering people. In world affairs it's been let down a time or two by some other countries it thought were its allies, like France particularly I'd say. But we're big enough to take things like that, and that's another great thing about America, that we don't go around looking to make enemies because we'd sooner be friends with everyone. Except the Commies.

Larry Manders, store manager

– Where I live it's not considered to be very sophisticated to say you're patriotic: and it does, that truly gets me sometimes. I don't see there's anything all that wrong in saying you love your country, you're proud to belong to it, and you're grateful for all the good things in life that being an American brings you. You have free speech, you have democratic government, you have high standards in public life, most places you can walk safely on the streets without fears of riot or revolutions. There's hundreds of thousands of places all over the world where people have no hope ever in all their lives of getting to have the kind of life we've got for most people in America. OK sure it's not a one hundred per cent perfect country yet. But everyone knows that, and the really good and marvellous thing about it is everyone's all the time trying to make it better. Like I say, I don't think we're proud enough of it, not as proud as we should be that we belong to the best country in the world that there is.

Marilyn Ryman, visitor

– When I said I was glad being an American and I couldn't imagine being something else or living somewhere else, what I meant was I wouldn't ever want to. I've read books, and we have lessons about other countries at school, and you see all the programmes on TV, and I've never read or seen or heard anything about anywhere else that's half as good as the things we have in America. Our system of government's better than anyone else's and everything about the whole country makes you feel you're a real lucky person to live here. I wouldn't like to live in a country where you all the time were frightened if you stepped one foot out of line you might be taken away in the middle of the night and never heard of again. Or that you didn't have freedom of religion and that kind of thing. We have a good government that tries to do its best for people, and if people don't think its best is good enough every four years they can vote to change it. This is a great great thing we have, and I think not sufficient people appreciate it.

Karl Gidman, High School senior

– America? Well I think it has to be the greatest country in the world, without argument and it's as simple as that. I mean we're the biggest, strongest, powerfullest nation of all, pretty near aren't we? I mean you watch the Olympic games on TV, we do pretty damn good I reckon. Those Soviets, they take their people right from when they're kids, and they put them in camps and train them every day of their lives and don't let them do anything else, they've no free choice about it. But we, well we just let our best people come to the top naturally, they don't have to do things they don't want to, just for the glory of their country. And then when it comes to the Olympics, then they can still beat all the others when it comes to most things. It proves which system is best, no one can argue about that.

Darrell Greaves, college student

– As an American citizen I'm very proud of my country. I'm not one of those who doesn't see anything wrong with it, but all the same I still think it's got more going for it than any other country that there is. I think it's a wonderful country to live, and most of its people are honest decent upright people who've every reason to be proud they're Americans. The greatest gift we have is our freedom of speech, and the way we stand up for other people and their rights, wherever it is in the world. I'd say the biggest wrong thing we have is we don't always make it clear to other countries that although we'll help them, give them food and aid and money and all the rest of it, that doesn't mean we don't expect decent behaviour from them in return. It's like with your kids, you'll give them food and shelter and pocket money, but in return you expect them to behave around the house and be polite to people and the rest of it. You don't give them money so they can start a war against you, or give help to other people to start wars against you. So I'd say that's a big fault, we're too soft sometimes. But I think that's because we think others will be decent with us the same way we are to them. Maybe that's the price you have to pay for being generous: and if it is, well I guess I'd still say I wouldn't want for us to be any different.

Irene Finney, housewife

– You know I think a lot of people in the world get it wrong about America. Because we're a country that loves peace, and that would every time sooner settle for a peaceful solution to a problem, a lot of them do get the idea that in some way this makes America a weak country and one which is going to go on and on putting up with provocation and aggravation. And I think there is, there's some justification for seeing America like that. We stand by and we watch these countries one after another taken over by communism, even right in our own backyard here in central and south America, and we do nothing about it because we hope they'll sort it out for themselves. Well the biggest threat to the world that there is is communism, everybody knows it: and America's foursquare against it, but doesn't always make it plain. There's more than one country where to my mind we should just go right in there and clean it up, to make it an example and to show the world we mean what we say about communism, we're not going to give it houseroom.

Dan Forgan, teacher

– I'm a loyal American and I respect my country, I love my country, and I'm proud of it. That doesn't mean I regard it as beyond improvement: I don't, I think in certain respects it's got a long way to go, say in such areas as eradicating poverty for instance. We haven't totally achieved that, but then what country is there anywhere that has? And I don't think in international affairs we're always totally right in everything we do. But what I do believe, and believe very sincerely, is that we always at least try to do what's right. We don't go out looking for trouble, we're looking for the best way to solve things: and sometimes before we know where we are, we find we've gotten ourselves into trouble and don't know how to get out of it. We have a government though that believes in honour and integrity, and in filling its obligations. If we tell a country we're not going to let it be taken over by communism, then we stand by our promise to that country and we go on and on trying to keep our promise however unpopular it makes us. It grieves me very much when I hear our own American citizens saying we should pull out altogether of countries we've promised to help: I'd say that was anti-Americanism, and that it comes from Americans themselves is shameful. How can you have any pride in yourself when you don't stand by your own country? That's what matters, to stand by your own country always, at all times, everywhere.

John Stone, Attorney

– I would say I'm probably not a very American person when it comes to patriotism. Like everyone else we think our country's the best, and I don't see anything wrong in that. It's OK, but what we don't seem to see is other people think their country's the best and America isn't. Maybe it's because America's a young country and hasn't realised, because it's big and powerful that won't necessarily get other people standing up and cheering for you. I think a lot of the fault's in the schools: they teach the kids to salute the flag and sing about the land of the free and America the beautiful and all the rest, but what isn't taught to them properly is how other kids in other countries feel it just as sincerely and deeply as they do, only about their own countries.

Calvin Hughes, VFW

– You know I think there must be something in the character of a lot of the inhabitants of the United States, I don't know what it is but it makes them hit out first without thinking. You see this in international affairs and then afterwards they start making excuses for it, because they find not only hasn't it brought the results they intended, but what's worse is it's lowered their standing in the eyes of the rest of the world. They want other people to like them, and then here they are and other people don't like them. They go around behaving big and tough and shoving anyone in front of them out of their way, and then they get all hurt people don't admire how strong they are. People don't trust them in their living rooms as it were, they'd sooner keep them out in the yard in a cage on a chain. You see most Americans, they've never grown up in world affairs at all, they've never learned how to behave with dignity and respect towards the rest. Tread on their foot, the first thing they think of is to punch you on the nose.

Michael Dormer, visitor

– Well just about the worst thing you can be in USA is non-patriotic. It's somewhere way down below being a drug addict or a felon. Least if you're a drug addict you can go on a treatment program, or if you're a felon you can be put in jail: but if you're a non-patriot you can't be treated and you can't be punished and so wow, you're going to get clean away with it and maybe the wrath of God won't fall on you either which is plain downright terrible. So I have to say it very very quietly: I'm non-patriotic, in fact sometimes I think I'm worse than that, I'm anti-patriotic. I like America, I think it's a good country, and in a lot of ways: but that's not the same as saying I think it's the greatest in the world. Whoever I was, wherever I'd been born and lived, I'd probably feel a fondness and a liking for the place. But no more than that, not all this 'my country right or wrong' stuff, frankly I think that's childish. There's some things other countries do better than we do, some things other countries do worse. I'd say most the time our government tries to do what it thinks best – but what it thinks best for America that is, not best for the world in general. It's the same everywhere, other countries do what they think's best for them.

Fanny Petersen

– I don't know why our rich powerful country America has got the idea it's some kind of world policeman with a God-given mission to stop the spread of communism, and do it by killing people for believing in communism. The idea of it spreading frightens us to death, and yet we're the ones doing more to spread communism than the communist countries are. Because what do we do, we send billions of dollars to guerrilla fighters to fight their own governments, but we do nothing at all to prevent communism finding a breeding ground in all the poverty there is there. I'm no communist myself, but it's an idea: and the only way you'll beat an idea is with another better idea. Killing people who believe in it, that's just helping more folk to believe in it.

Lucille Richmond

– I'm not a specially religious person, but sometimes I say a prayer when I see the news on television, I do. I pray to God to give peace to the world: I hate the idea of war, and when you have a child of your own you don't want them growing up into a world where everybody's fighting all the time. I've never been there and I don't suppose I ever shall, but I think there must be lots of women in say Russia like me: and they don't hate me any more than I hate them, we just want to live in peace and bring up our children if our governments'll only let us. I think most Russian people are the same as we are, they want peace. They had some very hard times of suffering in the last war did the Russians, much more than we did: we didn't have our country invaded and millions and millions of people killed. That we should be threatening them with bombs and rockets and things, I think that's terrible.

Betty Holt

– It sometimes makes me real mad, the way our government behaves. We only know what they tell us. Well I don't believe everything our government tell us, and other people don't believe everything their government tells them either: people aren't that stupid. And what also makes me mad is I don't have any control over what the government of my country's doing, I mean in international affairs and to other countries. And I know a lot of kids like me feel the same way. Sometimes we'd like to say to our government No, I don't want you to do that and then say you're acting on my behalf: I don't want to be claimed by the government as a supporter, not when they never even asked me. If they had asked me sometimes I'd have told them don't you do that, I don't want it done.

Debbie Potter, High School senior

– What I want for America is what I've wanted all my long life, and that's peace, not war, and love, not hate. I want to see my country at peace with every other country in the world, all living together in peace and all one big family, which is what they are. And in my country I want all people to live together in love as one big family too: black and white, yellow and brown, everyone together. The Lord didn't make us all to be quarrelling and bickering with one another, he made us as His children to help one another. America, this is a big country with a big heart and millions of decent folk who've done a whole lot of things they can be proud of, like freedom and emancipation and such things as that. So sure, let's be proud of ourselves: but proud for the right things, not proud because we can win wars, there's nothing in that to be proud of. To be peaceful and gentle and kind, that's what we should be proud of.

Dinah Johnson

– What I'd like most is two things: if Americans could try harder to understand other people, and other people could try harder to understand Americans. But I guess maybe that's asking too much. Most, I think Americans should get the idea out of their heads that everyone else would really at heart like to be American, and to take it on the chin that to some folk that idea'd be pure poison. And if other people could see Americans aren't all the same, noisy and loud-mouthed and talking big, and that those who're making all the noise aren't necessarily in the majority in America, then I think that'd be real good.

Jenny Ash

– I sometimes think the rest of the world must see us like we seem to want them to, in those television series we keep on putting out and proudly selling all over the world: rich, sophisticated, empty-headed monsters with no morals and no interest in anything but power and money. Or if not like that, then we show ourselves as small town hicks riding around on horses, spitting tobacco and saying things like 'Well I'll be darned!' every other sentence. The idea most of us are just ordinary everyday people, some good, some bad, and most a mixture of the two – well it's almost like we didn't want that idea to get around at all.

Linda Burns, housewife

But the stars burn on overhead,
Unconscious of final ends,
As I walk home to bed,
Asking what judgment waits
My person, all my friends
And these United States.

W. H. Auden (1907–73)
From "A Walk after Dark"

Acknowledgements

The idea for this book originated with my editor, David Godwin. He's been a steadfast guide, supporter and counsellor about it ever since, and I'm deeply grateful to him. I must also thank Helen Fraser at Heinemann for making my decision to follow him to Secker & Warburg far less awkward than it could have been; and both Georgina Capel and Maggie McKernan for all their subsequent help to me there. Constant as ever, my agent Gill Coleridge of Rogers, Coleridge & White, has worked tirelessly for me, always giving me encouragement and, most importantly of all, her friendship. No one could have a better representative or a more sensitive friend.

During complicated and long drawn-out preparations for my travels to and in the United States, Louise Castro of Hogg Robinson made all my arrangements for me with patience and expertise. After I returned to write the book, yet again Genevieve Broad typed and retyped the manuscript with the reliability and accuracy which I now almost take for granted; and Carol Moy of the Leiston Bookshop was endlessly helpful with all the labour of photocopying and collating. As usual, Josephine Hugo corrected the proofs impeccably. My thanks are due also to Cliff Evans at Lowestoft Central Library for his ready assistance in providing prompt information and answers to queries. I must acknowledge too supportive help from another source: like many authors I suffer the vagaries of delayed payments and other financial uncertainties, and my Bank Manager, John Studd of Barclays at Saxmundham, has never been other than understanding and helpful, taking interest not only in one sense of that word.

I hope my wife Margery will know what wider and deeper expressions of my gratitude for her love and help are implicit in the dedication. And so too, I hope, will all the kind and warm-hearted people we met in 'Bird', and among whom we lived so happily while we were there. We thank every one of them for so quickly making us feel at home; we arrived as strangers, but left with a host of wonderful friends. While I was in America I was able to achieve my long-held ambition of going to meet the great Studs Terkel. It was an experience

I shall always cherish the memory of: he and his wife Ida extended boundless hospitality to my wife and me, and gave me most generous encouragement in what I was doing.

Tony Parker
Westleton, Suffolk,
England.